Aristotle in Africa

Ethics and the
African Philosophical Tradition

Patrick Giddy

UJ Press

Aristotle in Africa: Ethics and the African Philosophical Tradition

Published by UJ Press

University of Johannesburg
Library
Auckland Park Kingsway Campus
PO Box 524
Auckland Park
2006
https://ujpress.uj.ac.za/

First published 2025

https://doi.org/10.36615/9780906785799
978-0-906785-78-2 (Paperback)
978-0-906785-79-9 (PDF)
978-0-906785-80-5 (EPUB)
978-0-906785-81-2 (XML)

This publication had been submitted to a rigorous double-blind peer-review process prior to publication and all recommendations by the reviewers were considered and implemented before publication.

Proofreading: Mike Leisegang
Cover design: Hester Roets, UJ Graphic Design Studio
Typeset in 9/13pt Merriweather Light

Contents

For Marianne

Acknowledgments

Some sections of Chapter 1 were originally published in *Social Dynamics* 21 (1995):117-131. Chapter 2 is a reworked version of the article, "African Traditional Thought and Growth in Personal Unity", *International Philosophical Quarterly* 42 (2002):315-327. Chapter 3 is a slightly altered version of Chapter 4 in J. Chimakonam and L. Cordeiro-Rodrigues (eds) *African Ethics. Guide to Key Ideas* (Bloomsbury Academic, 2023). Chapter 4 was published in A. Attoe et al. (eds) *Conversations on African Philosophy of Mind, Consciousness and Artificial Intelligence* (Springer Cham, 2023):79-94. Chapter 5, slightly altered, appeared as a chapter in A. Shutte (ed) *The Quest for Humanity in Science and Religion* (Pietermaritzburg: Cluster, 2005), Chapter 6 was published under the title, "A Communitarian Framework for Understanding Liberal Social Practices," in *South African Journal of Philosophy* 16 (1997):150-157. Chapter 7 appeared first in *Acta Academica* 46 (2014):18-34. Chapter 8 was a contributing chapter to M. Chemhuru (ed) *African Environmental Ethics. A Critical Reader.* (Cham: Springer, 2019):47-58. Chapter 9 (co-authored by Markus Detterbeck) was published originally in *Transformation* 59 (2005):26-44. Chapter 10 appeared first in *Ethique et Economique* 4 (2006). Chapter 11 was published as part of a collection edited by R. Barreto and V. Latinovic, *Decolonial Horizons. Reshaping Synodality, Mission and Social Justice.* (Palgrave, 2024). Chapter 12 was first published in *Method: Journal of Lonergan Studies* 14 (1996):133-153. Chapter 13 appeared in P. Bessinger et al. (eds), *Humanizing Higher Education Through Innovative Approaches to Teaching and Learning* (Bingley: Emerald Publishing, 2021): 117-129. Chapter 14 was published in *Acta Academica* 45 (2013):154-172. Chapter 15 appeared in *South African Journal of Philosophy* 31 (2012):504-516. Chapter 16 was published originally in *South African Journal of Education* 32 (2012):15-25.

About the author

Patrick Giddy studied philosophy at the University of Cape Town and Stellenbosch University, and theology at Blackfriars College, Oxford. He taught philosophy for some years at the University of Lesotho before joining the University of KwaZulu-Natal where he is currently a Senior Research Associate. He recently edited a collection of theological essays by Augustine Shutte, *The Christian God* (AFT Press/UJ Press, 2023).

Preface

The Aristotelian background

'Aristotle in Africa' as unifying theme in these discussions requires some brief preliminary remarks.

This is not a book on Aristotle, nor on African philosophy as such. Rather, it pursues one line of thought, namely that the tradition of philosophy associated with Aristotle - it is a distinct tradition - has something of value to offer in thinking through ethics in the context of the African traditional thought-world.

The Aristotelian tradition in philosophy was for many centuries the mainstream frame of thinking in European culture. For Thomas Aquinas, Aristotle was simply, 'the Philosopher'. This tradition was overthrown in the modern period, through the influence on philosophy of the rise of science and scientific method, as well as the turn to a greater appreciation of individual freedom. Copernicus had undermined the 'cosmological' frame of thinking through bringing to the fore our earthly, or human, perspective on things. The Protestant Reformation, likewise, drew the individual conscience into the centre of people's outlook. These shifts were to be definitive of the modern consciousness.

Every culture has its shadow side and it is no different with the modern period in European history. The fascination with science and scientific method has led to an oversight of the person of the scientist as agent, as the one doing science. An unhelpful reductionist view of the world would see human persons as fully explicable in terms of biological, or sociological, determining factors. At the same time, the greater appreciation of individual freedom has led to the idea that there is no objectivity in ethics, that all ethics is relative to one's culture.

As I understand it, such conclusions are alien to the spirit of the African traditional thought-world. How to regain a sense of the human person's capacity to know things more or less as they are, and to judge what is of true value? It is in this context that Aristotle's approach again comes into play This whole book articulates a way forward, based on a reworked Aristotelian philosophy and drawing on the insights of the African traditional understanding of the person.

A very brief background to the Aristotelian philosophy is necessary. The classical Greek thinkers are credited with a breakthrough in moving from a common-sense way of dealing with the questions of life, to a more self-reflective one: the 'discovery of mind', of a capacity to think about how one is thinking. Famously, Socrates made his interlocutors aware of inconsistencies in their answers to his questions. At the same time, this capacity for transcendence, to go beyond how things simply appear to one, to how they are in themselves, was seen to be in conflict with all the determinations of one's attachments, in particular one's natural desires. For Plato, the real self was the mind or the soul, not the bodily being.

Aristotle, Plato's pupil for many years, took issue with this. For him, the mind or the soul was simply the way the human being has its being, its 'form' of being, the kind of being it is. For a plant, for example, its kind of being is the capacity for living; for an animal, it is sensitive living; and for the human being, it is reasoning sensitive living. The human being enacts its nature, and develops skills or virtues appropriate to its nature, through its typical acts of sensing and reasoning. The human being is most adequately understood through these metaphysical categories.

It is easy to see why Plato's philosophy was, at first, an attractive framework for the emerging Christian community to articulate their own spirituality. Nevertheless, the deep insight of the Hebrew and Christian vision was of the basic goodness of all of creation, in all its aspects, both bodiliness and spirit. The real me is equally my mind, equally my sexuality. Aristotle was, finally, adopted by Thomas Aquinas as an appropriate vehicle for the philosophical grounding of Christian theology.

The modern period introduces a new kind of questioning. What actual evidence is there for Aristotle's - or Aquinas' - understanding of the human being? This kind of questioning is characteristic of Descartes' 'method of doubt', putting the emphasis on observation and ushering in a new period in philosophy - along with the neglect, referred to above, of how the human person is a 'subject' and 'agent', able to do science and carry out the scientific method. This neglect provoked a reaction in the twentieth century existentialist revolt against an impersonal kind of philosophy, in Kierkegaard, Kafka, Sartre, Camus and others.

The solution proposed in this book is a recasting of Aristotle's metaphysics of the human person in a framework that begins from any person's experience of being a subject and agent, the starting point for any philosophy that is going to find traction in the modern period. This experience includes the event of going beyond determinations in an act of self-reflection to reach a reasonable assessment of how things really are. A further oversight in the modern period has to do with the widespread assumption that all ethics is relative - the upshot of a greater appreciation of individual freedom of choice. And again, Aristotle's normative vision of our common human nature can be recast in a frame of thinking that incorporates the findings of the social sciences circumscribing any person's action. Two contemporary writers, in particular, are central to this reworking of Aristotle: Bernard Lonergan and Alasdair MacIntyre. This very sketchy description will be unpacked in detail in the chapters that follow.

The context of the discussion in this book is that of the African traditional thought-culture. The genius of the African philosophical tradition comes into play in countering the unhelpful tendencies in modernity, as sketched above. In addition, it foregrounds the original idea of the intersubjective facilitation of personal growth - both in how we come to greater self-knowledge and how we become more integrated and consistent in our actions.

In this respect, Aristotle's philosophy, suitably updated, is arguably of great benefit in framing a dialogue of the African tradition with modernity. This book shows how both Lonergan and MacIntyre, contemporary thinkers in the Aristotelian mould, can help in articulating an ethics that is open to the African tradition and can indeed help to take it forward. Lonergan and MacIntyre are both counter-cultural in delinking scientific method from a scepticism about human transcendence, and the liberal ideal of individual freedom from an ethical relativism. What this means exactly will show itself in the discussions that follow.

The starting point of this book is, thus, a dominant global culture emanating from the modern European tradition of thought, alongside an African traditional culture that still has purchase. Its aim is to think through the strengths and the shortcomings of that global culture. It is a culture marked by secularity, science, commerce, democratic social arrangements, and the values of procedural equality and individual choice.

Neither Lonergan nor MacIntyre are intent on simply repeating the philosophical approach of Aristotle. Rather, what we have in their writings is a reconfiguration of Aristotle in the context of science and the greater degree of individual freedom that characterises the modern period in European and global history. The key idea in the book, to say it again, is that one counter-cultural philosophy in the dominant European tradition of thought can offer a way towards a fruitful dialogue with African cultural ideas, that is to say, the neo-Aristotelian, as articulated by Lonergan, MacIntyre, and others. One pioneer of African philosophy, Placide Tempels, uses an Aristotelian-Thomist metaphysical framework to unpack traditional African cultural ideas and to see how the latter challenge modern Western ethical assumptions. Similarly, a pioneer in the South African context, Augustine Shutte, draws on similar philosophical ideas, reworked through the phenomenology of intersubjectivity, to promote African ethics. My focus in this book is on Lonergan's contribution to facilitating a dialogue with African traditional patterns of thought, and, so far as concerns ethics, on MacIntyre's communitarianism, which I show can facilitate a dialogue of African thought and European philosophical ethics.

No culture is an island, entire of itself. But how is one to sort through the blind spots of a culture, and to judge which changes would bring out the genius of that culture? In academia, African philosophy is flourishing. But is it going to make its proper impact on global thinking? Kwame Appiah's

(1992) classic account of the challenge to African thinkers, *In My Father's House: Africa in the Philosophy of Culture*, bears repeating:

> Because they are Africans rooted to at least some degree in their traditional cultures and, at the same time, intellectuals trained in the traditions of the West, they face a special situation. They may choose to borrow the tools of Western philosophy for their work. But if they wish to pursue such conceptual inquiries in the thought-worlds of their own traditions, they are bound to do so with a highly developed awareness of the challenges of Western ideas ... They are bound also to make choices within Western traditions (Appiah, 1992:137).

This question motivates my research. MacIntyre and Lonergan are thinkers who run counter to the dominant approach of the contemporary European or Western framework of philosophy and ethics. In this latter culture, an instrumentalisation of life is almost unconsciously fostered by a fascination with the technologies issuing from scientific research but which is unable to articulate the foundational value of the human person and to make thematic human transcendence. Lonergan is counter-cultural in delinking the value of greater individual freedom from a relativism that is so taken for granted in a culture of human rights. In his contemporary classic, *Insight* ([1957] 1970), he invites the reader to appropriate their capacity for intelligence, reasonableness, and responsibility. The norm of 'being a person' is at the heart of his thought.

MacIntyre is counter-cultural in uncovering the incoherences of the liberal ideal. In his classic of contemporary ethics, *After Virtue* (1981) he builds a framework for a more communitarian ethic that, in our understanding, is cognate with the African traditional understanding of the human person.

This book aims to synthesise an extended argument, which I have made in a series of journal articles and book chapters over the past three decades, on how these writers can help in thinking through an ethics that is open to the African tradition and can indeed help to take it forward. In a culturally plural society such as our own in South Africa, such an attempt is not only desirable but indeed inevitable. The point of view taken in what follows is that in this attempt Aristotle, now in contemporary guise, has a not insignificant role to play. Aristotle, in my own judgement, 'belongs' in Africa.

Chapter One

Introduction. Towards a Fruitful Dialogue

Any attempt to bring the African philosophical tradition to bear upon the global understanding of ethics is bound to be controversial. My mentor in my attempt is the South African philosopher who initiated me into the discipline of philosophy, namely the late University of Cape Town academic Augustine Shutte (d. 2016). The relevant texts here are his *Philosophy for Africa* (1993) and *Ubuntu. An Ethic for a New South Africa* (2001). I begin, however, with an account of the opposition he faced in his (pioneering, in the context of apartheid) work in this regard. I will refer, in particular, to his use, in interpreting the African philosophical tradition, of his own Aristotelian philosophical background as reformulated in a different cultural frame of thinking by the neo-Hegelian phenomenologists. In Chapter 2, I draw on Shutte's analysis of the intersubjective transactions that facilitate personal growth and, arguably, bring into play the empirical findings of psychology into an elaboration, in a post-traditional culture, of the ethics of *Ubuntu*.

No tradition is static. All traditions grow through their encounter with new situations. But how is one to judge what developments genuinely bring out the real genius of the tradition? In this regard, as mentioned above, I bring in two counter-cultural Western thinkers as guides for the journey, namely Alasdair MacIntyre and Bernard Lonergan. MacIntyre is acutely conscious of possible cultural bias in philosophical ethics (the topic of Chapter 3), a bias uncovered by what one may call the sociology of ethics as a discipline, and which he executes brilliantly in his celebrated *After Virtue* (1981). Being aware of those factors that form the background to ethics as a social practice is, I think, crucial for any attempt to develop an ethics in the context of the African philosophical tradition. The hybrid frame of thinking that will result is what one hopes for - an approach that I develop in the final chapter of the book, on teaching ethics and philosophy to school learners.

Lonergan and MacIntyre are broadly speaking in the Aristotelian tradition in ethics, a tradition that runs in some ways counter to the modern liberal approach. Similarly, one pioneer in African philosophy, the Belgian missionary Placide Tempels (see below, Chapter 3), in articulating the African genius as he sees it, is drawing on his philosophy background in this premodern tradition - that of Aristotle and the Christian philosopher Thomas Aquinas - for whom Aristotle is referred to simply as 'the philosopher'.

This is a book on ethics, with one eye constantly on what is called for in my own cultural milieu, namely an ethic that can also speak to the African traditional thought-world. My concern is not to develop an 'African ethics' as such - this is something done by a number of excellent philosophers in this part of the world - but rather to focus on how to grow an integrated hybrid form of ethical thinking that corresponds to our hybrid culture. In this project, I want to draw attention to the work of the Washington DC-based Council for Research in Values and Philosophy, in promoting this hybrid kind of thinking over the past few decades. See, for example, Cochrane and Klein (2000), Walmsley (2011), Etieyebo (2018) and Mangena and McClymont (2018).

In my own contribution to this project, I find Bernard Lonergan as someone who has thematised the world of subjectivity and interiority in a way that is an invitation to any person to take up their own personal intellectual journey. Such journeying will inevitably build on the riches of their cultural milieu. In the global situation, this is a milieu which is scientific and secular, which is aware of a historical positioning and of the pressure of the urge to greater individual freedom of choice. The challenge for a philosopher in Africa is to forge a path that recognises the excesses of individualism but embraces the value of the individual subject in taking up the tradition. Lonergan is counter-cultural in showing the incoherences of a relativism that has often seemed to go hand in hand with greater individualism and indeed with the tradition of human rights - enshrined so definitively in the Constitution of the Republic of South Africa (RSA, 1996).

Modern philosophical thinkers in the European tradition tend to be grouped as empiricist or rationalist, as sceptical or realist. Lonergan's reworking of the Aristotelian approach can be described as a 'transcendental Thomist'. Very briefly, this refers to a non-sceptical approach to philosophy, affirming our capacity to know the truth and the idea that it makes sense to try to do what is good. These are points of view assumed by Aristotle and Aquinas but Lonergan casts these ideas in a modern frame that sees itself articulating not 'natures' but the structures of the intentional subject and agent. The 'bird's eye view' assumed by a Plato or an Aristotle has been, famously, thrown into doubt in the modern period, in the first place by Descartes, and then by Kant. Lonergan has learned from Kant, grounding his non-sceptical approach not in a metaphysics but in our cognitional operations, hence 'transcendental'. The transcendence is discovered in the process of reflection on how we know anything at all and how we come to decide what is good to do. This philosophical approach is one trend amongst others but its importance for philosophical articulation of African traditional thought is immense; at least this is what I will argue, simply by showing how it can cut through those frames of thinking destructive of - rather than reformative of - traditional-religious thinking.

These two thinkers form the backdrop to the foundational chapters of the whole book. Lonergan's influence on Chapter 4 is evident, introducing a metaphysics that can embrace the African thought-world, as well as Chapter 5, on Lonergan's idea of the 'differentiation of consciousness', key to any appropriation in our own contemporary culture of the African tradition. Once one turns directly to ethics it is the communitarian approach of MacIntyre that can help interpret African ethical culture in a way that is in dialogue with the liberal ideal (Chapter 6), and that, through a virtue ethics approach, can furnish a critique of the shortcomings of an excessively commercialised society (Chapter 7).

Part Three gathers together various publications applying these basic ideas to particular ethical issues. In Chapter 8, it is argued that the modern Western dichotomy of person and nature – so destructive of environmental value – does not pertain to the African philosophical tradition. Chapter 9 (co-authored by Markus Detterbeck) argues that the commercial pressures on an ethical tradition (in this case, that bound up with the black male choral practice, *amakwaya*) must needs be resisted, and being conscious of what is at play here is the first step in such resistance. Chapter 10 looks at the ethical challenges to do with the norms of professionalism in developing countries and judges the practice of mercenaries, not uncommon in Africa, to be destructive of the broader ethical tradition. Chapter 11, stepping into the intersection of theology and ethics, takes issue with the type of secular public policy that has been adopted, largely uncritically, by independent African states; again, an awareness of the history of such policies and the implied understanding of religion is the first step in growing a public policy appropriate for the African cultural milieu.

Finally, Part Four is a collection of papers written on the direction forward for philosophy and ethics in the university curriculum. In these more programmatic discussions, much of what has been developed in the earlier foundational chapters is repeated in summary form.

The whole book can be read as kind of background material for the way forward. No culture is monolithic, and this is also the case with the European tradition. It is important, for the purposes not of scoring points but of building convergences, to follow threads in European thought that can be seen as cognate with African tradition. It is important to work with, and at the same time against, dominant institutional practices. The European (and global) tradition can and must develop (hopefully through the benign influence of the African perspective, as I emphasise in this book). At the same time so too the African tradition, and it is important to thematise this in particular with respect of the growth of science. The African ethical tradition gives us a framework to appropriate science critically, and to resist the unhelpful aspects of the scientific culture.

I begin with a simple example of the task of capturing a tradition. When Augustine Shutte published a book on something called 'African philosophy' he nailed his colours to the mast: it was, he argued, the Aristotelian and Thomist tradition of thought, predating the culture of modernity, that could usefully be seen as a partner to thinking through African tradition. He was immediately shot down by a prominent colleague at the University of Cape Town. Philosophy is not about any particular culture, argues Holiday (1994), but is critical and universal. Holiday nevertheless affirms the importance of relating European philosophy to the African context. But he betrays a conception of academic inquiry so narrow as to make the project impossible of execution. There is, he contends, a set of topics that are definitive of the discipline of philosophy, arguing that Shutte diverges from this, failing even to mention Descartes and preferring to see merit (and usefulness) in the contemporary reworking of the tradition of Thomas Aquinas. Shutte's intuition is that it is through this tradition that we can see how African ideas of humanity and interpersonal influence, originally articulated in a non-philosophical image, can be given a philosophical framing and so influence the broader global practice. However, for Holiday (1994:131), these ideas do not merit to be called 'philosophy'. Basically, he says, Shutte chooses to sidestep the content of what counts as important philosophy. The critic is concerned that, for example in the matter of 'truth', Shutte simply gives a summary account of what it is to judge that some idea truly represents things as they are. But this account is "a hotly contested set of postulates", the critic complains. And Shutte fails to address these debates.

The point being made by the critic points to the priority of philosophical *method*. How valid is this criticism? There are indeed African philosophers who lay the emphasis on method (Bodunrin, Wiredu, Oruka and Hountondji are cited by Shutte); this emphasis, however, goes along with a tendency to adopt an already established *content* to philosophical topics (more about this in Chapter 3). Shutte chooses rather to follow those who are more concerned with the actual content that is drawn from traditional African thought-patterns and systems of value (Gyekye, Kagame, Tempels, Ruch are mentioned by him). The point is very well put by Gyekye, who writes the starting points, the organising concepts and categories of modern African philosophy [should] be extracted from the cultural, linguistic and historical background of African peoples, if that philosophy is to have relevance and meaning for the people, if it is to enrich their lives. (Cited in Shutte, 1993:17)

Shutte adds that there is no route to philosophical truth except via reflection on one's own cultural milieu; that some or other philosophical idea is true or not must necessarily be "tested against the reality of one's own experience" (1993:20).

Here we get to the core of the problem: how one is to understand the relation between ordinary experience (including that of African traditional culture) and the sciences. The dominant philosophical tradition that Shutte has identified as a problem for the project of engaging with African traditional thought has a conception of science as disqualifying that ordinary experience of oneself. Here, the dominant tradition has a sensitive spot and Holiday immediately attacks Shutte as being "hostile to the methods of the natural sciences." He links this to Shutte's supposed neglect of the proper standards of academic inquiry. We need therefore to say something about this very central philosophical issue, a key to our whole discussion of ethics, philosophy and the African tradition. I judge Shutte's contribution to be of major importance, as will be evident in the course of my discussion. But before that, Shutte's final retort to this criticism is worth noting. It is that, as he says, "academics are also human beings, and it is more important to be good at being human than good at philosophy" (1993:6). It is worth the effort to turn to an engaged inquiry even if it stands as less 'academic'.

Our concern is with engaging the African tradition of thought. In his foreword to Shutte's (1993) book on the African-influenced approach to philosophy, Denis Hurley puts his finger on the central (or one of the most central) topics: the interaction of African traditional thought with science and scientific methods. "Africa must adopt a scientific culture if it wishes to develop but, in doing so, is it inevitable that it should sacrifice such profound truths as those contained in its own traditional ideas of vital force and community?" (in Shutte, 1993:2). Shutte, he adds, is offering a way through this. Accompanying the emergence of a scientific culture has been the myth that the only proper knowledge is that gained through the sciences. And this implies a sidestepping of the human capacity to go beyond any final determinations, natural or social; it implies a constricting determinism in philosophy and is linked to a reductionist materialism in ethical thinking.

If engaged philosophy is to get underway it is important, then, to show we can trust our ordinary experience. What the myth accompanying the growth of science and the rise of Western culture misses, however, is the person of the scientist himself, "as one who knowingly and deliberately produces science, and with it the scientific picture of the world... the scientist as a thinking and choosing subject, that is as an agent" (Shutte, 1993:35). Understanding *that*, is the matter of philosophy. Of course, science studies human beings. But the activity that actually is science is a normative set of procedures "always presupposed to the body of knowledge that it produces and not included in it". Any philosophy that misses this point will be out of touch with ordinary experience, the ordinary experience that one is trying to draw on in doing philosophy in the context of the African tradition. Those "profound truths" Hurley mentioned above are truths about our experience of ourselves. And this experience is that of not, in the final analysis, being fully determined by the causes uncovered in the sciences. We are talking here of experiencing our capacity to know the truth and our sense of responsibility. "In everyday life we take both for granted. We would be stupid not to... However much we believed in the truth of determinism... we would still retain this sense of responsibility for those acts we had deliberately decided on" (Shutte, 1993:71).

What is important is that the philosophical framework cannot shut down the African experience of human persons transcending the realm of the merely material and the idea that in order to develop we need to be empowered by others. These two ideas are connected. The whole approach of this book is concerned with developing this point of connection, hence the focus on how we understand science in the context of an ethical tradition of intersubjectivity. Something needs to be said about this at the beginning, and it is important to recognise here Shutte's account, influential in all that follows. Shutte points out that science uncovers the role that some or other cause plays in determining the nature of the thing under inquiry. This is not the case with the human person insofar as it can be affirmed to have the power of self-possession. What does this mean? We refer here to the capacity of the person to be aware of and act upon itself as a totality, in the classical terminology of Thomas Aquinas, the power of *reditio in seipsum* (turning back on itself). Shutte (1993:67) explains that this power is

> revealed in the peculiarly radical self-awareness and self-determination of persons, could not be a characteristic of anything material since it involves the presence of the intellect, as a whole, to the whole of itself, not of one part to another as, for instance, in a self-scanning computer. This capacity of the intellect to be present to itself and act upon itself thus shows that it is simple, in the technical sense of having no co-existing parts, and so immaterial.

Why is this important for the development of an ethics that takes forward the African tradition of thought? Self-realisation, in this tradition, comes about through being powered by another. But is this not simply an ethic restricting each person to the role ascribed by their society? On the model of a scientific explanation, the more one person acts, as the cause of the other, the less the person acted upon. Seeing the person's fundamental capacity as, strictly speaking, non-material opens up a different perspective. This freedom is enhanced not restricted by a certain kind of influence of other persons.

Perhaps the easiest way of seeing this is to take the example of the newly born infant. In the absence of the mother's benevolent influence on the neonate, and not simply the fulfilment of its biological need for food, for example, the child fails to show proper development. This is termed 'hospitalism'. The kind of causality operative here is not strictly speaking of a scientific nature, but rather is thematised in philosophical inquiry into interpersonal transactions. Non-scientific yet crucial for an adequate account of ethics. In the African cultural tradition we have a framework that can give the necessary impetus to follow this up in our post-traditional context. This is what I will suggest in the course of the book, returning to these underlying themes in a number of different topics.

Part One

Ethics and the African
Philosophical Tradition

Chapter Two

Being a Person in the Context of African Traditional Thought

In the Bantu linguistic groups, the key metaphysical and ethical notion is that of 'being a person', the root *ntu* (pertaining to the human person) being common to a number of languages, as in *muntu* (Shona) or *umuntu* (isiZulu, isiXhosa), or *motho* (Sesotho, Setswana). This is a normative idea: a boy or girl is initiated and develops, through progressively more responsible participation in society, into an adult man or woman. "The word 'muntu' includes the idea of excellence, of plenitude of force at maturation," explains Menkiti (1979:158). In isiZulu the popular saying is *umuntu ngumuntu ngabantu*, a person is a person through persons, similarly in Sesotho *motho ke motho ka batho babang*. Quoting Tempels, Shutte (1993:57) notes the fundamental norm of African ethics is human nature itself: "It is the living *muntu* who, by divine will, is the norm of either ontological or natural law."

The aim in this chapter is to move this idea forward, by posing to it questions arising from our own context of global modernity. More specifically, this is by unpacking what is involved in the growth in motivational integration. As mentioned in the Introduction, I will draw on the writings of Augustine Shutte on the necessary conditions for personal growth – this includes, apart from the books mentioned above, his unpublished Ph.D. thesis (Shutte, 1981). My aim is to highlight certain ideas in Shutte's account which answer directly to the question I pose to African ethics.

In African traditional thought the idea of our spiritual nature goes hand in hand with the notion of the intersubjective conditions for growth as a person. In the contemporary context, however, culturally pluralist and with a technocratic and individualistic mentality, the concept of spirituality is interpreted dualistically, and intersubjectivity reduced to the notion of social conditioning, entailing an ethical relativism. The challenge then is to reformulate these ideas so as to bring out their original challenge to the dominant materialist metaphysics and utilitarian moral thinking of contemporary society. In the first section below, I suggest traditional African ethics, focusing as it does on the community, gives inadequate attention to growth in personal unity, in integrity. It does however indicate an effective motivational source for good action, a problem I illustrate through a brief discussion of Derrida's attempt to reintroduce into ethics the centrality of personal integrity. I then turn to a contemporary personalist version of the Thomist conception of the unity of the person, which I judge to answer to the problem at hand.

An ethics of respect (*tsika* / *isihlonipho*)

An often-remarked phenomenon about African morality is its emphasis on respect (Shona *tsika*, Zulu *isihlonipho*). It stresses conformity and respect over and above principle and conscience, shame more than guilt. And this does not, according to the Swedish anthropologist Jacobsen-Widding (1997), at first sight even *look* like morality, which she thinks of in terms of norms embodying a concern for the well-being of others. *Tsika* (and the same is true of *isihlonipho*) can also be rendered as 'good manners', or 'the proper way to greet people'. And how could concern with *appearing* respectable (a self-centred concern) be thought of at all as an *ethics*, in the European conception thereof?

A radical explanation of this phenomenon is given in a well-known article by Menkiti (1979), cited above. In the African conception, Menkiti argues, the community in a sense *confers* personhood on individuals. He quotes John Mbiti: "I am because we are, and since we are, therefore I am." The person is not defined by some or other property (reason, or the power of choice) but by a set of relationships. Compared to Western thought, the individual is not as distinct from others, but also not as unified. Concern for solidarity overrides concern for what is due to the individual. Menkiti goes further and points to the fact that the newborn baby - before its ritual incorporation into the community - is referred to as an 'it'; and while in the common European outlook the title 'person' is removed at death, this is not at all the case in African thought: the ancestors, the living dead, are properly speaking persons since they continue to play a role, and this is even increased. However, Menkiti (1979:161) does not want to speak of 'collective immortality': once the community has forgotten the individual name of an ancestor, that person reverts once again to an 'it': personhood is no longer conferred on that entity by the community. And this would indicate that the regard of the community, of others, is not something valued simply as giving us a certain status, but rather as more than this: as giving us our very being. We are only what we are in the eyes of the other. And this would seem to put an arbitrary limit on what a person can grow into. Indeed it throws into question whether persons are really by nature self-transcending and free. As Shutte (1993:56) puts it: "If the self is constituted by its relations with others, what are the relations *between*?" This then is the first question to be kept in mind as we turn below to the Thomist understanding of the person and of the natural capacity for growth in freedom.

Jacobsen-Widding's analysis of African thinking on morality brings out a further question central to a critically developed African ethics, and that is the need for the more developed person to be motivated to *concern themselves* with the less developed. Further reflection on the ethics of *tsika*, respect, brings Jacobsen-Widding to the conviction that her first impressions were wrong: what is at stake in the rituals of respect is the expression of 'social personhood', affirming the set of rights and obligations recognised in that culture. What is different here is simply that while in her own Swedish society (egalitarian, Protestant) this set pertains to the individual, in African culture it accrues more to particular social categories, father (*baba*), elder brother, wife, mother, first-born son, and so on. So it was mistaken to think of African 'morality' as self-centred: it is, she concludes, "a matter of recognition of the social value of both the Self and the Other" (Jacobsen-Widding, 1997:51).

Jacobsen-Widding points to the importance of hierarchy in African society, social interactions being marked by such distinctions of relative status in all kin relations except for those between joking partners. It would seem to be worthwhile to suggest - Jacobsen-Widding does not - an explanatory link between these two central ideas - morality in terms of *tsika*, and hierarchy. According to the African conception, we need to see the actual social connectedness as primary. Underlying moral prescriptions lies the fundamental power or 'vital force,' *serit'isithunzi*, which is the source of the dignity of the persons and of the attitude of respect amongst them (Sesotho *hlompho*). *Seriti* (Sesotho) or *isithunzi* (isiZulu) - words which can also mean the person's shadow, and hence the *effect* of the individual on the world around them, their effective influence - is manifest in bodily strength and power but encompasses the whole person at their most intimate. It is shared through sexual transmission as well as interaction between the more developed (the elders) and those still developing members of the community. Ultimately all forces reside in God who causes things to be and to grow, and thereafter in the ancestors, elders, and so on. Life is an exchange of influences amongst hierarchically ordered persons and powers, giving and receiving. All evil is diminishment of force. And the affirmation of this social and metaphysical hierarchy is the most important thing in any social interaction, and each agent should govern their behaviour with this in mind. Hence the importance of *tsika*.

Jacobsen-Widding gives an entertainingly honest account of herself being tripped up, in her dealings with the Manyika people of Zimbabwe by the African concept of morality. There is a certain white farmer 'Mr. George,' whom she considers as possessed of less integrity than, for example, herself, in other words promoting his own interests (fencing off his farm) at the expense of those of the Manyika people, still the people accept him as a good man. She voices her objections, thinking along the lines of an abstract equal treatment of all, while he, as the people say, has no such conception of equality (he seems not to consider the individual Manyika his equal) but still includes those he deals with - embraces them - by greeting and acknowledging them in the proper way (i.e. not simply proceeding immediately to the business at hand). He is a "big man", they explain, and: "He makes us big" (Jacobsen-Widding, 1997:63). He makes other men grow.

What is interesting here is that Jacobsen-Widding seems not to be acquainted with the literature on the African metaphysics of vital force referred to above. And yet the congruence of conclusions is clear. Underlying the importance given to respect lies the aim of developing persons to their fullness of power. How can this be possible unless one person has the fullness of power and confers it on others who can develop in no other way? Social hierarchy (grounded in hierarchy of personal power, *isithunzi*) is seen simply as a fact. Recognising the inferior person is the way of including them, making them a part. And here we have a reason, at least in germ, for the more developed person taking regard for the less developed - the problem mentioned above. It is that by doing so, one affirms the social connectedness that underlies both my own power and that of the other, to the extent that he or she possesses it. This would seem to be the meaning of the popular saying, 'A king is a king through the people.' As she says (1997:55), "the Manyika regard the recognition of an inferior person's social personhood as equally important as the recognition of someone's superiority."

Yet there remains a problem. Jacobsen-Widding observes, without passing any value judgement, that in Africa social personhood submerges the individual, which is less the case in, for example, Swedish society. She quotes the strange-sounding but important Fulani (West African) saying: "Three things are indignities for a respectable person: I have lied, I have farted, I have stolen." How are we to make sense of this; to us, confused juxtaposition of incommensurable categories. What is evident here is that the stress is on the indignity of *having to say*, 'I have lied' and so on. And it is undignified because it shows, like the other two instances, an inability to be in control of one's life and surroundings: 'lying' is shorthand for making any mistake, even unintentional, and 'stealing' indicates that the person "has failed to manage his own life circumstances" and also, in the case of stealing food, to control his appetite (Jacobsen-Widding, 1997:50-51). This example highlights a problem in traditional African ethics not brought out by Jacobsen-Widding, namely the fragility of the operation of the system of social personhood. This system - the proper hierarchical social arrangements - is in part maintained *by its public confession*, in the correct greeting rituals etc.; in the instances cited in the Fulani saying however they are flouted by the transgressions being *revealed*. Concealed and nonmanifest the individuality of the person nevertheless remains, the ever-present possibility of mistakes, of tripping up in the face of social demands and so revealing the still-developing individual underneath, and in particular the individual *with a mix of motivations, both social and selfish*. And with this problematic actual individual submerged, so too lies undeveloped the set of virtues needed to sustain integrity. The details of the *development* of one's motivational structures need to be clarified if ethical reflection is really going to make an impact on how people in the long term behave and hence on the quality of social life.

We are suggesting then the dangers of a notion of *Ubuntu* – humanity achieved through others – without an adequate articulation of the conditions for growth in personal integrity. "What falls on one, falls on all", says one writer (cited in Magesa, 1997:66). Many of our students from the Zulu community, women in particular, welcome the advent of an individualist mentality as a positive, liberatory change from the traditional social norms. It will be important, then, to distinguish the *measure* of greater individual freedom that goes along with the emergence of a plural society, from a complete loss of the tradition.

Jacobsen-Widding does not really bring out why we should take African conceptions of morality seriously, i.e. *for our own understanding of morality*. By virtue of the nature of their discipline, anthropologists would seem committed to an ethical relativism. But we do not have to go all the way with Jacobsen-Widding. Morality, we can say, includes not only as modern European thinking would have it, norms regulating our dealings with others (contractualist ethics), but concern for the well-being of persons, both self and others. This has been stressed in the revival of the virtue tradition in ethics. Here, in the African conception, is suggested an effective motivational source of good action, i.e. action that promotes the well-being of self and others. This contention can be supported with an illustration from one contemporary attempt to reach beyond individualist subjectivism in ethics.

The inaccessibility of an ethic of personal responsibility

The whole trend of modern thinking about the person lacks a grounding for understanding how 'personal integrity' could have a concrete normative content, and not simply mean sticking to your principles, but could grow in its depth and quality. In the analytic philosophical tradition we find the idea of the 'self' very problematic - the self is the person, says Kenny (1989:87) for example, attributing the mistaken notion of the self in part to the influence of our grammar (i.e. in saying 'I kicked myself' and then supposing that the 'self' must differ from 'me'). No concept of growth here, and the reason is easy to find: no content is prescribed for the person and their commitments, so there can be no idea of approaching this content in an ever-fuller way. Self-knowledge is not given the centrality that we will here, in constituting how one understands the person. But we can begin to build on a different tradition, deriving from the Hegelian concept of the person as self-expressive, as relating herself to herself. I focus in particular on the concept of authenticity.

In Western personalist thinking since the nineteenth century the notion of authenticity has come to the fore with Kierkegaard and then Heidegger, as a way of stressing the ideal of the integrity and wholeness of the person grounded in being true to their inner or given nature, rather than being false - in some way betraying what one is - or divided. It is related to 'wholeheartedness' (Harry Frankfurt) and also to personal responsibility. Derrida (1995) too, has returned to this idea in his book *Donner la Mort*, translated as *The Gift of Death*. He takes the much-discussed example of 'the binding', Abraham's decision to sacrifice his beloved son Isaac in order to fulfil his obligations to Yahweh, his calling. Derrida refers in particular to Kierkegaard's use of this as a case study in *Fear and Trembling* (1843 and 1986). Abraham "assumes the responsibility that consists in always being alone, entrenched in one's own singularity at the moment of decision" (Derrida, 1995:59-60). And this implies an inability to articulate one's reasons for one's action: any articulation would be in public terms. True responsibility implies secrecy.

If we keep in mind that Kierkegaard is benefiting from Hegel's critique of Kantian ethics, we can explain this point of view as follows. Because each situation is particular, special, the question always arises as to how and to what extent any moral rule is, here, actually applicable. To answer the question, I must make my own judgement. But I am not master of how what I do is *classified*. The standard moral categories, the only ones available through which to articulate my reasons for action, might not be exactly applicable. But they are used and I am judged. And the courage to face this misunderstanding - as Abraham does - is given, as the 'religions of the Book' tell us, in my personal confrontation with the absolute other, which opens me up to greater willingness.

Derrida concludes that the generality of ethics incites us to irresponsibility, impelling one to employ inappropriate categories in a situation which calls for creative singularity. He quotes Kierkegaard: "the ethical is the temptation". The paradox of absolute responsibility "remains irreducible to presence or presentation" (Derrida, 1995:61-64). It must be accepted in silence, and this is reinforced by the 'secret' nature of the relation with the absolute other, who is "absolutely transcendent, hidden, and secret in this dissymmetrical alliance." In this sense, each individual is "inaccessible, solitary, transcendent, nonmanifest" (Derrida, 1995:73-78).

But is there not a danger here in too much silence? How does one, in a society without the benefit of a common religious tradition, avoid a subjectivist interpretation of such ethics? Do we not need to develop - for example in order to form the most sensible public policy in the context of developing nations, balancing individual freedom with the promotion of social participation - what precisely growth *as a person* consists in, growth in that uniqueness in each person's 'singularity' in the free acceptance of responsibility?

There is the notion here that our moral source, or springs of action, flow out of our participation in an intersubjective relation with a personal other, one who possesses, and is able and willing to communicate, a fuller unity of individuality than we have. I have suggested that underlying Kierkegaard's (and others') attempts at ethics lies Hegel's critique of Kantian dualistic morality, an attempt to restore the wholeness of personal response, to see the integration of the person effected through their own powers, in a process of development. We have suggested above that traditional African thinking about ethics, with its emphasis on interpersonal causality, could well provide the insights needed to complete this account of personal responsibility. But a more adequate account has to be provided of the development of one's motivational structures. My suggestion will be that the kind of philosophy developed by Shutte has something of genuine value to contribute here.

Shutte: The psychology of personal authenticity

We have been suggesting that true integrity and authenticity is not simply a matter of being consistent. It is a matter of growth in the scope of one's willingness to follow the insights into the truly desirable or worthwhile – and such expansion of one's horizon of willingness must come about through being inspired by another, an influence which is less controversial in the case of growth in self-knowledge. Our understanding of how persons are mutually influenced, however, is conditioned by the presuppositions of the social sciences, namely a reductionist and materialist conception, and it is significant that John Macmurray's (1961 and 1999b) classical account, *Persons in Relation*, was preceded by a critique of the social sciences (Macmurray, 1939 and 2018). The notion that an increase in personal freedom is brought about in direct (and not inverse) proportion to the increase of conditioning influence of another is only plausible on the assumption of the self-transcending nature of our personal powers. Social scientists would routinely interpret such influence not in terms of a growth in integrity but rather simply as conditioning. This is not the case, on the other hand, if agency is spelled out in terms of self-transcendence.

For my account of growth in personal unity I am going to draw almost exclusively from a section of Shutte's Ph.D. thesis, *Spirituality and Intersubjectivity* (1981). Indeed the idea that self-realisation comes about through empowerment by others is central to Shutte's thesis: he calls it "the law of growth". Shutte uses John Macmurray's account of agency and personal growth as a model for his own (Macmurray, 1999a and 1999b), which is based on the Thomist tradition in its contemporary personalist expression particularly (but not exclusively) as developed by Rahner. As Shutte points out, in order for personal growth to occur, two basic conditions need to be met: there must exist the *capacity* to rise up to the level of meaning, to live by meaning and shared meaning, to live by the motivations and understandings common to oneself and the other. And there must exist the power of unselfish love. These two questions can be addressed to any version of how personal growth occurs, including the African. The first question concerns the autonomy of the individual: we have already pointed to this issue in traditional African thought - if we are constituted by relations, what are the relations between? What exactly is our nature? This question determines *what we are able to grow into*. The second concerns the rationale for committing oneself to the other at all, in particular for the more developed person to concern themself with the less developed.

Why is a fresh philosophical psychology needed? Self-determination understood by means of a faculty psychology, the mind operating on the will, does not make clear why interpersonal causality is at issue at all. It does not really raise the question about the kind of causality that is operative in explaining the occurrence of personal growth. Popularly understood, the mind simply determines the will. The question of the *unity* of the person is not raised, or at least not brought to the fore.

But it also fails to answer the critique of those who would unmask morality as simply ideological, not entailing genuine personal and interpersonal growth. The self is determined, or determines itself, according to some or other limited ideal or self-image. Ethics as based on the classical notion of rationality as constitutive, seems unable to avoid the critique of a certain stultifying ideological side to it. Karen Horney researched how neurosis blocked human growth, proposing, for this reason, an ethic of personal growth beyond "morally right and wrong" (Horney, 1950:13-16). The failure to integrate normative personal growth (which is not far from Aristotle's understanding of ethics) with the human sciences, remains something of a philosophical scandal, as already pointed out with respect to MacIntyre's critique of the ethics of modernity. African culture, with its affirmation of a normative *Ubuntu*, forces the issue to come to a head. Thus, the radical unicity of the person, and its self-transcending nature, needs to be clarified by a more adequate psychology.

This absolute unity of the person is manifest in themselves enacting *their own* powers (the idea of self-transcendence), and so bringing about their own development. Such self-transcendence is most clearly manifest in the common act of coming to know the truth and even more so in our sense of responsibility. When I judge something to be truly so, I reflect on the applicability and adequacy of my idea about, my insight into, the matter at hand. In concluding that it is indeed adequate (or only partly so, or not at all) I *myself* determine what I should believe. In this respect I am free from conditioning influences and I enact myself. Similarly, in making a deliberate decision I consent to, or withhold consent from, a particular desire in the light of other competing desires (perhaps judged of more intrinsic worth). A desire I have consented to is more my own than one not consented to, and in this way I come to be more myself. I act for a reason. In both cases I am present to myself and it is myself (not a part of me) that acts on myself. This is the notion of self-transcendence (Shutte prefers to speak of self-enactment) or spirituality.

But while the classical texts in the Thomistic tradition develop this idea in terms of the metaphysics of 'rationality', Shutte draws more upon phenomenological accounts of intersubjectivity to explain the same point. He comments that:

> The metaphysical understanding of spirituality, which refers to all cognitive and volitional acts indiscriminately, though justified in absolute terms, is too abstract to guide our understanding of the actual dynamics of personal development... it leaves the content or object of self-enactment open and undetermined, so that there is no way of assessing or assisting the actual development of a person (1981:125).

The classical accounts were always open to being taken as a dualism of two substances, soul/mind and body. The African traditional ideal of *Ubuntu* is, similarly, not immune from this kind of interpretation. Here, on the other hand, we have a duality of relations: relation to self (self-consciousness, self-determination) and relation to other, dependence, manifest in our desires as given. And, paradoxically, the one relation is seen to be achieved *through* the other relation (thus preserving the fundamental unity of the person). In his later publication, *Philosophy for Africa*, Shutte (1993:69) comments that the freedom "that characterises persons as self-conscious and self-determining beings, is found to develop in direct and not inverse proportion to the degree of strictly personal dependence of persons on other persons. Put more simply: the more I am subject to a *certain kind* of influence of other persons, the more (and not the less) self-determining I become." We have now to see how this insight into persons impacts upon our understanding of the unity of the person.

Growth in personal integrity

The individual is one. Yet, as developing it is necessarily described by three distinct elements. Since the unity is one of self-reference, it must be internally differentiated. In other words, it is a unity which goes out of itself and returns to itself. We speak here of the 'moments' of self-knowledge and self-affirmation. In order to grow as a person - to reach the "plenitude of force at maturation" (Menkiti) - to be less divided in myself and my motivations, I need at least greater self-knowledge, insight into which of my pressing desires are the more fundamental.

Understanding the person as self-enacting, i.e. in terms of agency, entails therefore, a genetic account, and this accords well with the approach to personhood in African traditional culture. The bulk of Shutte's thesis consists in the analysis of the three necessary facets of personal becoming, which he finds it useful to think of as 'stages', the emergence of our personal powers, their development, and their fulfilment. The discussion of each of these takes the form of a model of ideal interaction between just two persons, in the first place the 'child' (representing the bare natural capacity for agency) and the 'mother' (representing whatever is necessary for this capacity to develop, its personal milieu). We are talking here about the emergence of the sheer capacity for self-realisation, of the "consciousness of oneself as self-determining, an origin of free action" (Shutte, 1993:79). The second stage has to do with the development of this capacity, with personal or moral growth, and the model here is that between two friends, one fully developed and the other developing. We can speak in this context of self-knowledge and self-affirmation. This entails growth in integration, of their cognitive, volitional and emotional lives. Finally, the fulfilment of our capacity for self-enactment is discussed within the framework of two 'lovers', fully developed, and in this case, Shutte speaks of self-transcendence and self-donation. In each case it is shown that spirituality (self-transcendence) entails intersubjectivity. Perhaps this is obvious in the case of growing self-knowledge, but it is not so obvious in the case of our sheer *possession* of self-consciousness, nor is it self-evident that we have a *continued* need for the other in the fulfilment of our personal powers.

The first stage clarifies the exact nature of our personal capacities or powers. The appearance of self-awareness in the child is a forever-astounding fact that can only be accounted for by the existence of a natural potential for such self-awareness. Only if (a) there is this potential; and (b) there is a personal environment containing unselfish love, will this occur. Only if the child is regarded as *in itself* of value (not as a 'task' within the achievable projects of the mother), will it properly develop this self-reference. Otherwise, there will be stunted growth, or - as in the famous cases of 'wild children', nurtured perhaps by a she-wolf - no coming into being of self-awareness of the radical kind at issue here, at all. How the nature of our capacity to be a person *entails* at the same time its absolute dependence for its emergence on the action of another, is well brought out by Shutte in his Ph.D. thesis (1981:88):

Whatever the particular content or character the self has, there is over and above that the reference of itself to itself in all its acts. This self-reference is neither conscious nor consented to in the case of a child. Yet no particular set of aspects of the child's life could lead to its emergence later on; it is a totally indeterminate relation of a whole to the whole of itself. Hence if it is not present at the start it will never be present at all. It can therefore only be present in the beginning as pure potentiality. For this reason it is wholly dependent for its exercise, parasitic one might even say, on the personal activity of another.

The capacity we are talking about here is then fundamentally different to other natural capacities (say, for walking). Firstly, it is non-specific, i.e. self-referring capacity - adapted only to *communicating* as Macmurray (1999b:51) points out. Second, it can enter the self-consciousness of another since it is not naturally oriented to any specific object. A correct description of the growth of a child will thus include not only how one is socialised but how one is valued.

We are, however, concerned with growth in this unity of self-reference, treated in Shutte's second 'stage' of personal growth. A variety of scholars are drawn on by Shutte in his nuanced treatment of this topic - it has to suffice simply to mention, for example, Cirne-Lima, Farrer, Johann, Nedoncelle, Macmurray, Toner, Rahner. What is important is to note here a shift from speaking of the person in terms of intellect and will, to the corresponding but more explanatory terms, self-understanding and self-affirmation. The latter terms of themselves indicate a *process*, and thus growth, as part and parcel of the meaning of these powers. They also point more directly to the problematic unity of the self. Here we are concerned with how the individual develops "so that one becomes progressively more able to fully accept and express the person one is becoming" (Shutte, 1993:80).

What would such growth entail? First, one would have to grow in self-awareness and understanding of one's real desires; secondly, one would have to accept and fully affirm this and so come to possess oneself more fully. This can be illustrated through one 'technique' for personal growth, that of psychoanalysis, which aims at facilitating insights into one's deep motivations (causing compulsive and disturbing behaviour), and the gradual acceptance of these insights so that one becomes 'more oneself', happier.

Shutte thinks of the self in terms of three related systems, the belief system, the value system, and the system of desires. Each contains a multitude of objects very scantily unified, but nevertheless in each (perhaps most evident in one's belief system) there is "a pressure towards unity and coherence, consistency and order" (Shutte, 1981:81). To understand a person is to know what they believe, especially what they believe about what is of true value, worthwhile of effort. One's beliefs may, and do, conflict with one another. Clarity on such conflicts is needed, greater self-understanding. Secondly, one has a hierarchy of commitments and values, choices habitually made which make one one kind of character rather than another. Again, there can be conflicts here too, and conflicts between one's beliefs and one's habitual choices. One's self-affirmation is half-hearted because of such conflicts. Finally, since we are talking here about an essentially (if not actually) radical *unity* of personhood and not two externally related *parts*, there is the element which is "the origin of the inner movement of the self", and this Shutte calls 'desire', "the fundamental desire to be, to be a person, to be myself, that wells up in the center of my being and shows itself in the never-ending quest for happiness and fulfilment."

> Ultimately what is most fundamental and central to the self are my desires. So real self-knowledge must be based on an insight into what I really desire, which of my desires are the most central to and important in my life. True self-affirmation, on the other hand, will consist in a whole-hearted consent to these desires and the attempt to realise them in my life (Shutte, 1993:81).

The state of incomplete development is characterised by contradictory beliefs, incompatible choices, and warring desires. There are also conflicts between what I believe I ought to do and what I choose to do, what I want to do and what I judge or choose to be right. It is clear that personal growth must entail an increase in unity. In fact, the problem of growth as a person is really one of division more than lack of any particular quality of character, of mind or will. Personal growth will not be brought about by any drug, or even with self-improvement courses. Shutte (1993:83) puts the problem well:

> If my self-knowledge is incomplete then I do not know what I really want. I will not know which desires to consent to and which to inhibit. Insofar as I encourage the superficial desires I will increase the division in myself since the deep desires which I am suppressing will not go away but instead persist in growing opposition to the rest.

Genuine wholeheartedness will be impossible. Nevertheless, the desire for such integrity persists. Affirming a *false* self makes matters worse.

> In order to maintain the illusory harmony and identity I have constructed I suppress all awareness of my real desires and all recognition of beliefs that contradict my illusions. So it is a vicious circle: lack of self-knowledge makes genuine self-affirmation impossible, the inability to affirm oneself wholeheartedly prevents real self-knowledge.

My heart is not really in the project of getting to understanding myself better.

How then can the Other inspire me to greater willingness (Derrida)? We intend here, unlike Derrida, to point to a psychological reality. I am able to affirm my friend - my blocks apply less to him - as a whole, with his set of beliefs and desires ordered in a more integrated way. And in getting to know and affirm him I affirm the deep desires that pertain to the human nature we both share. I can continue quoting from Shutte's own summary presentation (1993:85) of how this transaction occurs.

> Insofar as I really come to know him as he know himself, I come to share his own judgement of their relative importance. Moreover acquaintance with them in him puts me in touch with them in myself.

What needs to be pointed out here is that the transaction only occurs if my friend enables it. He has greater insight into our common nature.

> He is able to affirm me in a way I cannot affirm myself. He affirms my deep desires in spite of the fact that they are hidden.... And since, deep down, this is really what I want too, his affirmation of me will enable me to "open up" to him. Insofar as I open up to him I will begin to affirm him.

In the final section of Shutte's analysis of personal growth, the third stage, the desire for personal growth is seen to be one with the desire for the reciprocity of personal communion. For our purposes, this points to a way of establishing the plausibility of the more developed person having the motivation to promote the growth of the still-developing individual.

The unity pertaining to persons is a precious insight. It cuts through any dualism of reason and desire. For the person is defined in terms of a developing unity, and the powers of self-enactment - understanding and the power of choice - are united: the self that is known *is just* the self that is affirmed and vice-versa. And at a further level, the self that is known and affirmed is affirmed precisely *as a unity* of this self-knowledge and self-affirmation. So our personal growth occurs insofar as we fully affirm our deepest desire to be ourselves, to make ourselves. Our personal powers of self-enactment are also the content of this enactment.

> As the actualisation of the distinctively personal powers they are simply the subject, the person, in act. And as the central tendencies, the ultimate values, of his nature they are the object, the content, of this act (Shutte, 1981:125).

It is this turning back on oneself "that gives the unity of the person its peculiar absoluteness". The subject, and the object acted upon, have only a formal distinction. There is no separation in reality. Self-enactment constitutes a norm for us. And this undercuts any attempt to say that the normative morality is an arbitrary superimposition on persons.

> The self-enactment is thus an occurrence in the sphere of being and not only in the sphere of ideas: the self-knowledge and self-affirmation constitute the person's self-enactment of his nature.

And here we come to the point of this lengthy analysis. With this understanding of the spirituality of the person, of our personal powers, there is no danger of a dualist interpretation being seen as a reasonable approach to recapturing what is of value in traditional African thought and ethics. At the same time, we are making sense of how interpersonal causality is a reality at a trans-cultural level and is not at all a question of social conditioning: such interaction - which is also a transcultural ethical norm (understood in Africa in terms of *Ubuntu*) - makes possible the ever-deepening self-possession of individuals.

What this analysis shows is that the growth in personal unity, in motivational integration, which we identified as a largely undiscussed problematic in African traditional ethics, depends on (a) the existence of a nature of the self-referring (self-transcending) kind, which is empowered *only* through the interaction with the other of the kind we have been describing; and (b) this empowerment being actually facilitated to occur, people understanding its place in our lives, and society providing the kind of environment which supports such close, intimate, self-sacrificing relationships which are at issue here. The first condition is not fully expressed by African traditional thought, as we have argued; the second is more likely to obtain under African cultural influence than modern European.

Chapter Three

Basic Intuitions in African Ethics

Introduction

In 1981 a number of South African philosophers published a collection, *Basic Concepts in Philosophy*, edited by Zak van Straaten at the University of Cape Town. No reference to Africa was mentioned, nor indeed to any cultural context. In the Ethics section, the basic distinction was between custom (uncritical) and reasoned-out principles that are universalisable. It went without saying that such reasoned-out ethics contrasted with any African traditional or perhaps religious view. But the historical and intellectual context was shifting. Steve Biko's proscribed writings on basic African cultural concepts were already circulating clandestinely (Biko, 1978). And in the same year, Alasdair MacIntyre published *After Virtue*, a demolition job on the purported universality of the reason-based ethics at issue here; rather, he showed that the 'basic concepts' are only basic if you go along with the unstated premises. But different premises are possible, and equally 'rational'. The different sides to the debate argue from 'conceptually incommensurable' first premises, each employing "some quite different normative or evaluative concept from the others..." (MacIntyre, 1981:6-9).

Various examples illustrated the point. In the case of abortion, an act in accordance with the rights of the mother over her own body could, contrariwise, be seen as violating the fundamental principle proscribing the taking of innocent life. Both positions would seem to be legally enforceable. The rational foundation of the first would be the trump value of individual autonomy, the rational foundation of the second would be the telos of human nature. Which is more 'rational'? A third rational foundation could be the Kantian principle of universalisability: putting myself in the position of the individual to be aborted, I would be unable to will it in my own case. And this being the case, the debates are going to be interminable and unresolvable. So much for philosophy as reasoned-out ideas.

To understand how, once the African cultural context is introduced, the perspective will shift, it is useful to compare and contrast four central debates in African ethics with the debates highlighted in the ethics section of *Basic Concepts of Philosophy* (Van Straaten, 1981:163-192), hereafter, *Basic Concepts*. The first point of debate, as mentioned, concerns the nature of ethics, contrasting practices and precepts that are simply customary, for example associated with African traditional culture, with universal principles. The second focus of debate concerns the fact/value distinction. No 'ought' conclusion can be deduced from 'is' statements only because the conclusion would then contain something that is not in the premises. This would apply to factual knowledge about the telos of human nature, a central element in the *Ubuntu* idea, which does not see facts about human nature in that value-free way.

The third point of debate contrasts the role of absolutes versus that of consequences in ethics. This reflects the familiar division of ethical approaches into deontological (Kantian) ethics and utilitarian or consequential ethics. Kantian ethics seeks to secure the dignity and freedom of the person in the face of what science saw as a deterministic universe where every element is subject to a calculus. But what if freedom is achieved precisely through insertion in the world outside the individual, as in the African traditional outlook (which predates the rise of modern science). There are important implications here for business ethics and professionalism in general, giving a broader framing of an ethic of rules and, indeed, of human rights.

Fourthly, *Basic Concepts* points to the different approaches of externalism and internalism in ethics; that is to say, between seeing values as determined by the external evolutionary, biological and social environment, and seeing human behaviour as explained only by the agent's internal 'reasons-for-action'. The whole idea of the will, and of agency, is problematised, being cast as something intangible and 'ghostly'. It is also seen as 'anthropocentric'. Value, in the internalist view, is said to be simply what it is from the point of view of humans: should not other beings be taken into account? But the African traditional metaphysics sees human telos in a continuum with the telos of all of beings. Being is 'living force', running through all nature. There is no radical discontinuity between the external and internal points of view. Again, we can see implications here for an environmental ethics influenced by an African cultural context.

In what follows, each of these points will be discussed, concluding in each case with suggestions that further research might take. Finally, something must be said of what is completely left out of the picture of ethics in *Basic Concepts*, namely the historical context of resistance to the very existence of an authentic African culture, the struggle against political and cultural colonialism. Freedom, in the sense of autonomy, is a central theme in modern European ethics, but the communitarian emphasis found in African voices, such as that of Biko, sidelined or silenced in the past, will necessarily shift our understanding of the ethics of liberation. Contemporary African culture has its unique contribution to make here, exemplified, perhaps, in the way South Africa was able to transition from apartheid to democracy. The continuing debate around this, and the contrasts between the approaches of Desmond Tutu (1999) and that of Frantz Fanon (cf Pithouse, 2001), needs some mention.

Universality through an inclusivity sourced in the moral order

The first area of debate concerns the nature of ethics and the distinction, as mentioned, is between custom (localised) and morality (universalisable). Ethical judgements go beyond any parochial approach, and being reasoned out can be contrasted with religious ideas based on faith, or with custom; ethics, in other words, is secular. The shift in African ethics is to point to the dependence of such 'reason' on premises that are largely unarticulated and hence, perforce somewhat arbitrary. The question for debate is now that of the appropriate religious and metaphysical framework for ethics, casting doubt on the secular humanist assumption, which sits uneasily with African traditional culture. The debate here concerns the possibility of a spiritual reality but not one that is seen as rivalling the ordinary framework of human reason. Bénézet Bujo remarks that "it is hardly conceivable the African, whose thinking is always set in a religious context, could have a morality without God" (2009:114).

We can draw again on our summary of the findings of anthropologist Jacobsen-Widding. As we saw, the emphasis, in her research, was found to be on respect and conformity rather than conscience, shame more than guilt. And this can be contrasted with her own Swedish cultural emphasis on egalitarianism and on rights - an attitude of impartiality regarding the status of the person, disregarding, which would be shocking in the African culture, whether the person was family member, elder brother, and so on. The power hierarchy is taken for granted but this does not necessarily imply domination, and the recognition of the inferior person's personhood is fundamental.

The community, not the individual, comes first. It is only because of the community that I am who I am. Here one could pose a critical question: what if the custom is that the correct way to greet people be structurally different according to the perceived 'race' of the person being greeted? It is clear that custom is not an absolute: an inappropriate greeting based on prejudice (through a greeting that sidelines the person) would go against the principle here, excluding rather than including. This indicates that not only is sympathy with others needed, but also impartiality, as argued by Wiredu (1992).

As we saw, the ethics is framed around the value of social connectedness and underpinned by the idea of an order constituted by the fundamental power or 'vital force', the source of the dignity of persons and of the attitude of respect amongst them. The debate, then, turns on the question of the best way of re-expressing this traditional intuition in the conditions of a scientific and plural culture. Should one attempt to express it simply in terms of an exclusive humanism, shorn, as one writer puts it, of its "cloudy supernaturalist assumptions" (Farland, 2007:356). This is an attitude of those more influenced by the Analytic approach to philosophy (Gyekye; Wiredu; Metz;

Matolino). In objecting to any pretention to knowledge beyond empirical evidence, some African thinkers object to the project of delineating some supposed 'African essence', and this could apply also to the project of African ethics. In the section titled 'Critique of Ethnophilosophy' in Section 1B of Mosley's collection, *African Philosophy: Selected Readings* (1995), one finds essays along these lines by Houtondji, Appiah, Mosley, Owomoyela and Irele.

Or, contrariwise, is the religious/metaphysical framing a foundational element in the ethics, not just as a matter of fact but as a matter of logic. It cannot simply be stated that in African ethics the moral order over and above the social nexus is vital, an other-worldly reality, as Bujo seems to do, adding that God, as creator, "has to intervene in the moral order if the human person does not follow the laws set by him" (2009:114). A more extreme view is that of Sophie Oluwole (1995), who defends the reality of witches as an integral part of the world, a supernaturalist approach which would seem to undermine normal individual responsibility. Chemhuru notes, more moderately, that "beings or existence in general and morality are closely intertwined among... most African communities" (2019:60). Bidima, in support of a metaphysical grounding of African philosophy, mentions as sympathetic to this line of thought, Tempels, Diop, Senghor, Kagame, Mbiti, Mulago and others (Bidima, 1995:13). To this, one could add Magesa (1997) and Shutte (1993). Which of the two approaches, or some combination, is true, cannot be decided by counting cultures in Africa, by majority vote, because all cultures are dynamic and developing, dropping some elements and incorporating others, but would have to be argued for.

Human nature and its telos both a fact and a value

In accordance with the 'is-ought' dichotomy, values have to do with your commitments and with the principles governing this. Critics term this the 'free-floating ought', the moral imperative being somehow imposed from above, in a kind of fideism, Kant's categorical imperative. Philippa Foot (1978), famously, argued that there is no such thing, and that all moral imperatives are hypothetical, not categorical: in other words, what one should do is determined in accordance with what one aims at.

The African intuition, in contrast to any strict separation of 'is' from 'ought', is that morality is about the development of natural tendencies towards fuller being and more abundant life, this being at once a fact of our nature and a basic value. In the words of Menkiti (1979:158), as already noted, "The word *'muntu'* includes the idea of excellence, of plenitude of force at maturation." The end is assumed, but this does not imply that the ethics is uncritical, simply a cultural assumption. The ethics is grounded in a metaphysics of being, being as 'living force', and it is the same force running through all things, and ultimately not material and deterministic but spiritual, transcending social determinations. It is important for this pre-modern intuition, if it is to have purchase in our own times, to be critically developed and re-expressed can be re-expressed beyond a normative idea of culture. Tempels, as we saw above, identifies a critical viewpoint, that of "the living *muntu*", furnishing the norm of all ethical judgements (Tempels, 1959:121).

This idea is common amongst commentators. But importantly, the human nature being drawn upon here does not refer to some fundamental property or set of properties (say, reason) asserted of individuals in an uncritical and premodern way. For example, Achille Mbembe writes in *Le Monde* (December 15, 2019) (my translation) that

> Western philosophers of the subject... start from the idea that there is something that is intrinsic to us, fixed and stable and unvaried. Creator of himself, a person gets his identity from himself, and because he has a reflexive consciousness and an interiority, he is distinct from all other living species.

In contrast, the identity of the person in African traditional thought was more dispersed. What was important

> was not the self as such, but the manner in which one composed and recomposed oneself, each time in relation to other living entities. In other words, personal identity was nothing other than the process of becoming, within

the tissue of relationships of which each person was the living sum.

There is an important point here. The procedural approach to ethics, grounded on the is/ought distinction, takes any substantive notion of human nature, its telos, as culturally arbitrary. The latter, as Smith (1994:91) put it some years ago, amounts to "simply a mob forcing its commonly agreed standard on another group whose agreement they do not have." But this overlooks what is being put forward here, namely an ethic not founded on some or other normative property definitive of the person but on the norm of active participation. In the African traditional approach to ensuring that human freedom is respected and developed, the idea of freedom is not that of refusing any substantive specification of this freedom, a freedom floating free from human nature, a 'for-itself' cut loose from any 'in-itself', to use the existential terminology of Jean-Paul Sartre . This point will have implications for how the struggle against colonialist structures of domination is conceived.

The debate then, is not how to spell out the principles recognising individual autonomy (the fictional discussion of persons 'behind the veil' in John Rawls' political ethics). The debate is rather on the conditions for the enactment of the power of being for the other, the ideal expressed in the proverb alluded to in Chapter 2, *motho ke motho ka batho babang* (Sesotho), *umuntu ngumuntu ngabantu* (isiZulu): a person is a person through other persons. An important point would be to turn that idea into a psychological reality, specifying the requisite virtues of character.

Whereas the framing of morality in terms of an 'ought' abstracted from any substantive human values, the question arises as to motivation for following this moral imperative. Of any such ought, one can always ask, Why should I? Why honour the implicit contract with others if in any particular case I find I can disregard it with impunity? In contrast, the African ethic encompasses the motivational dimension, there being no radical distinction or antithesis between the good of oneself and the good of the other. The centrality of this idea of a shared human good means society may even be seen as something like a single person.

But it is important, for further research, to spell this out in terms of the actual interpersonal transactions that bring out personal growth, an idea that can be traced to Hegel's phenomenology of intersubjective recognition, and drawn on, as we saw in the previous chapter, by Augustine Shutte. This will obviate any dualist misinterpretation of the African ethic.

Ethics as recognising autonomy versus ethics as building community

Whether deontological or consequentialist, the *Basic Concepts* approach to ethics is founded on the idea of individual autonomy. In the consequentialist frame of thinking, it is the autonomous individual who must perform a calculus on pleasures and pains in deciding on any course of action. Kant's approach is likewise instructive: it is an attempt to rescue morality from a Newtonian deterministic world, positing persons as ends-in-themselves, of absolute not calculative value. Ethics, in Kant's view, is absolutist, grounded in this affirmation of freedom from determination. Any calculation of consequences will be a reasoning that disrespects this freedom, source of human dignity.

But the African traditional cultural framework predates the rise of science and the split between free persons and a deterministic world subject to instrumentalist attitudes. The African ethical absolute, in contrast, lies in affirming the other and responding to the other's affirmation of oneself. It centres on building up a shared space of common values, more concerned with the achievement of community through dialogue than with the purity of one's moral conscience or a focus on rights. The starting point of ethical reasoning is that shared norm of our common human nature. Since this norm is realised only through interpersonal transactions (the 'mother' through her attentiveness bringing the neonate to the beginnings of self-consciousness, for example), it is not an obstacle to our free self-determination. The focus of ethics is not, as in the European tradition, individual autonomy, but community. As Metz (2009:343) notes, "like the utilitarian, the Kantian places no fundamental moral value on identifying with others. A Kantian can respect others by being distanced and not including them in any 'we'." The African intuition is, however, that personal growth and effective freedom are brought about through other persons, and in no other way, through the building of personal community.

In the context of a culture of science and its operative picture of causality, however, a further point must be made. This is that growth in personal freedom is, paradoxically, brought about in direct, and not inverse, proportion to the increase in the conditioning influence of a beneficial other. This is only plausible on the assumption of the spiritual, rather than simply material, nature of the agent's powers. The bias of the social sciences, by contrast, by virtue of their being limited to empirical observations, is that such influence simply amounts to conditioning. In the background is the idea of an ideal of human being, the telos of human nature; if this is thought of as the possession of some properties, then we have a dualism of these properties and the actually existing desires and inclinations of the person. There would be something arbitrary about compelling the preferencing of these above the person's inclinations. But this is not the case in the African ethical frame of thinking. The ethical task for the person is thought of as unifying the different relations constituting one's identity. There is a duality, but it is a duality of relations: relation to self (self-determination) and relation to other (dependence, manifest in our given desires and inclinations): and the first relation is achieved through the other. I can repeat the description given by Shutte, unpacked in greater detail in the previous chapter, The freedom that characterises persons as self-conscious and self-determining beings, he writes, "is found to develop in direct and not inverse proportion to the degree of strictly personal dependence of persons on other persons. Put more simply: the more I am subject to a certain kind of influence of other persons, the more (and not the less) self-determining I become" (Shutte, 1993:69).

This shift in emphasis from principles to community has implications for ethics in the field of business practice. The metaphysical background to the ethics is, strictly speaking, the idea of an operative spiritual dynamism, but this is not understood as opposed to materiality. In a sense, however, this can be seen as eminently practical, even utilitarian and materialistic, as pointed out by Gyekye (cited in Murove, 2009a:230). In a secular and commercialised global culture there is a danger here in the emphasis on the group, on kinship and family. For, it could lead to a neglect of the internal, constitutive goods of the professions, legal, medical, teaching, and so on, in favour simply of success in a competitive sense, maximising prestige rather than excellence. Apart from the internal goods of the social practice, there is always the need for institutions to frame the practice: teaching needs administration, rules for promotion and for the allocation of salaries, and so on. But in a commercialised society, these are in danger of simply overriding the internal values that are valued by society: justice in law, health in medicine, and so on. As MacIntyre (1981:181) argues, "the ideals and the creativity of the practice [and] the cooperative care for the common goods of the practice [are] always vulnerable to the competitiveness of the institution". Without the virtues of character, "without justice, courage and truthfulness", the practices could not resist the corrupting power of institutions. This point will be taken up in greater detail in Part Two.

Taking the short cut to prestige and success is taking the path of corruption. In the face of African traditional culture at least one development expert has suggested, in the title of his book, "working with the grain", cooperating with systems of patronage, rather than emphasising principles and human rights. "Manichean campaigns," he writes, "to root out corruption polarize: instead of bringing people together they demonise potential allies [...who] may be key parts of any effective change effort" (Levy, 2014:94). This would seem misguided. The African traditional frame of thinking has a good standard of excellence in the growth of the person and building community, and these entail truthfulness and courage. These are part and parcel of the professions and good business practice. And such values are not equivalent to success in material terms; the latter, pursued for its own sake, would be a betrayal of the values.

At the same time, one could point to the neglect in the dominant global culture, of the basic human needs for bonding and for meaning. Individual autonomy is emphasised at the expense of these equally foundational needs. Persons enter the global society not as members of particular cultural traditions but as units of production and consumption, 'atomised', in the title of Michel Houellebecq's (2001) pessimistic political novel. Here, African business ethics could contribute a valuable counter view of the matter. A legalistic and contractual approach is not always the best way forward, and Mary Clark (discussed in Chapter 7) puts forward the South African Truth and Reconciliation Commission as an example of building community in a typically African attitude of inclusivity rather than procedural justice (Clark, 2002, Chapter 10).

Human agency as developed through the 'other'

So far as concerns the externalist/internalist debate in the standard *Basic Concepts* approach, the African intuition is to see values as explained in general by the agent's internal 'reasons for action' rather than simply by the sum of the conditioning biological and social forces. In the background to this debate is the so-called 'intractable problem of free will', 'intractable' because in a universe taken apart in science the assumption is that every event, including human action, has a determining cause. But the African intuition is that persons achieve freedom *through* their natural and social conditioning environment, and not despite this or by opposing it. The internal is enacted through the external. The *Ubuntu* idea, that a person becomes a person through relationality, is key to the whole approach of African ethics. It complements and corrects the emphasis on individual freedom that is the nodal point of the standard textbooks in ethics.

The implications are big for environmental ethics. Environmental neglect comes about from a disconnect between person and nature. If one capitulates to the idea of scientism, that only empirical science gives knowledge, properly speaking, then all living beings are seen simply as functional elements in an eco-system. In that case, fairness demands that one simply calculates and compares the quantity of suffering of persons with that of other beings. But this way of seeing things is not true of persons, nor of any living organism.

The typical African traditional approach, in contrast, sees persons as part of an encompassing reality of spirit or force, of *seriti* or *isithunzi* or *ukama* (Shona), referred to by Bujo (2009:14) as the 'moral order.' To see human beings in a reductionist way as simply functional elements in an eco-system would not resonate with African cultural thought. In a contemporary dialogue with the dominant frame of thinking in modern thought, African philosophy can find cognate ideas in the premodern Aristotelian and Thomist approach. Ndaba (1999:177) argues that the vitalist trend in European philosophy may well partner African traditional thinking in a positive way. In Chapter 8, below, this point will be developed at greater length. Timothy McDermott explains it well, taking, as example, the nature of a cow. Cows, he argues, should not be thought of as "simply implementations of a function that the eco-system demands of them. Rather, they are historical facts that have just proved to be viable in that eco-system..." (McDermott, 1989:xviii). Nature is not there as an object for our will (anthropocentrism). Rather, nature is equally ourselves as subjects and agents. African ethics has to counter the unhelpful picture of the person as disengaged from and indifferent to the natural world. It is not the case that humans are imprisoned in their subjectivity, unable to grasp 'what it's like' to be another non-human being - say, a bat, in Nagel's (1979a) famous example. Humans, through the spirit that runs through nature, can transcend their particularity.

This also applies to arguments that *Ubuntu*, as Theron argues, is simply an ethic that is that of the 'tribe' (cited in Murove, 2009b:328). Again, one can draw on the non-dualist picture of the human spirit that is developed in the Aristotelian and Thomist philosophical tradition. In the act of choosing, it is argued, it is not my social or biological or social determinants that act on me, as the pistons of a car cause the vehicle to move forward, one part determining another. Rather, it is I myself who acts on myself. The self that I choose and consent to (the more generous rather than the hoarding impulse that I have to own to) is the same as the self that does the choosing and consenting. It is not one part determining another part. In reflective deliberation I am able to take into account my biases due to my being a human (not a bat) or a Zulu (not a Spaniard), my 'tribe'. Freedom is not achieved through independence from what is other than me, but in interdependence.

Resistance to global neo-colonialism

Once the European humanist tradition lost its rational grounding (hence, its universal applicability), there could be equally no appreciation of the grounding of ethics in other different cultures. If human rights was a model for the world, and originated in Europe, this could only be because of the unique circumstances of that part of the world. Other cultures, the implication was, had, in the words of Samir Amin (1989:106) simply to eliminate "the obstacles posed by their particular cultural traits, responsible for their backwardness." A similar observation was made by Tempels (1959:110) in his pioneering study of African traditional thought; he realised his approach had to contend with a general notion of European culture as "an All against a Nothing", and of the ethical educator having to clear the ground of worthless notions so as "to lay foundations in a bare soil."

The global ethical approach has, in this respect, a blind spot. We take up this point later in our discussion of the ethics of liberal democracy as a much-lauded method for social arrangements. In Chapter 11 it will be pointed out that what is missed in the taken-for-granted public policy of secularity, attached to liberal democracy, is the inherited idea of religion. Once this inherited idea is properly articulated, the process can begin of decolonialising the democratic African state's policy with regard to religion.

A different angle on these issues has to do with how liberation and resistance to domination is understood. If we go back to the impact of the work of Biko, the context of acting from the principle that we are free, we find a way into moving to an expression of the traditional African ethic that has grown through the influence of the European 'discovery' of freedom. However, insofar as a major influence here is that of Fanon, via Sartre, we have a conflict with the traditional African idea of the person as growing through other persons. It is true that Sartre does not think of consciousness as 'internal', in a kind of dualism. Rather, consciousness is always 'consciousness of' something other than the self, always already directed onto the world. At the same time, for Sartre, freedom 'pour-soi', for-itself, cannot be captured in terms of any en-soi, in-itself. This means that there can be no directionality found in the pour-soi, in the telos of our common human nature. "There is no human nature, he writes, because there is no God to have a conception of it" (Sartre, 1948:28). As Fanon argued, "I am not a potentiality of something. I am wholly what I am" (cited in More, 2004:84). This is pure Sartre. Importantly, it does not allow for the normative directionality that is core to African ethical thinking. Sartre's rejection of any such norm corresponds with a contemporary trend to see identity as 'buffered', only constituted by being mobilised, as Charles Taylor puts it in his discussion of our 'secular age' (Taylor, 2007). While this approach might suit the framework of contestation that characterises public life in the USA, it fails to bring out the unique tradition of ethical thought in the African cultural world.

Ethics as resistance carries the danger that the 'other' is demonised. It is important to be aware of the gap (as in all cultures) between the ethical ideal and the actual practice. What do you make of Western civilisation, Gandhi was asked by a reporter. The reply expresses this gap well: "I think it would be a good idea", he answered. Realist, or even pessimist, portraits of actual ethical practice in Africa are given by V.S. Naipaul (2010) and, in a more hopeful vein, by Njabulo Ndebele (2012).

Chapter Four

African Traditional Philosophy of Mind: Facilitating a Dialogue

Introduction

We turn in this chapter from ethics to a discussion of the metaphysics that underlies the ethics. Our aim is to clear the way for the development of a philosophy of mind and world that has learned from the African traditional understanding of the human person. This is necessary if there is to be a real dialogue and 'African Philosophy' is not to be something simply added onto an already existing set of core ideas. At the heart of the discussion is the African cultural notion of the person - unpacked in Chapter 2 - as intersubjectively empowered.

This carries the implication that in the African approach, the philosophy of mind will always be framed by a set of normative ideas. This metaphysics of the person - for example, denying any determinism - does not at first glance sit easily with the dominant standard Analytic approach to mind and world. In this latter approach the influence is overwhelmingly that of science and scientific method, as French philosopher Luc Ferry, looking across the channel, has remarked (Ferry, 2011:202). Within the framework of science, there is, as argued above, by the nature of things, no resources for thematising the one doing the science, the person or agent treated precisely not as one object amongst others but, of course, presupposed to science as a human project. Without this awareness it is likely that philosophy will routinely overlook, or misinterpret as a dualism, the African traditional understanding of the spiritual reality of the person. Key to such awareness is a clarification of the notion of 'objectivity'.

For the one tradition to meet the other no dubious metaphysical leap of faith is here envisaged. In MacIntyre's uncontroversial notion of philosophy as a social practice - "a coherent and complex form of socially established cooperative human activity" (MacIntyre, 1981:175) with internal goods that operate as standards of excellence - we have a picture of the participant as tied into a normative journeying from apprentice to expert or 'professed'. This point will be explored below in Part Four, on the university curriculum. You cannot be a proper participant without appreciating those standards (easy in a practice such as the game of soccer, much more difficult in the practice of family life). Getting to this appreciation is a growth moment for the novice or apprentice to the practice. The ineluctability of the framing normativity here can be seen to be isomorphic with the normativity attached, in the broader context, to the African notion of the person or *muntu*. Denying this normativity, in the case of the philosopher, amounts to a performative self-contradiction, or self-stultification: you are in fact declaring yourself out of the game (see below, the discussion of self-appropriation in the philosophy of Lonergan).

I begin, in the following section, with an introductory sketch of how, within the frame of the standard approach to philosophy of mind, one can misconstrue the African traditional notion of the spiritual reality of persons as a form of dualism. The situation does, however, also make a demand on African philosophy of mind, a tradition of thought predating the rise of science, to re-express itself in our new cultural context. And this is to the good, as the insights from the social sciences may amplify the traditional intuitions concerning the intersubjective conditions for personal growth.

In presenting some foundational notions of a philosophy of mind that has absorbed the African cultural insights into persons, I return to the pioneering work in this area of Placide Tempels (1959) (ideas developed in greater detail in Chapter 14). There is a remarkable congruency between Tempels' version of African thought and some philosophical ideas of Thomas Aquinas. Tempels was a Catholic priest and would have studied Thomism at seminary. However useful we find the formulations of Aquinas' appropriation of Aristotelean thought, our very different context demands more, namely an approach that is self-consciously in dialogue with the culture dominated by science. For this reason,

I will introduce a version of the pre-modern approach of Tempels that has learnt from the existentialists' move, in reaction to the emphasis on science, to recapture the subject at the heart of philosophy. Following the lead of Bernard Lonergan, I focus on an ambiguity attaching to the idea of 'objectivity' and I outline a more nuanced understanding of this notion that allows for a proper thematisation of the person and subject. This is a key preliminary to the dialogue of the two traditions.

Contemporary European philosophy has not been completely unaware of the problems associated with the tendency to obliterate the subject and agent in the dominant philosophy of the modern period. Not all philosophy of mind is Analytic. An obvious example of this awareness is the existentialist approach, reacting against 'scientism', and it helps to see (very briefly!) why it does not get to the root of the problem. I introduce, with the African traditional notion of personhood in mind, a way of translating the ideas of Tempels (and of African thought before the encounter with European culture) into a language that speaks directly to philosophical assumptions characteristic of an age of science. The normativity attached to being a person is expressed, in Lonergan's thought, in the notion of the self-appropriation of the subject and agent. This fundamentally undercuts any dualist interpretation of the spirituality of the person.

In the final section, and anticipating the more detailed discussion in Part Four, I will suggest how the basic questions in the philosophy of mind could be restructured, to take into account the African traditional insights into the human person. As foil for the discussion, I take Nagel's (1987) classic of introductory philosophy of mind, *What Does It All Mean?*

An African traditional approach to human spirituality: Not a dualism

The central 'given' in African traditional philosophy of mind, to be further unpacked, is the human person or subject as able to take hold of itself. This is a crucial datum in African philosophy and in African traditional culture the person is seen, in the first place, within a normative frame of reference - a boy or girl is initiated into and encouraged to grow towards an objective ideal of what it is to be, for example, a Mosotho man or woman. Placide Tempels, as we have already seen, highlights the centrality of this idea: "It is the living *muntu* who, by divine will, is the norm of either ontological or natural law... [and] equally the norm of language, grammar, geography, of all life..." (Tempels, 1959:121-122).

In the absence of this crucial 'given', this idea could issue in the thought that the African understanding of mind and world is a form of dualism: there is the body, and there is also the soul or mind. But this would be to (mis)read the past through the lens of the categories of thought characteristic of modernity and associated with the rise of science. For this reason, one commentator suggests the neo-logical-positivist school of philosophy - the Analytic, to use a more general term - is unable to capture this life-world of the African (Ndaba, 2001:37). To appreciate this point, it will be argued that this philosophical school, the one most pressurised by science's self-understanding, disallows according the status of 'real' to anything not subject to scientific methods (cf Kim, 2005). By the nature of things, that includes the subject or self (the doer of science, presupposed to science itself) and the kind of self-knowledge that is at issue when one talks about growing as a person. Something like the soul, simply added to the 'bodily reality', is then seen as un-real, or at least of no consequence to our normal way of seeing things.

If only bodily things are real, the question arises as to the status of how we *experience* the world (the sunset as sublime rather than the sunset as refracted light), how to deal with the evidence of 'qualia'. This is termed by philosophers in the Analytic tradition, 'the hard problem of consciousness' (see Solms, 2019).

There is another reason for not interpreting African traditional thought as dualist. By taking on the task of breaking the reductionism that characterises the understanding of the intersubjective formation of the person, African thought can deepen its own insight into the fact and norm of *Ubuntu*, through the way the human sciences unpack the levels of interpersonality. Each person, after all, has a mix of motives, both other-centred (the *Ubuntu* ideal) and selfish, and unless bolstered by the concrete modes in which the former is developed and the latter inhibited, the ideal could seem simply of cultural interest.

The reductionism I am referring to, and its intimate connection to dualism, is familiar to philosophers. It is built into courses in introductory philosophy, perhaps in particular in anglophone cultures. It is 'in the genes' of modernity to think in this way, the securely true objective world out there, and the subjective world of my conscious experience. Factors outside this subjective world can and do influence me (my class positioning in society, or my gender, and so on) in ways that I might not be aware of, but it would be contrary to this received wisdom to think that they could in any way be thought to *enhance* my freedom to be myself.

This leads to a third point, not dealt with in this discussion but indicating the importance of following this line of research. The human person in the European - and, through cultural colonisation, to some extent global - tradition as it has come down to us, is characterised by the capacity for freedom, and the absolute centrality of this idea is given expression in the liberal democratic structures of government. Human rights are all about respecting the capacity of each individual for freedom. Yet because of the philosophical framework that has accompanied this valuable insight into human persons, the freedom remains at an abstract level, its ethical potential unrealised, the social structures of centrifugal individualism tied to a scepticism about human transcendence through growth in self-knowledge and in less conflictual habitual dispositions.

A new way of framing this tradition is needed, and I want to suggest here the potential of an African traditional understanding of mind and world to meet this need. That the latter predates the scientific revolution is to its advantage: it is not stuck in the problematic dualism of the objective world mapped by scientific theory and the subjective world that is the reality of the individual person as they experience themselves. Problematic because it seems to lead to at least two unhappy conclusions: the reduction of the subjective reality to determination by pre-personal forces uncovered by the sciences (giving rise to the 'intractable problem of free will'); or the dualism of the free subject alongside the determinism of the objective world, a view sometimes associated with religious faith, in the sense of hanging on to the reality of something more than the physical world. In contrast, the idea of growing as a person (subject) through the objective social and human environment of the subject is central to African traditional thought. It is an understanding of transcendence, but not at all implying a dualism.

The way forward for a metaphysics that has learned from the African tradition is to pull apart the standard introduction to the philosophy of mind that is caught up in a framing of philosophical questions that arise from the particular conditions of modernity but arguably cannot on its own terms challenge itself. I have pursued this latter point in a number of publications without particular reference to the African thought context (Giddy, 2009; 2016) and this has been paralleled by unpacking a cognate direction in ethics, virtue ethics, key to understanding how African tradition may influence, for the better, the dominant liberal frame of thinking in morals, and spelled out in Chapter 6. The clarification of a certain ambiguity, even incoherence, in the Analytic strain of thought concerning the notion of objectivity, will facilitate a non-dualist understanding of the person, or the mind, sourced in African traditional thought. This will, in turn, assist modernity to better frame its leading ideas and values.

Tempels' Bantu philosophy: Categories of mind and world

According to Tempels, the metaphysical substratum for the Western philosophical tradition is that of 'being', while for the African traditional mind, it is 'active force'. Force is not something 'out there' simply to be observed in a neutral way; rather it is at once a reality and a value: things find their fulfilment, their natural end, in the actualisation of what they potentially are. And since persons are part of nature - not standing over against nature - their actualisation is also a value for us. Union with how nature is, is a value. And nature tends towards the augmentation of force.

Nature and persons are seen as very much more integrated than is the case for the Western thinker. There is a spirit ('living force') which runs through the whole of the cosmos, as Matolino reminds us, the "divine force, celestial or terrestrial forces, human forces, animal forces, vegetable and even material or mineral forces" (2012:338). Things are thought of not in terms of what they are but rather how they act: force is not an accidental predicate of some or other static being, thought of in a neutral way apart from how it acts. Rather, "force is the nature of being, force is being, being is force."

Matolino, however, is critical of Tempels' approach to African metaphysics. "Whereas being is a fundamental category in Western thought," Matolino (2011:338) argues that "its equivalent in African thought is some dubious concept of force gleaned from magic and irrational fears" and that it is "illogical and mystified". There are basically two points of criticism here. First, in what way can we show that magic, and a fortiori witchcraft, are not implied by the logic of this way of thinking? Secondly, does not this whole idea of external forces operating on persons stem from primitive fears in the face of things beyond one's control? Would that not undermine responsibility and, indeed, ethics as such?

The first point seems unfair to Tempels. It is true that he uses the term 'magical' to describe the influences of forces upon one another. However, he clarifies that if we want to keep the term 'magic', "it must be modified so that it is understood in conformity with the content of Bantu thought" (Tempels, 1959:59). Such modification will show up, Tempels argues, that magical practices exhibit "contradictions of the healthy principles of his [i.e. the African person's] own philosophy."

Tempels himself doesn't allude to his own philosophical background but we can, as mentioned already, note a similarity of Bantu philosophy as he describes it with Thomistic metaphysics, originating in Aristotle's hylomorphism. Whereas Plato thought of things in terms of their (static) essence and their (changing) appearance, the essence lying behind the appearance, Aristotle saw that the essence (form) was what made the thing what it is, and to describe it is to specify what the form is a form *of*, i.e. its 'matter'. But matter is never something existing of itself, it is matter *of* a particular form. Every being is properly described in terms of how it is becoming itself, form out of matter, so that matter is the potential for that being to become actual. How it is becoming itself we call its characteristic 'act of being', for example growth in a plant, sensitive living in a non-human animal, knowing and responsible acting in a human being. The dynamic of all things can be captured conceptually by means of the categories of form, matter, and act. The African world of living forces has something in common with this strand of philosophy – hence not at all self-evidently irrational, as Matolino judges it to be.

This whole conception can be further clarified if we follow the strand of thought in the European philosophical tradition that has articulated, with Hegel and others, a shift from substance talk to subject talk. That is to say, a shift from the impersonal third-person description of humanity – characteristic of Caesar's own narration of his part in the Gallic wars, for example – to first-person descriptions that are, clearly, also intersubjectively accessible, as when one reads a contemporary autobiography. This will introduce the idea of fuller or more comprehensive levels of being. So far as the *substance* (the being) of 'human nature' is concerned, it doesn't matter if one is asleep, awake, inattentive or alert, exercising intelligence or looking blankly into space, considering carefully how best to act or reacting without thought. But from the point of view of the *subject,* this is absolutely crucial. One moves to a different level of existing, from asleep to being awake, to applying one's powers of observation, to asking intelligent questions about the data, to considering the plausibility of one's idea and so not jumping to a conclusion: these actions involve the virtues, but they are also one's very being, one's level of existing. That it is indeed a question of a higher level of being comes out clearly when one considers how, in coming to hold a new belief on the basis not of influencing factors but on the grounds of having a good reason for it, one achieves a 'new self': myself holding the new belief. And this is through my own agency, the exercise of my capacity to 'double' myself, to hold my own beliefs in consideration. Similarly, in the case of actions taken responsibly. This is, clearly, a notion very far from mystical or magical.

The second point raised by Matolino is that the metaphysics of 'force' is generated out of irrational fears. It is true that Tempels develops his ethics on the basis of how every person is always, as he says, "in intimate and personal relationship with other forces acting above him and below him in the hierarchy of forces. He knows himself to be a vital force, even now influencing some forces and being influenced by others" (Tempels, 1959:103). The growth of force occurs through the positive influence of others who are more 'persons' than oneself.

But Tempels emphasises the *normal*, not mysterious or mystical, nature of this transaction of forces, far removed from superstition. "One force will reinforce or weaken another. This causality is in no way supernatural in the sense of going beyond the proper attributes of created nature. It is, on the contrary, a metaphysical causal action which flows out of the very nature of a created being" (Tempels, 1959:59).

Nevertheless, it could seem that if a personal force outside me determines my very being, I am to that extent diminished, and I should fear this, as hostile to me. A writer who has expressively addressed this question is Augustine Shutte. Shutte's understanding of the key interpersonal transactions in personal growth was outlined in Chapter 2. Here, the implications of this idea are drawn for understanding metaphysics in general. If the transaction is envisaged on the model of the natural sciences, this will indeed be seen as something negative, to be feared, taking away one's freedom: the more A operates as a force on B, the less work B does. However, there are other models, in particular the way that one person influences another person so as to empower them: here, the *more* influence (of the correct sort) A has on B, the *more* work B is empowered to do in their own self-actualisation. Explaining the notion of 'interpersonal causality', Shutte (1993:92) writes: "The more you are involved *in a strictly personal way* in the production of my act, the more the act is my own." This is because the influence of the more matured, integrated personality on my own results, through my identification with that person, in myself affirming a less conflicted set of wants in myself.

Modernity, science, and the problem of objectivity

We turn now to the question of the encounter of this metaphysics of the human person with the more dominant tradition. It is quite common for African thought, out of fairness, to be allocated a place in the curriculum, the specialisation- termed 'African Philosophy.' This can happen while philosophy ('as such'!) goes its merry way, just as it used to. Our understanding of philosophy as a social practice is aimed at undercutting this tendency. Our suggestion is that there is a normative set of standards applicable to anyone participating in the social practice. If these standards are systematically obscured, as they arguably are in the dominant practice, this will disallow anyone from raising the question of a perhaps *better* set of foundational questions in philosophy of mind.

A confusion about objectivity is central to the failings, as we see them, of the dominant approach to the philosophy of mind. The subject - it is supposed - in general, experiences something different to what is actually the case in the objective world. The internal incoherence of this is immediately evident: the statement purports to say something objective here, and not just confined to the subjective world as experienced by the speaker. In this and the following two sections, this confusion will be carefully traced and unpacked.

To suggest there should be a norm of being human - even worse, an African norm - that frames philosophical questions would seem a case of reverse cultural imperialism. But this misunderstands what is being proposed. The problem is clear: when Plato suggested a normative human nature, his thought was that this lies in the role played by reason in a person's life, ruling over desire. His interlocuter, Callicles, was quick to respond: without desire you might as well be dead (*Gorgias*, 492e). The norm, in other words, seems to have something arbitrary about it. Why not opt rather for desire? 'Reason' as central to our human nature is not self-evidently true. Would this be the case for any suggested norm of being human?

On the other hand, let us return to the idea of a social practice. Practices do have framing normative structures. They have objective standards attaching to the realisation of their internal goods. You are not a proper soccer player if you think you can systematically disregard the offside rule. You are failing to be a true participant. And in our own case, we are suggesting the set of standards simply to be a participant in the practice, a normativity transcending any particular way that one might participate.

In a sense, the move being suggested here goes back to the origins of philosophy in classical Greek thought: in his celebrated cave metaphor Plato describes human knowing as an existential journey, a journey of personal growth. What obscures this framing of philosophy is the idea that, as personal, it is seen as not something 'objective' or of metaphysical import. Wittgenstein famously believed that there was nothing of philosophical interest in this line of questioning, in other words only empirical psychological facts: "the will *as a phenomenon* is of interest only to psychology" (Wittgenstein, 2001, para. 6.423, emphasis added).

However, Lonergan has put his finger on the root of the problem: the ambiguity in the notion of what 'objective' actually means. This ambiguity stems from an unavoidable duality in human knowing. He notes the kind of 'objectivity' relevant for any biological organism confronting and tasked with dealing with what's out there, not flying into a windowpane, in the case of the ibis. And he contrasts this with the attainment of objectivity through our capacity to reflect on and evaluate the accuracy of our ideas, how we suppose things to be. The organism - and this is the case with the new-born infant too - lives in a world of immediacy, dominated by biological ends. With the acquisition of language, we however also live in a mediated world - encountered not in terms of biological needs but through meaning. We can think, because we can unlike the pre-linguistic toddler grasp things in the mind without grasping them with the fingers or the mouth. By invoking their names, we can simply hold them in mind without them being present. When your dog pricks up his ears on hearing your name spoken in a conversation while you are still at work, he looks around to identify you. But your name is being used here not at all to point to you but to bring you to mind. The dog plays no active part in this conversational world.

Someone might object here: "We cannot know what it is like to have a dog's subjective experience". This viewpoint is standard in the dominant tradition of the philosophy of mind: it refers back to Nagel's famous essay, *What is it Like to be a Bat?* (Nagel, 1979a). An objective description, Nagel says, can only abstract from the particularities of the organism's subjectivity. But this shows a confusion about 'objectivity' that supposes we have immediate subjective knowledge of our own selves which we can then infer of other selves, but this does not apply to organisms with different sense apparatus. In fact, all we have in our own case is an immediate awareness: *knowledge* of ourselves, just as knowledge of others, is a question of making sense of the data, and judging the possible accuracy of our grasp of how things are. Because we can use our imagination and intelligence a woman can enter into the subjective life of a man (the great novelists!), an ethologist into the subjective life of a dog, or a lioness. See, along similar lines, Mary Midgley (1995:231-232) and JM Coetzee (1999:54).

If we focus only on the former sense of objectivity, we might think what is real are 'bodies', i.e. 'out there'. But more coherently, what is real is whatever we come to critically judge actually is the case on the basis of the evidence - 'bodies', to be sure, but also, for example, minds, atoms, transactional forces, personal growth, and so on.

A key factor in this whole historical development is the shift - unpacked by Lonergan (1972, Chapter 4 and 1988a, Chapter 16) - from what one might term a common-sense culture to one in which meaning is 'controlled' not by sheer volumes of additive experience (the sage) but by theory and science. As an example of this shift, we can take the classic case of Newton's dissent from the common-sense idea that bodies have a natural tendency to fall down. Newton disagreed: all change - whether from a stationary position to movement or from uniform motion in a straight line to something else - must be explained by the intervention of outside forces. The key idea is that of inertia. Treat all physical reality, he suggests, as nothing like our experience of intentionally aiming at something (the stone 'wants' to reach stability) but as inert. The upshot of this new approach is the contemporary conventional wisdom that sees the universe in terms of a dualism of the purposive, end-directed, reality of free personal subjects choosing for themselves and the non-purposive causally determined reality of objects that is the proper domain of science.

Such major cultural shifts can lead to widespread scepticism about truth and value objectivity. Common sense is discredited in favour of the real, scientific facts of the case. But even science is seen as socially constructed - for example, Boghassian (2006) - and by this is meant, not objectively true, but relative to some person's viewpoint.

Common-sense relates things to us, from our perspective, while theory, science, relates things to one another, the difference between saying 'it is heavy' and specifying the weight in kilograms. In a sense, the latter can be termed, in the title of Nagel's book (1989), *The View From Nowhere*. But it is not really a *view* at all. Newton struggled with the problem of relative and absolute motion; he postulated an absolute space-time viewpoint. But we don't need this absolute point for viewing the world. Viewing, or touching, or sensing do not give us knowledge, but only evidence. We need an insight into the evidence that yields how things actually are. The rain falls and the sun dries out the rain. But only insight into what is captured in the concepts of evaporation and precipitation give us an understanding of what is actually going on. Objectivity is not a matter of having the perfect (detached!) view of things, but rather of continuing to ask further questions until the evidence is accounted for and a reasonable judgement can be attained). A fuller account of this is to be found in Lonergan's classic work on cognitional theory, *Insight. A Study of Human Understanding* (1957 and 1970). in particular, Chapter 10.

Having this kind of consciousness or awareness of ourselves, implies an ineluctable tendency to ask questions. This posing of questions, an openness to my reality, is emphasised by existentialists. And this implies that there is a transcendent normative framework that makes me me. When I judge some understanding as probably true, it is I myself taking hold of myself; similarly, a considered action marks me as the one who chooses that kind of action, as responsible. The conditions for rising up to this set of standards that mark what we are, furnish the normative framework for philosophy as a social practice.

Contemporary European thought on 'the subject'

Existentialist philosophy is the most well-known of the reactions to the thinned-out philosophical agenda of modernity, and an obvious candidate for framing a future philosophy of mind open to the African traditional insights into the human person. For Kierkegaard (1968:181), the highest truth is what he terms 'subjectivity'. In the existentialist approach, philosophy needs to say something about what it is to be a self-conscious subject faced with the need to make something of oneself, to 'be oneself'.

The name Sartre is synonymous with the idea that no objective account of the person can replace the existential awareness of one's open choice to determine one's own life. This openness, the *pour-soi* or 'for-itself', is defined by the phenomenon of being conscious. But this determining of oneself seems doomed to be frustrated, as Sartre (1948 and 1969) explains in the opening section of *Being and Nothingness*. Here, Sartre argues that consciousness, as consciousness *of* something, is always directed towards an object, and being directed outward, contains nothing - in the sense of having as it were *another* object 'in the mind'. At the same time, he says, it is clearly *conscious* of itself as being conscious of the object - the contrary would be 'absurd' (1969: xxviii). However, since consciousness always is directed upon an object *other* than itself, it cannot grasp itself, because it is not itself an 'object': "there is no inertia in consciousness", as there is in bodily things (Sartre, 1969:104). For this reason, we are not able to take hold of ourselves in the way that we have outlined above, become more of a person, more consistent in our choices of action, for example.

This idea that we do not have the ability to objectify ourselves, and so the possibility of making something of our lives, can be traced back to Hume and Kant. Hume discredits the idea that one can come to a belief on the grounds that one's reasons for the belief are, in fact, sound. As he explains "When I give the preference to one set of arguments above another, I do nothing but decide from my feeling concerning the superiority of their influence." The belief "arises immediately, without any new operation of reason or imagination." (Hume, 1740 and 1969, Bk 1, Part 3, Sect. 8). Kant, objecting to Hume's reductionism, puts the spotlight not on passive sensing, feeling, but on our active capacity to formulate ideas. He argues, against Hume, that there is a reality that is the mind or the self, the 'transcendental unity of apperception', as he phrases it in his *Prolegomena to Any Future Metaphysics* (1783 and 1966). The mind, however, is framed by a finite number of structures determining how those ideas are formulated. Kant has forgotten the element of holding our ideas reflectively, judging their possible objectivity. All we can hope for is 'universal necessity', that is to say, agreement (Kant, 1969, para. 19).

This approach continues to the present day. So far as concerns contemporary Western philosophy, Kitcher (2006:199) mentions those writers who remain followers of Hume's denial of any reality to 'the self', such as Derek Parfit and Daniel Dennett. For an account of how Kant's account of subjectivity differs from that of Lonergan, see Lonergan (1993a, Chapter 7), and Lonergan (1996, Chapter 10).

Lonergan and self-appropriation: Framing a dialogue

It is Lonergan's insight into the ambiguity around the notion of objectivity that allows us to take forward the existentialist focus on the subject or person. Our target is framing a possible dialogue that undercuts the practice of side-lining African traditional thought. For this, a normativity transcendent of particular cultures needs to be put in place. This is done when one thinks of this normativity in terms of the internal goods of the social practice.

The technical term for the kind of argument used in establishing these 'rules of the game' is 'retortion'. The argument turns, Lonergan remarks "upon what no subject can avoid":

> You cannot avoid experience. You cannot avoid trying to understand... If you want to play the fool, to play being stupid, still you do that intelligently. Again, you cannot avoid the exigencies of your own reasonableness... If you were to renounce your reasonableness you would find yourself asking reasons for it (2001:317).

There is an internal demand of the subject (the participant in the practice) to bring these norms of intelligence and reasonableness to conscious awareness, to appreciate and 'appropriate' this way of being.

The existentialist turn to the subject is thereby amplified, to its benefit. The questioning characteristic of the new openness to becoming oneself, has a natural end. *Being self-conscious* does not imply I lack a human nature, as Sartre thought. I can develop in accordance with my nature as a questioning being, faced with obstacles or blocks or tasks to be met well or badly. The activation of my questioning is not without an effort. My judgement of the adequacy or otherwise of my insights has to overcome pressures towards laziness or failing to admit the possibility of an oversight. It is always a struggle to accept, from anonymous journal referees of one's manuscript, that sections could be better expressed. This struggle is even more pronounced in the case of my judgement that such-and-such is the best course of action, all things considered, and of course it takes effort to conform my will to that judgement. The motivation of that effort is a further interesting question.

The foundational question in the philosophy of mind is not:

> What are the conditions of possibility for knowing anything at all?

which seems to invite a too static set of conditions, whereas we are trying to capture what it is to be the dynamism - the norm of *muntu* - somewhat enacted but not at all fully so; but

What am I doing when I am knowing?

In other words, we do not pretend that we are not already aware that we do make judgements about our own ideas, and come to own our beliefs, or at least some of them. This undercuts the conventional starting question in the philosophy of mind: How can I be sure that I know anything at all (Is it all a dream?). Now, on the contrary, we can see there is, in the reframed question, a necessary normative dimension.

Philosophy of mind and world - shifting the questions

We can now give an example of how, with this normative framing of the philosophical practice, an African-influenced philosophy of mind will shift the fundamental questions.

It is convenient to follow some of the issues put forward in Nagel's (1987) classic of introductory philosophy in the English-speaking world. The first three topics are: How do we know anything; other minds; and the mind-body problem. This is followed by discussions of the meaning of words and of free will. Similarly, in other textbooks, for example, Pinchin (2005) and Salazar (2019). The first question concerns the problem of knowledge, framed as: Can we get from 'in here' - our mind - to 'out there'? This is only a coherent question if we assume the aim of knowledge is to get to what is 'out there'. If, by 'out there' is meant simply what is the truth of the matter (rather than simply imagined), then the problem dissolves into the development of reasonable judgements. However, if by 'out there' is meant what does not involve the subject, it is a misleading concept of the real. In the process of trying to reach knowledge, the aim is a reasonable judgement of the accuracy or otherwise of our ideas in the light of the data furnishing evidence. The aim is the appropriation of our capacity for a heightened self-presence and cognitional self-transcendence. In other words, the framing question has to do with the fulfilment of our humanity - in our African suggestion, this is captured in the term *Ubuntu*. How is this possible? How is it linked to the human sciences? How has our understanding of it changed since the rise of modern science? These are, contrary to Nagel, the more interesting questions.

Nagel asks whether other minds exist. This is an offshoot of the above problem: if we assume, with Descartes, some special exceptional inner knowledge of our own self, then we might ask what about other selves (as opposed to their obviously real bodies)? But if the capacity for self-consciousness develops only through others, the reality of my own self is not at all something like an inner 'thing'. It is affirmed simultaneously as real and as a norm (I can achieve it more and more). We discover our own self in intersubjective causality, in the sharing of ideas and the personal influence of one person on another.

Is there an intractable problem of free will? If every event has a cause, then so too must so-called free choices. If an action is caused, it is determined. The problem lies in the fact that our entire social set-up, in particular our legal system, seems to *assume* the capacity for free choice and responsibility, that is to say, precisely *not* being determined. But how is this explained? It is implausible - an anomaly - to suggest that that there is a magical power of choice operating apart from the conditioning factors uncovered by the human sciences, by psychology, sociology and ethology.

Our normative framing of philosophical discussion on the human person can clear this up. The norm of 'having a good reason' for an action is a constitutive ('internal') element in philosophy as a practice, and it is similarly constitutive of doing science, when one determines (reasonably!) the particular cause of an event. The two 'causalities' are not in conflict. There is, however, a real, though not 'intractable' problem of free will, and that is the problem of how the essential human capacity for free self-disposition translates into a real, effective freedom. In the philosophy of mind, this would be the more fruitful question.

I mentioned at the start that an African philosophy of mind, in contrast to the more dominant tradition, will always be framed by a set of normative ideas, focused on what it is to be a person. We can, finally, suggest something of the background to this conflict between the two traditions. It has to do, to simplify, with a general understanding of modernity in terms of simply subtracting from the whole set of objects of belief (spirits, gods, miracles, myths, and so on) of a previous age, to reach the natural (material, bodily, scientific) residue underneath. It is that previous age that is the cultural milieu of African traditional philosophy of mind. The feeling is, however, that we are now free from this, we are enlightened. Putting aside that world of transcendence as a matter of principle would seem to be largely a prejudice. On the contrary, I would suggest, along with Taylor (2007:151-154) and Gauchet (1997), for an understanding of modernity as deriving from an appropriation of human subjectivity that has its roots in what Taylor and others term the 'axial age' of the major religious traditions (the prophets in the Hebrew religion, the Upanishads and Gautama Buddha in the Indian culture, for example), where outward conformity is criticised in favour of an inner authenticity of human faith and the norm of self-appropriation developed above (Taylor, 2012).

African philosophy of mind can point to a recovery of human transcendence, and this is big with implications for broader matters. To give just one example, which we noted in Chapter 2 with reference to Jacobsen-Widding's research, in the African traditional thought-world social connectedness is a higher value than that of procedural equality. This is because, as we have seen above, the effective human ability to act ethically (to be a full person) is dependent on the action of others on one, and one's own receptivity to such action. Again, it is Matolino (2011:340) who expresses well the response of modernity: could Tempels not see, he asks, that all peoples, in this case African peoples, can indeed "go beyond their culture to see timeless values such as equality, justice and fairness"? Whatever one's answer, it is clear that changing the metaphysical agenda allows for these kinds of interesting questions, in the context of a world opening up to a plurality of cultural ideals.

Chapter Five

'Differentiation of Consciousness': A Conceptual Tool for Unpacking African Traditional Thought

Introduction

I am concerned here with the effective impact of African traditional thought on global trends in philosophy. The former tradition of thought predates the rise of science, and it is these pre-scientific formulations that furnish the source material for the discussion of African philosophy. In the modern European philosophical tradition, on the other hand, adjustments have had to be made in the face of the dominance of the methods of empirical science: Kant's critical philosophy and his 'transcendental' method is a good example. So at first glance, it seems likely the two traditions are simply going to talk across one another. This is a pity, and it would seem prima facie of great importance to unpack the conditions for a fruitful encounter of a pre-scientific culture, with its own particular genius, with a culture in which science is institutionalised.

I am not ranking the written tradition over the oral, an issue recently canvassed by Graness (2022). It would seem uncontroversial that a person's facility in standing back and critically evaluating a set of ideas and beliefs is enhanced when those thoughts are objectified in writing. But, as the slide into textual fundamentalism shows (evident in some of the major world religions), there is no automatic or necessary connection between written ideas and thinking that is truly critical. My focus, rather, is on the interaction between a culture with what Voegelin calls a 'compact consciousness', and one in which the theoretical point of view has been institutionalised; The difference between the two, very briefly, can be indicated by the awareness, in the latter case but not the former, of the person begins to be aware, in grasping the object, of something in his or her own subjectivity, "and he finds such words as psyche or pneuma or nous to symbolise the something" (1974:8). I argue that a proper dialogue here can be beneficial to both traditions.

The encounter of this theoretical or scientific frame of thinking and common-sense or traditional-religious one has often been thought to be necessarily destructive of the traditional culture. More recently, however, there has been a development amongst anthropologists, showing greater appreciation of the interpretative schema of primal societies, seeing the mythic consciousness as a way of making sense of the world and as governed by a certain kind of logic. I refer in particular to the discussions around the classic of such texts, Winch's *The Idea of a Social Science* (1958 and 2008). Of course, various philosophical influences are at work in Winch, in particular that of Wittgenstein and his uncovering of the way in which the position of 'scientism' - the view that only the products of the special sciences are worthy of being considered true knowledge - is itself unsupported by reason. Unless the African philosopher comes to terms with and critically evaluates such influences, African philosophy - and any traditional-religious frame of thinking - would seem fated to remain strictly on the margins of the practice of the discipline, of no effective influence on those various trends. In this respect, African philosophy shares in the same condition as the religious traditions in a culture in which the authority of science is dominant.

The more sympathetic approach to pre-scientific culture, however, has its own problems. Western scientific rationality has been unable to ground its own project or relate it to the new openness to traditional-religious thinking. The tendency is to cultural relativism. Some commentators have indeed objected to comparing the two cultures, for example Horton (1995) and Wiredu (1995). I argue that the received idea of scientific rationality needs to be critiqued in a more comprehensive way, and I point in particular to Lonergan's attempt to root scientific practice in a wider framework that introduces the notion of the differentiation of consciousness. For Lonergan, in short, both scientists and those in traditional cultures dominated by common-sense and symbolic ways of understanding – the 'compact consciousness' – are subject to the same dynamic norms for knowing and for responsible action. This is of overriding importance for the whole project of a philosophy which draws from African traditional culture. In this chapter I draw on the discussions around 'understanding a primal culture' in the last three decades of the last century as a useful foil for unpacking the conceptual tool introduced by Lonergan.

The received idea of scientific rationality, in positing the disengaged subject over against the object (whether natural or cultural) is bound to lead to the destruction of the traditional or primal society with which it comes into contact. The answers given by primal societies to unwanted chance events, for example, pointing to certain malicious intentions of a member or members of the community, could be misunderstood as bad science. Lonergan, however, distinguishes between a common-sense knowing (relating the object to me) and a scientific (relating the objects to one another). In addition, he differentiates from both of these the self-reflexivity that characterises the sphere of interiority (Lonergan, 1972:85-100). The appropriation of this capacity for self-reflexivity is productive of what we call the differentiated consciousness. The chance events mentioned above clearly ask for an answer in accordance not with the scientific question; that is to say, seeking a practical answer, a particular cause (say, witchcraft), but with this third kind of knowing: they are 'wrong to me as a person'. Similarly, in distinguishing the two kinds of question, Ramose (2006) argues for the priority of the more fundamental 'why' question over the practical one.

Howsoever one makes sense of the 'supernatural' in our universe, this cannot consistently be thought of as in any way in opposition to, or destructive of, our own self-determining powers. This is a point well made by Shutte (2006), in his contribution to the collection of essays he edited on *The Quest for Humanity in Science and Religion. A South African Perspective.* The dialogue between scientific and traditional cultures must proceed in accordance with overarching norms of knowing and acting revealed in the experience of the life-world common to both the member of the scientific culture and the participant in traditional society. In the mythic consciousness, as in the scientific, there is an intention of truth. For an undifferentiated consciousness the distinction of the kinds of knowing in these, mythic and scientific, is obscured; a differentiated consciousness, on the other hand, is aware of and assents to the criterion of what is real as residing in their capacity for reasonableness in their judgement. The mythic and symbolic kind of knowing point to the personal frame of reference at stake in this interior development of one's consciousness; the scientific kind of knowing, when sufficiently philosophically enlightened, unpacks the conditions - psychological, social and so on - for such development. This developmental stage can be blocked, it goes without saying, in persons in the scientific culture. One only has to think of the contemporary religious fundamentalist.

The received picture of scientific rationality and its critique

We can start from a well-worn example. When a barn wall falls on a passing man and kills him, a variety of questions may arise. The observing scientist and the man's family agree that the cause was the termites that had eaten away the support. But the family questions why it was their father in particular who was killed; the scientist's answer, 'chance', or 'statistical probability', does not satisfy. What is being sought is an answer in terms of personal meaning, how our set of motivations for living our individual and collective lives should incorporate this event. The family could suggest the action of some enemy, through witchcraft. The aim of this suggestion is, ultimately, not so much reparation to the injured party, but rather restoring meaning, chiefly through the reconciliation of the hostile persons.

Is this answer irrational? Oluwole (1995:369) argues that "the existence of witches cannot be ruled out on purely logical grounds". Agreeing with this, anthropologist Evans-Pritchard adds, however, that although possessing a kind of logic, this answer does not correspond to 'objective reality' (cited in Winch 1972:11). The clear implication is that eventually the scientific objective picture of the world will triumph over the other one.

Would this be a loss to global culture? John Horton (2000:33) thinks not, complaining that Winch has too much of a 'romantic' attitude to the primal culture. The approach I am taking in this chapter is to turn the spotlight back on the scientific culture and to argue that far from being triumphant over the traditional culture, it is itself profoundly dysfunctional, at odds with itself. We cannot, in other words, simply use empirical methods to refute Oluwole's affirmation of the reality of witches, as Bodunrin (1995) suggests we do.

The received picture of science is, however, not the only one possible and has come under fire for a number of years. In their classic critique of modernity, *Dialectic of Enlightenment*, Horkheimer and Adorno (1944 and 1972) take the positing of the disengaged subject over and against the natural and social other, as engendering a new myth, that of the unquestionable good of sheer domination and manipulation, for whatever end. The subject taken out of nature to lord over it, constitutes, they say, the nucleus of so-called 'civilizing rationality', but engenders in fact a 'mythic irrationality' (1972:54). In the 'enlightened' world, as they put it, "the reality which has been cleansed of demons and their conceptual descendants assumes the numinous character which the ancient world attributed to demons" (1972:28).

This blind spot in the European thought-world, its inability to give a foundation for itself, and its alienating abstraction from the broader concerns of people, can lead to a scepticism about the human capacity for self-transcendence in general. The whole domain of our values, commitments and concerns, whereby we are connected into society and to nature, is since seen as ineluctably experiential and subjective, unable to get a foothold in the rational enterprise.

Rethinking the person/nature dichotomy

Reversing the usual direction of inquiry of the anthropologists, we start from the self-understanding of scientific culture itself. Here, we are helped by some recent developments in the philosophy of science. Polkinghorne (2003) points to the twin factors of temporality and contingency as constitutive of science today:

factors previously falling on the 'person' rather than 'nature' side of the divide. The geological formation of the earth, the insight of biology into the evolutionary character of the history of life, and the discovery by Hubble of the recession of the galaxies, freed science from the static picture of reality. At the same time, Polkinghorne notes, greater recognition was given to "the role of contingency in the unfolding coming-to-be of the world".

> In the aftermath of Newton's great discoveries in mechanics, it seemed to his successors that science was committed to the necessitarian picture of a tightly deterministic physical process... The discovery of quantum mechanics, and subsequently of chaotic dynamics, showed that there are widespread unpredictabilities present both at the microscopic level of subatomic phenomena and also at the everyday level of macroscopic processes (Polkinghorne, 2003:114).

Biological evolution came to be seen as actuated through a combination of chance and necessity, historical contingency and lawful regularity. This is important, for, as Polkinghorne comments (2003:115), real novelty can only emerge "in the region where order and disorder interlace each other". World system is not closed or deterministic.

In a similar vein to that of Horkheimer and Adorno, Stephen Toulmin (2001:13) writes of the 'wound' inflicted on rationality by the dream of seventeenth century natural scientists of uniting rationality, necessity and certainty into one package. Contemporary debates on rationality, he observes, very often issue in a scepticism about people from different cultures being able to understand one another's science. Toulmin seeks to clarify that not one, but a multitude of procedures characterise our rational activities and research - for example, social and historical studies work with generalisations postulated from the evidence gathered about how people live together and see themselves, and this does not emulate the level of abstraction found in the physical sciences. He argues a change is warranted in how we think of objectivity and in particular, scientific detachment. Whereas, in ornithology, the researcher needs to find a 'hide' from which non-intrusive observation may take place, in anthropology, on the other hand, the scientist aims at entering into the life of the community so as to read it from within.

Retrieval of traditional thought

More recent accounts by anthropologists of primal societies depict their typical 'non-scientific' accounts of phenomena not as bad science but rather as ways of making sense of the world. Winch argues that science cannot be taken as the benchmark for objectivity as such. The member of the traditional society may seek a different kind of meaning to the destruction of the crops due to a natural disaster.

> He may want to come to terms with its importance to him in quite a different way: to contemplate it, to gain some sense of his life in relation to it... He must see that he can still go on even if he is let down by what is vitally important to him... (Winch, 1972:39).

Winch sees the general context of the persons seeking explanations as a vital mixture of personal and natural events, a "drama of resentments, evil-doing, revenge, expiation, in which there are ways of dealing (symbolically) with misfortune and their disruptive effects on a man's relation with his fellows, with ways in which life can go on despite such disruptions" (1972:40). When one understands this, the answer given in the primal culture becomes more intelligible.

According to Geertz (1994:89), the problem is that we need a rethink of the division between the two kinds of science, natural and human:

> one driven by the ideal of a disengaged consciousness looking out with cognitive assurance upon an absolute world of ascertainable fact, the other driven by that of an engaged self, struggling to make readable sense of intentional action.

This critique is repeated by Descombes (1994). The neutral observer standpoint misrepresents the primal culture, mimicking a scientific explanation, but also implying the misleading idea that just as in the natural sciences one seeks a cause; here, one seeks an intentional 'super-subject'. In other words, the model of explaining the individual's behaviour by his or her intention is mistakenly transferred here to the society as a whole. Rather, Descombes suggests (1994:117), the anthropologist's explanation is referring to the way we can share a common intentionality through our capacity to share a world. The 'social' always implies an internal relation between the activity one person undertakes (speaking to someone, selling a product, ordering) and another activity which is necessarily called for on the part of someone else (the listener, buying the product, obeying). The paradigm case is that of having conversation, and this brings out a crucial dimension:

> In order to be able to say of two people that they are speaking with one another (rather than both simply speaking at one another) there must be a *langue*, in the sense of a normative rule authoritative for the meaning of the words uttered, in terms of which this 'speaking with one another' occurs (Descombes, 1994:118).

The normative rule, of course, does not secure its own authoritativeness: this is achieved only through a moral commitment of the participants to the community of dialogue, which is to say a commitment to the other persons involved. In the present context, this will involve the differentiation of consciousness - a developmental ideal. But impeding this development is a fixation on the dichotomy, subjective - objective. Our first task is to suggest a way around this.

A common normative framework for scientific and traditional-religious knowing

Scientific knowledge, in the received view, is understood to be objective, impersonal, factual, rational, predictive, and testable. Knowledge of our subjective reality, on the other hand, is considered untestable, personal, emotional, non-factual (evaluative), intuitive, and non-predictive (Maxwell, 1987:181–184). Nagel has given a clear articulation of that dualism. In arguing against any reductionist programme, he points out that a scientific description of our subjective reality can never capture the essential nature of the experience of subjectivity, 'what it is like' (to me). He uses the example of tasting chocolate: no investigation of the neural patterns in the brain which are necessarily involved with such tasting, is going to capture the taste itself, what it is like (Nagel, 1987:30). Or, to use his more well-known example, for each kind of organism, there is something that it is like to be that organism, for example, a bat.

> It is unlikely that we will ever come closer to the real nature of the experience by leaving behind the particularity of its point of view and striving for a description in terms accessible to beings that could only imagine what it was like to be that organism (Nagel, 1979a:174).

How sound is this argument? If we understand - as Lonergan (1970, Chapter 6) suggests we do - that 'experience' is not all of one kind, but variously patterned, we can see that while we can grant that we do experience a reality circumscribed by the sense-capacities unique to our species, and not intelligible without those capacities, yet this can be seen to be just one patterning of experience amongst others. Nagel's example is a special case of conscious experience. We can also have the conscious experience of coming to a more or less objective understanding of things. An example would be when we affirm our understanding of something as probably true (we are not saying it is probably true to us with our sense limitations, but *really so*). In order to understand 'the mental', one needs to consider the active agent. In particular, one can refer to the experienced fact of sometimes actively 'standing by' certain standards of reasonableness as appropriate for the purposes of considering rival claims to truth. In taking responsibility for one's own contribution to the common growth of knowledge and understanding, one is becoming more present to oneself as being under certain normative demands - basically, norms directing one to make something of one's intelligence.

The kind of experience Nagel evokes in his argument is described by Lonergan in terms of the biological pattern of experience, which is characterised by extroversion, knowing through sense and imagination. Various patternings of our experience can be distinguished, according to how we are intentionally oriented.

The biological pattern of experience is pertinent in Nagel's Cartesian construction of the dichotomy of the external and the internal (subjective) points of view (Nagel, 1979b:202). Such a patterning has as its object, in Lonergan's felicitous phrase, 'the already out there now real'. This refers to an object of extroversion, out there resisting, as it were, our sensible probing of the world: it is there and now, i.e. possessing a spatial and temporal reality; and its reality is of relevance to the biological success or failure of the organism: in that sense it is 'real'. This is what Lonergan (1970:252) terms 'elementary knowing'. But the internal/external dichotomy is not, however, of relevance to another patterning of experience, the intellectual, which aims at another kind of knowing, not simply through sense experiencing but also intelligent understanding and, finally, passing a reflective judgement on the adequacy or otherwise of one's understanding. In the latter case, 'sensible', 'realistic' concerns of the biological organism are put aside in favour of the demands of the enquiring mind. 'Objectivity' now comes to mean the goal of dealing with (raising and answering) all the questions relevant to the enquiry.

The intellectual pattern of experience does not eliminate the biological pattern. There is, of course, the issue of the scope of one's willingness to allow questions for intelligibility to be raised. This is especially pertinent in areas of one's life that such questioning would, or might, challenge habitual ways of behaving. Nevertheless, we have here - in the plural notion of experience - a foundation for seeing how the members of two very different cultures can engage in fruitful dialogue. For, experience does not only connote that which it is taken as by the scientist operating as scientist, but also, for example, that which is taken as data for the person interested in a common-sense understanding (whether scientist or member of the traditional culture). Dialogue can take its starting point from the normative structure common to all these instances, whereby the experience is taken up under the demands of our intelligence and reasonableness.

This enables us to counter the argument of those who define modernity as necessarily undermining of all tradition, whether of one's own culture or that of another - as well as those who would argue the only path to preserving the traditional culture is through mobilising, making it an issue for human rights. John Horton is astonished that Winch would find it a cause for regret if the scientific perspective came to dominate and exclude other ways of thinking. Why, Horton asks, can't Winch accept the possibility that "the Azande (and if them then we too) come to see witchcraft practices as involving false beliefs and misconceived practices so central that they deny the validity of that whole way of thinking?" (Horton, 2000:33). But our plural concept of experience has enabled us to see how we could have a framework for the traditional culture to resist this aspect of the scientific *culture* while absorbing the requirements for scientific *method*. This is key to the whole discussion at issue here.

Knowledge, for Lonergan, is a matter not of disengaging the subject but rather of heightening one's presence to oneself. Objectivity is properly understood not as extroversion but as the self-appropriation of subjectivity in its capacity for reasonableness in pronouncing on alternative theories or hypotheses as true, or probably true, or false, and so on. At the heart of knowing is the act of understanding, the insight that grasps the intelligibility in what is presented to the senses. Finally, there is the element of judgement. To understand but not to subject one's understanding to critical judgement is, as Lonergan says, "quite literally silly": "it is only by judgement that there emerges a distinction between fact and fiction, logic and sophistry, philosophy and myth, history and legend, astronomy and astrology, chemistry and alchemy" (Lonergan, 1988b:206).

Following on from this, we can see that growing self-awareness is a necessary norm for all human societies. Traditional African culture, in alerting us to how such growth is engendered through the influence of certain others, can contribute something of real value to the health of the global scientific culture. The scientific culture can in turn alert the traditional culture to the key fact of differentiations of consciousness; in particular, the common-sense attitude, relating things to us and to our concerns, and the very different scientific attitude, relating things to one another.

Applying the concept: Dialogue between science and traditional-religious culture

The notion of knowing through the self-appropriation of one's various patternings of experience allows one to see that the primal culture and the scientific culture can dialogue in accordance with overarching norms of knowing and acting. In the mythic consciousness, as in the scientific, there is an intention of truth. This final section applies this schema more directly to this problematic.

Garett Barden's essay, *The Intention of Truth in the Mythic Consciousness* (1972), points to the intentionality which applies both to the mythic consciousness and the scientific, and which encompasses both wonder, opening out onto the infinite, and also the precise questioning which issues in a judgement that such and such really is so. This implies the distinction between the known and the to-be-known, and only an acknowledgement of this reveals the subject as one who knows *progressively*. In contrast, if reality is simply 'out there', then no progress or development is envisaged on the part of the knower but rather the disengaged subject operates *on* reality. The acknowledgement that one's further growth into the territory of the to-be-known is not assured or fully controlled, undercuts the surety of the disengaged subject operating on reality. There is space for another kind of knowledge or wisdom.

This understanding of mythic consciousness allows one to appreciate how development can occur in the traditional culture without the entire destruction of the local tradition. The myth is not simply a theoretic distortion. The distortions that do exist in mythic consciousness can then be seen for what they are, namely, not as unnecessary excrescences that have to be pruned away to reach the real world of ordinary things and ordinary rational causality, but rather in terms of the difficulties in actualising the intention of truth in both mythic *and* scientific consciousness. This point corresponds to Charles Taylor's critique of the 'subtraction story' of the move in the European tradition to secularisation: simply take away the whole canopy of supposed sacred entities, witches, ancestors, gods and so on, and what is left is our ordinary normal selves (Taylor, 1997 and 2007:22-29). The drive towards truth and clarity is always subject to distortions through the interference of the need to quell anxiety about one's lack of control over one's further cognitive and moral development. The answers given in traditional-religious cultures, needing not discarding but reformulation, correspond to questions that make sense, in any culture.

The myth, then, is performed in a context in which its truth is assumed: unlike dreaming consciousness, mythic consciousness must convince - one is not in the realm of suspension of disbelief. Thus, as Barden points out, "the myth is subject to a critique: the conviction must be achieved by the power of the expression to evoke enthusiasm and loyalty." We call this the sacred quality of the myth, and because of this, the affective elements in the myth override the demands of the inquiring intellect. "A spurious and premature conviction is achieved, and the subject is blocked in his position by the pressure of tradition and the lure of symbol" (Barden, 1972:12). However, the myth possesses its own vulnerability: from the side of the intellect there is the possibility of the emergence of questions which would undermine the basis of mythic questions; from the affective side there is the possibility that the old images may no longer inspire. Needless to say, this applies not only to cultures that struggle with identity in the aftermath of a process of colonial imposition of the European culture: for some commentators - Tillich (1962:55) is an example - it is the Christian mythic symbols that no longer inspire in the culture in which they once dominated.

The development at issue here is not to be thought of as the emergence of logic. There is a perfectly competent sort of practical logic operative in some contexts of everyday life of the traditional pre-scientific culture. What needs to be explained, argues Barden, is why this is not operative in *other* contexts.

What is happening, in our understanding, is that the criterion of the real, in the pragmatic context, is not the critically judging subject aware of their judgement, but rather an acceptance that 'reality' is ascertained by a sufficiently repeated and convincing flow of sensitive representations, feelings, or words. A particular statement "is accepted as true because it is obvious; it is obvious because it is unquestionable; it is unquestionable because it is expressed." What reinforces this view of reality is, furthermore, the very self-correcting process which through the pressure of actual events is at work in practical matters. Barden explains it well:

> One may, and commonly does, learn by trial and error without ever coming to note the role of either direct or reflective understanding in the activity. Human intelligence and reasonableness is revealed in practical activity; the actor's understanding of his own intelligence and reasonableness demands a shift in viewpoint that itself requires the slow development not merely of the individual but of the community... Doubtless he understands, judges, feels, decides; doubtless these activities are distinct, but he does not know that they are distinct and so fails to grasp the implications of his intelligent inquiry and reasonable assent. This subject is conscious in his activities but since these are undistinguished by him, he is present to himself as an undifferentiated subject (Barden, 1972:8-9).

What 'undifferentiated' means here is an inability to appreciate that the truth evoked by the symbol or myth is addressing something other than the truth evoked by the scientific explanation. And this developmental stage can be blocked, it goes without saying, in persons *in* the scientific culture. One only has to think of the contemporary problem of the confused consciousness of the religious fundamentalist.

We can return to the problem of dealing with unpleasant chance occurrences. In his book-length expansion of his earlier essay, Barden (1990) takes the primal Azande culture as his example. Amongst Azande, these occurrences are thought to be due to witchcraft. In the modern Western culture these are variously explained: providence, astrology, or just a blank, inexplicable, statistical probability. Barden turns our attention to how, although their answers differ, by their questioning Azande and Europeans reveal themselves to share the same basic operations of rationality. Azande injured by a falling barn wall will ask, thinking that this is due to some enemy's witchcraft, who is it? But it is not the proposition that unpleasant chance occurrences are caused by witchcraft that defines the tradition, but rather the *questioning* which gave rise to this particular answer. By their answers, argues Barden (1990:92), they live in a different world. But, by their questions they live in the same world. Looking for an explanation, the injured party in Azande society must suggest a name from amongst his enemies: his suggestion might then be tested through the oracles, and Barden mentions that there is a series of tests to establish the truth: the rubbing board, the chicken oracle, and, finally, the prince's chicken oracle.

Barden's point is the following. If I suspect someone of a crime, I may ask him. Since his answer is likely to be biased in his own favour, we may invent a method to circumvent this problem. In a small society, there is no one who is without some personal interest in the outcome, and so the method will have to be such that no one can be accused of bias. In the days of apartheid, the organisers of the all-night *amakwaya* male choral competitions - as will be discussed in Chapter 9) - used simply to find a homeless white person and bring them into the hall to pronounce final judgement. Everyone could be assured that this person had no personal interest in the outcome. The method for deciding on guilt or otherwise can be developed: cross-examinations, the right to be represented at one's trial, and so on. As we are too well aware, no method is absolutely foolproof, and in the case of trial by jury the resort to plea-bargaining in the USA is an open admission of this doubt. Because the method is designed to solve a common and inevitable problem, namely that no interpretation is so self-evident that no judgement is needed as to its adequacy or otherwise, that truth is found always in judgement, by which one answers, 'Yes' or 'No', we can see that it is reasonable, and can develop towards adopting some other technique, as Europe indeed dropped trial by ordeal. The facilitation of the requirement of reasonableness is always social: there are certain tools available in the culture. The society is not *held together* by the particular method or technique that is current, and it will not fall apart if the technique is challenged.

Conclusion

We can now see how an interaction of scientific and traditional culture can be fruitful. Robert Doran, a Lonergan scholar, puts this well. "Conflict within a culture", he writes, "is partly a matter of persons of variously differentiated consciousness" (Doran, 1990:537, cited in Walmsley, 2004:248). Whereas the picture of science handed down can do nothing or little to help, in its interaction with the traditional society, this is not the case for a philosophically informed scientific culture. In affirming the developmental efficacy of participation, the primal culture is expressing an idea that is consonant with a wide range of religious expressions. For the ordinary human project of scientific enquiry requires, as we have seen, a quality of presence to self that is a matter of degree, and is actualised to a greater or lesser extent in any particular case. But such development is only actualised through the assistance of another, only through cooperation and participation.

What science can do, when sufficiently philosophically enlightened, is to help objectify the conditions for such fruitful interaction, for human and personal development. Empirical studies can identify trends - say, in the medical or psychological arena - that circumscribe conditions for a flourishing human life. Authentic participation, for example, cannot be achieved through repeating certain ritual or customary phrases which are prescribed for relations between various categories of more powerful or less powerful members of the community. Such phrases affirm ontological interrelationships amongst members but do not of themselves bring out a deeper intention to affirm the other as interior to one's own self-affirmation, the true meaning of participation. (The continuing use of terms such as 'Father' or 'My Lord' for greeting officials in the Roman Catholic religious community is an example). The customs can therefore degenerate into 'mere custom'. In order to meet the challenges presented to a culture by the ever-closer proximity of other, alternative, cultures and ways of doing things, what is needed is the differentiation of consciousness which crystallises a more theoretical intention to complement and critically secure the symbolic and common-sense approach of the traditional culture.

Science, then, expresses a differentiation of consciousness, but cultural development is not to be equated with technological advance: science and technology are one aspect of the development, and they can indeed be accompanied by a culture that is basically off-course. This is because the various patternings of experience and their interrelationships are not clearly appropriated. Furthermore, as we are arguing, one kind of society lends itself more to growth in personal integration than another. Using our critical faculties to discern what is truly of value in any culture, its traditions and wisdom, does not mean using the criteria appropriate simply to the theoretical differentiation of consciousness. In each case - common sense, theoretical, and so on - there are the self-assembling requirements of the inquiring mind heading towards reasonableness in opinion and responsibility of decision and action.

Our discussion can help us to understand what is entailed in capturing indigenous knowledge. The Kenyan philosopher Odera Oruka was concerned that our philosophical reflections do not simply dismiss traditional wisdom. 'Philosophy', as presently understood, seems to be a block to this, for while philosophy takes its stand on the critical use of reason, traditional culture is taken (although we have argued against this) as being uncritical. Oruka tries to refute this by means of interviews with persons in rural Africa who, in spite of having little contact with European culture, exhibit critical thinking. It is debatable whether he is successful in this: in her useful discussion of Oruka's method, Presbey (2002) points out that many of the answers given by the interviewees do not show these characteristics of philosophical method: they would not be able to answer questions to do with consistency and coherence of the ideas put forward.

Our discussion has shown that any such demonstration of logical coherence is not strictly necessary: there is an isomorphism of questioning in science and in pre-scientific approaches, and in both, the critical question of reason is catered for in some or other way. As we have argued, there is a development in cultures of the ideal of reason and knowledge, from common sense through theory to the framework which takes its stance on the set of operations basic to our being subjects and agents. To look for marks of consistency, coherence, and systematisation (marks of the philosophical discipline) might, in our case, be inappropriate. As phenomenologists argue, the typical experiences and intuitions contained in the natural life-world do not constitute a closed, logically articulate system. "The deficient agreement of the components of my stock of knowledge does not fundamentally compromise its self-evidency, its validity 'until further notice'" (Schutz and Luckmann, 1973:8). This contrasts with science with its postulates of logical congruence regarding valid theories. Furthermore, what is taken for granted as determinate and straightforward is surrounded by uncertainty: what is given is given along with a horizon which is indeterminate. And this is a spur to further development and growth. John Horton asked, as we saw above, why science 'as a whole way of life' cannot be adopted by the traditional culture. But science does not play this kind of role such that it could replace tradition. For it, that is to say, science, is only one way of actualising our powers of self-appropriation and must be complemented by others, for example, common sense. It forms a part only of our life-world, which is always presupposed by the scientist and the scientific procedures. It is only when this point is lost sight of that - as Verney says in respect of objectifying the world in writing - "this process ... separates our being in the world and we can lose touch and become isolated from all our relations" (cited in Graness, 2022:190). In line with our analysis of the framework for dialogue between a person from a culture with science, and one from a primitive society, the authentic philosophical re-expression of the tradition will inevitably be a synthesis of the views held by the philosopher in dialogue with that of the informants. In other words, Giddens' (1990) contention that modernity wipes the slate clean regarding traditional cultures, is misconceived. Oruka's objections to the efforts of the early 'ethnophilosophers' such as Tempels, Anyanwu, Mbiti and Ruch would seem unjustified, and similarly Bodunrin's dismissive attitude, reported by Presbey (2002:180), to any expression of the interviewee which has been "shaped by Western philosophy through the background of the interviewer."

What one needs to develop is not so much science, as persons motivated to adopt the goals of science as congruent with the spectrum of goals which have to do with self-appropriation and identity. One could point to the notion in the Africa tradition of a power which enables this growth in responsibility to occur, for the person to be healed. This is properly speaking a religious dimension and our discussion thus links in with the question of how contemporary versions of the traditional culture will interrogate Western practices of secularisation. This is a topic which will form the subject matter of Chapter 11.

Part Two

Virtue Ethics: An Africa–Type Response to the Liberal Ideal

Chapter Six

A Communitarian Framing of the Liberal Ideal

MacIntyre and a possible normativity overreaching traditions

We turn now to the second of our major interpretive frameworks for thinking through ethics against the backdrop of the African cultural thought-world. The communitarian ethics of Alasdair MacIntyre, it will be argued, resonates in important ways with the African tradition. Our aim is to appropriate this tradition in the contemporary global context; in particular, the context of the liberal ideal. Modern Western thought and practice has been guided by the central value of individual human freedom. But this notion has generally only expressed the bare notion of essential freedom: to such a notion one can juxtapose all those ways in which we are constrained by environmental factors of biological, sociological and psychological kinds, factors whose identification and verification is the meat of the social sciences. These constraints are, in the African traditional ethic, assumed within the *Ubuntu* ethical ideal. Although he makes no reference to the African ethical frame of thinking, in addressing the contribution of the social sciences to the ethical ideal, Alasdair MacIntyre adds to our understanding of how the bare notion of essential freedom can be made real.

The key idea in this project I take to be the normative notion of a social practice, as developed by MacIntyre. MacIntyre's communitarian approach takes seriously the findings of the social sciences as to the determining influences in human behaviour, and seeks to rethink the framework for moral discourse in that light. This seems to me a welcome shift in ethical thinking that can very well accommodate the insights from the African philosophical tradition, with the emphasis on community.

Contemporary liberal society is reluctant, as Charles Taylor (1989:10; also 75-90) has argued, to articulate the 'moral ontology' underpinning its values. The reason for this is clear. In the liberal tradition, argues MacIntyre (1988:210), reasons-for-action are formulated in a way which makes "no appeal to any agreed conception of *the* good for human beings". Earlier, in *After Virtue* (1981:147-149 and 178-180) MacIntyre had argued, as we shall see below, that this notion of *the* good makes sense only to those for whom the community itself is taken to be a social practice, i.e. normative - and that this is not the case in liberal conceptions. For this reason, the communitarian-type moral arguments, for example of Aristotelians, are found unintelligible in the context of a different tradition - the modern liberal, to be specific.

If this were absolutely true, it would suggest a cultural relativism and undermine our project of formulating an ethics which is intelligible within the African philosophical tradition. Is one simply going to favour one kind of social framework over another? In MacIntyre's view, the state of the debate at present does not display a genuine coherence. What is needed is a set of general criteria for evaluating the worth of any cooperative social activity. MacIntyre doubts any such set of criteria will meet general acceptance. However, I think MacIntyre's doubt is unfounded, and I seek here to show why. I will suggest a way of supplementing the notion of a social practice so as to provide a critical moral foundation to whatever is of true value also in the liberal social institutions - representative democracy and a free market, for example.

I suggest making an intuitively evident distinction between the fact of essential freedom and the question to what extent that essential freedom is in any particular case actualised, that is between essential and effective freedom. For example, the ideal of being faithfully married can be put alongside the achievement thereof, or one can think of the *wish* to be a good parent, rather than a rival of one's children and their demands. I am thinking here of freedom as the capacity to determine one's life. The bare fact of that capacity is termed essential freedom; the transformation of the capacity into an ability would be effective freedom. The appropriation of the capacity for freedom would entail a growth in self-understanding which could be illustrated in the examples above of marriage and parenting. It would also involve a growth in the extent to which one is able to be consistent in carrying through into practice one's understanding of what one ought to do.

One classical text for the discussion of questions such as these is that of Aristotle's *Nicomachean Ethics*. One thinks in particular of his analysis of the dispositions of character that lead to consistently good behaviour (Book II) and of weakness of will and strength of character (Book VII). Still, the growth of the social sciences has changed the shape of the relevant intellectual context for these questions. Our understanding of the regularities, social and psychological, which circumscribe and, in part, determine human behaviour, must now conform to the canons of empirical method. Furthermore, while for Aristotle, 'man' is used as a functional and normative concept, this is not the case in modern thought. MacIntyre (1981:56) writes that

> the use of 'man' as a functional concept is ... rooted in the forms of social life to which the theorists of the classical tradition give expression. For according to that tradition to be a man is to fill a set of roles each of which has its own point and purpose: member of a family, citizen, soldier, philosopher, servant of God. It is only when man is thought of as an individual prior to and apart from all roles that 'man' ceases to be a functional concept.

A reconsideration of the foundations for the moral evaluation of behaviour is therefore necessary if we are to use, in ethics, either the insights of Aristotle or the findings of a contemporary genius such as, for example, Freud. MacIntyre's notion of a social practice can be seen as foundational, I suggest, because it points at once to the fact of essential human freedom (the capacity to share a conceptual world associated with the practice and to act for reasons of its internal goods) and at the same time to the development of the virtues to make that freedom effective (which involves adhering to numerous principles 'of the trade'). However, I will argue that it does not quite do the job, and needs to be supplemented with an account of human rationality of the kind that takes into account the empirical method of modern science. For this purpose, I will once again draw on the ideas of Lonergan.

I turn now, first to the notion of a social practice and its possible use as foundational and normative; and secondly, to the inadequacies of the classical foundation of moral values in a kind of metaphysical knowledge of (rational) human nature. Lonergan's proposed foundation for moral values will then be presented. It will be argued that the latter framework provides for what in MacIntyre is not fully developed, a moral discourse that can in principle integrate the findings of the social sciences.

The frame of a social practice giving objectivity to ethics

In his classic critique of the liberal ideal, *After Virtue* (1981), MacIntyre argues that much modern moral philosophy - for example of the kind practiced by GE Moore, RM Hare and others - has by and large an ideological character, concealing non-rational choices behind an illusion of objectivity, manipulation behind a semblance of moral argument (MacIntyre, 1981:15-20). The basic (formal) principles (universalisability is a good example) lack proper philosophical foundations. MacIntyre's opinion is that this state of affairs is the consequence of the large-scale loss of cooperative social enterprises of the kind which supply the context in which moral reasoning makes sense. That context can be restored by linking the human good to historically conditioned social endeavours requiring particular cooperative skills or virtues. In this way a communitarian picture is painted (we are urged to form local communities with shared goods) as supplying that coherence, which, insofar as the practice of moral criticism is concerned, is lacking in a liberalist one postulating contractarian or utilitarian frameworks. Within the context of a social activity, a large part of whose purpose lies in goods internal to the activity, participants find meaning and reasons for achievement in ideals of character necessary to the success of the enterprise.

For example, participating in chess playing (mentioned by MacIntyre as an instance of such social activities, called by him 'practices'), requires attachment to the qualities (high analytical skill, and so on) internal to the activity, and requires the consequent development of such qualities. Someone who has learned to read, an example not mentioned by him, has become attached to the goods internal to the practice (the access to the worlds of fantasy and fact that are opened up) and reads no longer to please the teacher; she is also now attached to - and motivated by - the qualities of reading well (intelligently) as well as (perhaps implicitly) to the social arrangements that give us books - libraries, monetary rewards and prestige for authors, the removal of a luxury goods tax on books, etc.

By way of illustration, we can consider the principle of equality. In a predominantly liberal society in which moral values are in general considered as relative to culture, equality would seem to be the exception, supposedly of universal application. Yet, an ethic which focuses simply on equality as a principle, without making adequate reference to the structure of human motivation, is bound to fail. The achievement of ideals such as these, depends on people seeing the point of promoting them, and that means seeing how they tie in with their set of motivations. No doubt, legal measures are necessary. However, individuals and groups are notoriously able to circumvent legislation. How are people to be convinced to pursue goals that benefit not just themselves and their group but are beneficial in general, objectively so? In social practices, such goods are held to and do convince participants. The *means* used to reach the goals are themselves partly constitutive of those goals themselves. And those means include principles such as fairness. In these cooperative activities (chess-playing, sport, universities, family life), we are in agreement that the end does not justify the means. Of course, a goalkeeper can be bribed to let through goals but if our team wins in this way we do not applaud that goalie: we feel he has brought the game into disrepute. We want our team to win, but not by any means. The end to be achieved is winning, but the means taken to get there are also praiseworthy in themselves: the skills of dribbling, shooting, defending etc. We would not be happy with a highly skilled team that had a run of bad luck and failed to convert those skills into victory. But we would continue to praise their persistence. In the social activity, we are all united in pursuit of a common goal judged worthy of pursuit. We are lifted out of our prejudiced backgrounds into the higher plane of objectivity. We learn to make the values of the activity our values. Through commitment to the objective goods, our subjective biases are gradually undermined. To take a local example from closer to the time period of the publication of MacIntyre's thesis, should Bartlett or should Masingo be chosen as striker for the Africa Cup of Nations Finals at the FNB Stadium in Gauteng? Questions of race are irrelevant and should be set aside. The qualities needed are recognised no matter how they are packaged. Prejudices are overcome as one learns to enjoy the game more. The practice builds not just skills but virtues: cooperativeness, courage, patience, and so on.

Remove this context, however, and universalisability, or fairness, loses its power of motivation. Once the typical and central practices of a culture are no longer affirmed in this way then moral discourse loses its point. For there would seem to be nothing to *appeal to* in advocating a particular rule or principle. A practice is sustained by an institutional set-up with rules for the efficient allocation of the external goods of power, status and financial reward. The practice of chess needs chess clubs, that of reading and writing, academies of literature. A commercialised society is one in which the institutional goods have all but superseded the goods internal to the practices. In classical society ,the care of the institutional arrangements, facilitating the enjoyment of the practices by participants, was the most noble of activities, namely politics. The bureaucrat or functionary, on the other hand, remains unmoved by the normative idea of membership of a *polis*, the more or less coherent set of virtues which make up the ideal of being human and which ensure that the rules of the practice are taken in the spirit in which they were intended. In the absence of this, the practice as a cooperative venture is likely to be corrupted by the institution which sustains it. Only the bare shell of these activities - sport, family life, and so on - will remain (MacIntyre, 1981:179-181).

There is, then, something radically deficient in ethical theories which neglect to give due attention to the wide range of virtues needed to sustain those practices which make ethics possible - and also, therefore, something deficient in the accompanying notion of individual autonomy and freedom, in the name of which Kant proposed a pure formal principle of ethics, and Bentham identified what is concretely good with whatever individuals happen to *choose*. At least, that is what I am contending here. Apart from our essential freedom - pointed to by Kant and Bentham - there is also the question to what extent we are *effectively* free. One can, for example, freely choose fatherhood as a good, but fail to develop those qualities of character necessary to fulfil what the role demands, and so remain frustrated by one's own choices.

The classical model of society does not, to be sure, highlight a concern for individual creativity, nor for the egalitarian impulses characteristic of modern cultural institutions. Aristotle's ethics assumed a society in which individuals occupied roles with certain concretely understood social *functions* - a farmer, slave, soldier, wife, ruler, etc. Moral virtues were understood to be those qualities required to perform these functions well. One passage from Aristotle suffices to illustrate the problem with advocating such an ethics, given our present-day set of values. All people, writes Aristotle,

> share in moral goodness, but not in the same way... It is thus clear that... temperance - and similarly fortitude and justice - are not, as Socrates held, the same in a woman as they are in a man. Fortitude in the one, for example, is shown in connection with ruling; in the other, it is shown in connection with serving... (*Politics* I, 1260a).

The above passage is quoted by John Exdell (1987:178) apropos of his evaluation of the possibility of finding in MacIntyre's ethics criteria for evaluating and *reforming* social practices. The particular example of a practice he is concerned with is that of "the making and sustaining of family life". Exdell points out that MacIntyre by no means affirms all social activities and the implied role-qualities of the participants. To qualify as a virtue, a quality of character must sustain a practice in which "human powers to achieve excellence and human conceptions of the ends and goods" involved in the practice must be "systematically extended"

(MacIntyre, 1981:175). For MacIntyre, a husband/wife relationship which systematically involved the subordination of the one to the other, and hence for its stability, required qualities of character such as slavishness and docility on the part of the one, would not qualify as a practice, in MacIntyre's normative sense of the word. Nor would any activity that required on the part of a participant mindless drudgery: following Aristotle, MacIntyre holds that the exercise of practical intelligence is needed for a quality to be a virtue. Thus, returning to my concern in this chapter, there would seem to be scope here - i.e. in MacIntyre's framework - for the achievement of individual creativity and hence effective human freedom. For, the social practices involve, as equal moral imperatives, the following of all the particular rules and the development of the particular qualities of character that turn a good intention or a deeply held desire into a real achievement. My aim here, to repeat, is to outline a way in which we may understand the findings of the social sciences as contributions to our understanding of ethics, and by the same token, to the achievement of effective freedom.

MacIntyre presents a normative idea of a community of virtue-following persons as the soil in which particular practices might flourish and grow, and this of course entails a prescriptive notion of the human person as a *member* of that community. Needless to say, it is a controversial idea, and in MacIntyre's opinion, not universally justifiable. "For liberal individualism," he notes (1981:182), "a community is simply an arena in which individuals each pursue their own self-chosen conception of the good life, and political institutions exist to provide that degree of order which makes such self-determined activity possible." In a context such as this, the normative concept of membership makes no sense. MacIntyre's notion of a social practice, in other words, takes us only so far.

MacIntyre does furthermore suggest that the virtues (in our conception, facilitators of effective freedom) do necessarily form *some* kind of unity, but not of the kind that would serve as one single or unified critical measure by which to judge actions and practices (1981:147). Qualities of character do not come together as neatly as supposed by Aristotle: the virtue of courage, for example, might be incompatible with the full development of the disposition to be socially agreeable, which would be a rival virtue. Aristotle's picture of the harmonious self would mask such a conflict.

He concludes rather tamely that the only justified measure for 'the good life for man' would be that in terms of a quest seeking to realise ever more the good life for man, to realise the best in the tradition (1981:204). But this formula does not do justice to his argument. It is, as Collins (1985:103) has pointed out, a purely procedural ethic of the kind that has characterised liberalists (such as RM Hare).

MacIntyre is working from the backdrop of the classical foundation of ethics in a norm of human nature, and the same is the case in the African philosophical tradition. But how is this to be positioned, if at all, within the framework of the liberal ideal, which seems to entail an ethical relativism? Any prejudice, it would seem, could be justified by saying it is 'according to nature'. We are more than ever aware of different cultures (and different historical time periods) having different norms, in every case thought of as 'objective'. On the other hand, the popularity of Alan Bloom's critique of ethical relativism, *The Closing of the American Mind* (1987), shows that the liberal culture is open to self-criticism.

Classical Greek culture was thought of as normative, and the ideal of 'human nature' coincided with the best man of the society. But today our understanding of culture is descriptive. Stripped of this normative view of culture and in the face of an awareness of a multiplicity of cultures, this way of founding ethics, in what is 'rational' for human persons, seems simply wishful thinking. We tend to think 'sociologically'. Now, the notion of being rational has always gone hand in hand with the notion that we, or a part of ourselves, have the capacity to transcend the system of forces that would determine our behaviour without remainder. But the social sciences operate with the idea that human beings are part of the system of causes investigated empirically. In his critique of modern moral philosophy, it is this foundational question that MacIntyre has to address.

Given the determinism assumed by the social sciences, our ideals, and indeed the notion of free will that lies behind thinking of our behaviour in terms of our ideals, seem to be shown up as a kind of false consciousness. Furthermore, any form of dualism pitting our 'will' as operating free from the determining psychological and sociological conditions, seems to perpetuate 'the ghost in the machine' myth of the soul.

The social sciences: Against a strong determinism

It is not the case, however, that all social scientists conclude to a moral scepticism. What a scientist - a sociologist as much as a physicist - would need to assume is a degree of regularity in nature. This assumption - which Midgley (1984:94) is happy to call 'determinism', a usage we shall not adopt - should not be taken as incompatible with a belief in free will. Natural forces, once understood, can be used for the enhancement of human life (a farmer understanding the weather system, can adjust her planting habits, or a government understanding the nature of human aggression, can adjust the design of economic housing units). And this assumption of regularity, Midgley (1984:98) notes perceptively, is simply a willingness to accept certain limits as given. It is a notion as old as humanity, but in the seventeenth century was extended into an explicit general assumption about nature. All that is asked of the social scientist is that space is left for the further determinations of the kind suggested by Midgley, i.e. moral categories.

Much the same point of view is espoused by Hugo Meynell, who notes amongst social scientists, the tendency to give either a strong interpretation, or else a weak one, to the opinions of, for example, Marx and Freud.

> According to the 'strong' interpretation, human intelligence and reason are more or less a mere reflex of other factors: the economic and social environment on the one hand, and impulses of an organic nature on the other (Meynell, 1981:64).

In terms of the weak interpretation, on the other hand, human intelligence and reason, although *strongly affected* by such environmental factors, are not wholly *determined* by them. And clearly it is this latter interpretation that could accommodate objective moral values in the overall picture of human behaviour.

In favour of the strong interpretation, however, lies the grand scientific myth that what we are looking for in the particular sciences is the complete explanation of everything. One thinks, for example, of the programme to map 'folk-psychological intuitions' about our powers of self-determination to what are supposed to be the *scientifically* established truths of the matter (in one version, meaning brain activity). A milder version of that myth would have it that of the area (i.e. the realm of values) that science cannot ultimately claim as its proper domain, we should remain silent. But this moral coyness, argues Lonergan (1990:101), creates a vacuum likely to be occupied by a variety of uncritical viewpoints.

Midgley makes sense of the realm of values as follows. We are always motivated by a variety of motives, each one of which can be studied by the social sciences. We also, however, habitually construct our own personal identity by affirming some motives and inhibiting others, to some or other degree, and that is why it is reasonable and proper to attribute blame and responsibility to people. People judged vicious rather than virtuous do not have a balance of other motives to counteract ones that go out of hand.

> The natural method of investigation [in ethics] is, to my mind, to study directly the forms of inner conflict involved in temptation - the warring motives that take part in this conflict, especially those which actually tend towards evil - and the relation between this turbulent process and our personal identity (Midgley, 1984:69).

This distinction between the self-construction of our personal identity, and a realistic approach to the constraints on this, would tie in well with the point we have made about essential versus effective freedom. And Midgley uses it in a similar way: to allow for the insights of the social sciences to deepen our understanding of moral values. What I want to bring out is how this programme is *justified* (it is assumed rather than argued for by Midgley), by analysing the necessary structures in the construction of one's personal identity, and to do this by reference to Lonergan's concept of self-transcendence.

A 'transcendental psychology'

Meynell's argument is grounded in Lonergan's 'transcendental psychology'. We have already, in Chapter 4, drawn on Lonergan's cognitional theory in countering the dualism of subject and object that permeates modern Western philosophical discussions on mind and world. For Lonergan, objectivity is reached not through moving away from the subjective, but through the proper appropriation of our subjectivity. Objectivity is the fruit of authentic subjectivity. The findings of the social sciences can contribute to this appropriation, enhancing rather than detracting from our subjectivity, from our freedom of action. It is, arguably, more profitable to turn to Lonergan, then, rather than to a John Stuart Mill or a Rawls, for a defence of those values which characterise liberal democratic institutions. For our purposes as well, it is important not to leave behind the African traditional intuition into human transcendence. Lonergan's theory of knowledge helps us to place the findings of the social sciences within the framework of the set of values which define our human freedom.

His starting point is the practice of scientists, and his theory is then expanded to encompass moral understanding, too. Basically, to repeat here some of what has been unpacked above in reformulating an African philosophy of mind, he contests the picture of knowing as 'taking a look'. Certainly, attentiveness to the data at hand is a necessary element in knowing, and this has been stressed by empiricism. Equally clearly, intelligent conceptualisation, emphasised by rationalism, is a further factor. But knowing (rather than simply observing, or thinking about), reaches, to some or other degree, the truth of the matter. (In the popular definition, one's belief, justified by reference to the data, has also to be true). In the picture of knowing as 'taking a look', objectivity is thought of simply as taking a *good* look. What is missed in this picture is the point that it is one's own grasp of the matter at hand that is judged to be true, or untrue, or partially true, etc. In the judgement, one determines one's own orientation, at least to the extent of what one believes to be true. Objectivity is the fruit of attentiveness to the data, intelligent insight into the nature of the object in question, and reasonableness in evaluating one's own grasp of that object. In that final moment of evaluating, one has the conditions for *altering* one's given - environmentally determined - set of beliefs, by a measured estimation of their likely shortcomings. Scientific knowledge, Lonergan contends, presupposes - cannot deny without self-contradiction - a set of norms defining the human capacity to transcend, in the act of judgement, the determination of our beliefs through environmental factors alone.

Under the exigence of 'being reasonable' in one's beliefs, one stands back and interrogates one's own ideas. Similarly, under the more complex exigence of being responsible for one's behaviour, one consents to or withholds consent from any particular desire or motive according to one's judgement of its appropriateness to guide one's course of action. The implications of this are that any form of determinism is refuted: all the statements of the social sciences, to bring this argument back to our own concerns here, presuppose this normative structure, and implicitly affirm it to be true. Lonergan's term for the latter is self-transcendence, and it has a cognitive and a moral dimension.

Following on from this, Meynell proffers the argument that determinism (the 'strong interpretation' of the findings of the social sciences) involves what can be termed a performative contradiction:

> [a]ny account of human beings, from which it can be inferred that they are incapable of cognitive and moral self-transcendence, of getting to know what is true independently of their material and social milieu and acting in accordance with that knowledge, is self-destructive. On the strong interpretation no-one, including Freud or Marx, thinks or writes as he does because there is good reason for him to do so (Meynell, 1981:64).

There would thus be no reason for a serious consideration of their writings. And this difference is of crucial importance for our problematic. On the *strong* interpretation of Marxian theory (for example), truth and morality would be seen as entirely relative to class interests. On the weak interpretation, however, group bias due to economic and social class is seen not to determine but significantly to *condition* what people believe and value. Marxian theorists can usefully be classified in terms of this difference (Meynell, 1981:101-103).

The notion of a social practice has, in the light of the above, to be amplified. We praise skills by which internal goods are habitually attained, and it would seem reasonable to praise also those crucial qualities of character (to do with our powers of cognitive and moral self-transcendence) which enable one to attain a *balance* of motives (in Midgley's terms, overcome temptations). If a practice captures a part of our motivational structure, still one's participation is characteristically governed by a critical affirmation of its worth. Dedication to a practice (say, a profession) may override the sense in which a broader perspective on 'being human,' is also needed. Without this added dimension, judgements of moral value would not be properly founded.

Social and psychological determinants in ethics

We have now come to the point of this amplification of MacIntyre's attempt to integrate the human sciences into our understanding of ethics, without falling into a determinism. This is important for our broader project that looks towards a reformulation of the genius of African traditional thought. For, we are now in a position to appreciate the contribution of the social sciences to ethics, and in so doing, remove the objections brought by modern philosophy against linking moral values to a normative concept of human nature. For, these objections were twofold, to do with the proper scope of human knowledge - for some, restricted to the empirical sciences; and, secondly, with the morally overriding fact (and value) of freedom or autonomy. This whole chapter contests the dominant liberal conception of the latter; regarding the former objection to Lonergan's argument, given above, is crucial and offers a picture of the foundation of ethics different in an important way from the classical one from which modern philosophy diverted. For, in the classical conception, the laws of human nature remain unmodified by circumstances and context. Abstract and universal truths about 'man' are contrasted with concrete and particular instantiations. The particular, it is thought, is simply chance, how things happen to fall, and not subject to scientific explanation. There is a neglect of any account of the cultural and historical *variation* in the pattern of human behaviour. And this objection would, in the same way, be brought against the African traditional norm of being a person.

The genius of modern social science, on the other hand, lies in its ability to capture our *experienced* everyday reality. Its characteristic method is statistical, documenting trends which apply to some extent, although are not fully determinative of our behaviour. To be sure, the dominant conception of science in the modern age has been that of non-statistical causal laws determinative of actual events. On such a conception, the social forces can only be understood as operating deterministically. But besides the laws which can be discovered in nature and social affairs, there is the statistical residue which is not simply left to be thought of as chance circumstances but is subject to probability analysis. What is probable might seem from one perspective to be simply random occurrences. But, given large enough numbers and sufficiently long time-periods, what is probable sooner or later occurs. A different perspective, a higher-level viewpoint, can systematise what on the lower level remains only random. Classical ethics, based on a classical notion of science, remains unconvincing to the extent that under its ideal standard of rational human nature such 'random' phenomena as – to use Freud's famous example – 'slips of the tongue', remain unintegrated in the picture, rather than indicating a need for growth in self-understanding.

It is commonplace that the laws empirically established in the social sciences do not apply without remainder to human behaviour. Much behaviour seems to slip through the net of the conceptual apparatus built up by the social scientists. This would indicate that the data relevant to human behaviour are intrinsically open to fuller, higher systematisations. Human freedom and moral agency should not therefore be considered as epiphenomenal. At the same time, the terms and relations posited on this higher level, are not detached from the facts arrived at by social scientists. Probability fractions identifying tendencies at one level (say, to do with the motive of aggression), indicate a real potential for self-transcendence, the understanding of which is given through a higher systematisation (moral discourse). (The morally praiseworthy disposition, to stick to our example, not to shy away from the *unpleasant* task of confronting an injustice, would seem to build upon the aggressive instinct). These psychological factors, although not determinative of human behaviour, are nevertheless either integrated into our understanding of ourselves or else operate in a seemingly random fashion to upset our well-laid plans.

The human sciences and our capacity for moral objectivity

We suggested above that the classical conception of a normative human nature fails, in the face of wide-spread evidence of environmental factors determining both behaviour and beliefs, to establish our capacity in general for moral objectivity. In Lonergan's account, in contrast, no simplistic notion of the will following the 'higher' part of our human nature, our rationality, is assumed. There is the problem of converting one's essential freedom and rationality into effective freedom. An excellent resolution, for example, can be frustrated because one's imagination - the psychic level - is full of schemes of living that allow scant place for such an ideal, and one lives then, not a new but only a dual life. The practice of the virtues answers to the existence of relatively autonomous levels of operation (the level of 'instinct' for example) compounding the human self. To fail to acknowledge this tension between freedom and its constraints is to block any moral growth (Lonergan, 1970:474).

Each autonomous science helps in our understanding of the constraints on human development. But the empirical sciences need to be coordinated. As we learn more about the various factors - not rigid laws but real trends - operating in our own lives and the lives of others, we deepen our understanding of the obstacles to the free operation of our spontaneous drive to understand and know, and undermining our native willingness to do what we understand to be the right thing.

Chapter Seven

Virtues in a Post-traditional Society

Introduction

I am concerned in this chapter with giving a fuller account than is generally found in much social science studies of the conditions for good social development. Such an account, I claim, will necessarily be founded on an understanding of what makes for human flourishing. My starting point is an analysis of the conditions of modernity. I argue that the shift from a customary, tradition-based society to a commercial and law-based one tends to issue in an unhelpful oppositional dialectic pitting a reactionary conservatism against a dogmatic individualism prioritising rights. This is key to any plausible presentation, in the contemporary cultural context, of the African ethical ideal.

In her useful account of ethics thought of through the frame of a normative human nature, Mary Clark (2002) has identified the causes of this opposition between conservatism and individualism as lying in the failure of the new impersonal bureaucracy to meet the basic needs of the human psyche for bonding and for meaning.

In response, I argue that the values associated with this modern society, namely equality, fairness and individual autonomy, are, to bring in MacIntyre's concept once again, the internal goods of this particular social practice, and hence *virtuous participation* in such a practice can be seen as implicit in this outlook. What prevents this being *explicitly* fostered is the blind spot about agency that characterises modern global culture. This results in a systematic neglect of the conditions necessary to translate or transform our abstract freedom or autonomy (celebrated as a key value in modernity) into an *effective* freedom, a distinction we drew upon in the previous chapter. The latter bring into play the set of habits of behaviour, or virtues, to do with both intellect and will, that are the necessary conditions for any individual's self-determination and flourishing. However, contemporary culture is not without the resources, or social capital, to make such an ideal a real possibility, and I draw here on Jane Jacobs' revealing typological study of the actual operative value clusters in our modernity, *Systems of Survival* (1977 and 1994), subtitled, *A Dialogue on the Moral Foundations of Commerce and Politics*. The African ethical ideal is not alien to all aspects of modernity - an important point in presenting this ideal today.

The above summary determines the structure of my discussion. I first explain what is meant by characterising the transition to modernity in terms of a dialectic, and Clark's analysis of its basically destructive nature. I then introduce the Aristotelian-type engaged, rather than disengaged, inquiry into human behaviour and, in the following section, MacIntyre's way of explaining virtues not by reference to any normative idea of a human ideal or 'human nature' but in terms of participation in a social practice. The liberal ideal of individual autonomy, if *abstracted* from this context of growth as a person amongst other persons, growth in the virtues, can be contrasted to the idea of effective freedom, requiring growth in self-knowledge and personal integrity. I invoke evidence that the latter set of values does resonate with aspects of contemporary commercial culture, albeit in a secondary way. The whole discussion picks up on that in Chapter 5 on the confrontation of a traditional society with one in which the influence of science has been institutionalised. The genius of the African thought-world, if it is to have its proper global influence, needs unpacking in the terms of a transition to modernity.

A destructive dialectic of development

I need now to explain what I mean by the destructive dialectic of development and outline Clark's understanding of its basic etiology. The rapid shift from a customary to a law-based society has, she argues, through its radical erosion of identity created a level of personal stress that can only be harmful to the ideal of a good society. I will argue, in the sections following, that the dominant understanding of modernity - entailing a thin conception of value - needs a corrective, and that this can be plausibly found in the ethical approach of Aristotle and the Aristotelian tradition. In *After Virtue*, Chapter 14, MacIntyre (1981) has reformulated Aristotle's key concept of virtue through the notion of a skill or internal good of a social practice. This, I argue, can supply us with a way forward in broadening the dominant conception of moral values to include goods of personal growth and identity lost in, or threatened by, the transition to modernity.

My aim is to contribute to an interdisciplinary approach to social analysis. As a preliminary example, I can refer to the well-received analysis of Acemoglu and Robinson's *Why Nations Fail: The Origins of Power, Prosperity and Poverty* (2013). In this detailed and convincing study, the authors pay no attention to the conditions for developing virtues of character amongst the ordinary members of society. Sustained economic prosperity, it is argued, depends on the shift from extractive to inclusive political and commercial institutions. You cannot engineer prosperity; what is needed is empowerment of local groups. But that empowerment, I want to contend, has as integral component considerations to do with virtues of character and the type of self-conscious moral culture needed if the required shift is going to be effective. I want to suggest one way of framing development so as to foreground this ethical dimension. For these purposes I judge Clark's well-researched and wide-ranging volume, mentioned above, to be of ongoing relevance, in particular for interdisciplinary studies.

My basic idea would be to think of modernity - characterised by the kind of economy that emphasises creativity and enterprise - not as a clean break with tradition-based society, but rather as a development of this. For many people, however, modernity is valued precisely *as* such a break, sweeping away all such traditions. Similarly, others resist it for precisely these reasons, taking tradition as essentially and importantly not adaptable, and think that we need to turn back to tradition to give stability in an age of (for them, disvalued) change and upheaval. What is needed, I would like to argue, is to present a space for a plausible human vision, not necessarily at odds with the free enterprise model, of virtues as part of anyone's aims in their ordinary life. The greater individualism of the new social order includes, if thought through properly, a foundational virtue dimension.

As background to my argument, I take Clark's understanding of human nature (which she argues for over a number of chapters) in terms of three basic psychic needs, for bonding, for autonomy, and for meaning. Developing her argument, I arrive at the following likely dialectic of positions in the process of modernisation:

1. In a commercialised society, 'the bottom line' of policy discussions is largely economic development not meaningful lives. The neglect of this latter dimension results in the two psychic needs for bonding and autonomy being seen as antithetic, opposed to each other. (The meaning-giving traditions, based in general on an idea of how we are by virtue of our human *nature*, can explain how we can have them both, bonding *and* autonomy, being properly human through others. In this chapter I am assuming rather than arguing for this).

2. So, modernity is seen as breaking with traditions. A kind of procedural framework is offered, concealing the norm of being human it contains; I refer to the idea of autonomy as *trumps*, or - what amounts to the same thing - individual human rights as trumps, as operating not alongside other values such as participation, but at a different, higher level. In a thinker such as Kant, autonomy rather than heteronomy seems to define what ethics is.

3. As a result of the threat to the loss of identity brought about by this attitude (and the consequent neglect of the psychic need for bonding), a closing-down of minds occurs, increased authoritarianism, and fanaticism-fundamentalism as a strategy of defence. Clark mentions Hitler's Germany, and some Islamic states today.

4. In a further counter-reaction to this counter move, more than ever is emphasis placed on the inviolability, the trumping nature, of autonomy and individual rights, to check the seemingly irrational but passionately held views which resist modernity. This in turn generates resentment at what is seen

as an imposed and self-righteous insistence on individual human rights.

Clark on the harm of modernity

I now want to sketch a largely intuitive picture of why 'unchecked' modernity is destructive of the good life. Again, I take this from Mary Clark's study and in particular, her depiction of what she terms the 'technologized megamachines' that characterise our global culture. She points to the effective distortions of the ideals of modernity in contemporary society. Her analysis is worth quoting at length.

> By the end of the nineteenth century it was all too clear that the private ownership of wealth...was antithetic to the Enlightenment dream of equal rights and an equal say by all in the construction of social life... It was a new form of feudalism, but without the Church's moral teachings... to ameliorate its excesses... A new 'scientific' morality was conveniently invented to justify human inequality. Darwin's theory of evolution as a process of selection of the most fit individuals in each generation [showed] the superior fitness of the winners in the economic competition for power...

Clark goes on to emphasise the all-pervading influence of this economic culture on contemporary life.

> This mindset, this belief system, this new religion, she writes, is today more firmly entrenched than ever in the dominant social institutions of not only the industrialized world but also the now-global compass of transnational corporate capitalism. The drive for ever-more efficiency in production, for ever-more competition in the accumulation of wealth and the power it holds, and for ever-more rapid technological change is beyond the control of any single government, whether elected or not (Clark, 2002:309).

The last point is pertinent for the case of the rest of the world's attitudes to weak human rights records in developing countries. Clearly, a solution to the problem lies beyond simply the implementation of human rights.

Clark (2002:310) continues by pointing to the human costs of this situation.

> The psychic insecurities of having to compete throughout one's life; of perhaps becoming a 'loser' in the eyes of others; of having no stable future, no trusted, supportive community to contribute to and be accepted by; of being deprived of any familiar social story that gives one a meaningful identity and a realistic social goal to strive toward - all these wreak enormous psychic stress on people around the planet...

Some backing to this, on the surface pessimistic, view of things can be found if we simply list the changes that have accompanied the move from a customary to a law-based society, i.e. to one in which the contract between individuals (regulated by law) is most prominent. I summarise in my own words Clark's (2002:297) suggestive picture of this change.

Let us call these society A (customary) and society B (law-based). In customary society (A), the basis of social order lies in the beliefs of the community (common to rulers and ruled) expressed in value-laden stories, myths and such like. In 'modern' society (B) the authority for social order is distant - God, the king, 'the majority', and inflexible. In A, the judges / interpreters are the commonly acknowledged elders of the community; in B, it is the state judiciary or priests *appointed* from a central body. In A, 'wrong' is seen as personal harm (corrected by remediable compensation) or community harm (corrected by shame; exile); in B, all crimes are crimes against the state, which controls restitution. In society A, enforcement of social order is through disapproval coupled with the desire to belong; in B, it is fear of armed authority (police, military). In A, the goal of justice is apology, restitution, reconciliation; in B, it is whatever is prescribed by law. In A, the basis of social relations is trust, duty, customary kinship, family bonds, friends; in B, it is repression and punishment. In A, rules of social order are changed through group consensus; in B, through edicts, or majority rule.

Summing up, we can say that personal participation in the community has been displaced by a formal adherence to impersonal laws and institutional rules. Your individual character is now your private affair, not of public concern. Virtues of character are concerned with your internal attitude of meaningful consent to requisite kinds of behaviour. This is at least Aristotle's understanding, as he explains in Book I of the *Nicomachean Ethics*, of how virtues are taught: the commitment must already be somehow there, in the student of the virtues. But now, in society B, there is much less attention paid to the conditions necessary to *foster* such attitudes and behaviour. When authorities are distant, the emphasis is on conformity to procedures, and such conformity is measured through laws and rules administered legalistically.

Because the constrictions on your public behaviour are now deprived of the kind of support from others provided in the earlier social set-up, the *stress* to conform to those requisite behavioural principles is all that greater. Clark argues for the helpful role of religion in this regard, softening the psychic harm of modernity. Religion "helped offset the psychic stress civilisations created for such a large proportion of human beings" (Clark, 2002:298). But, one might object, are not religions, for good reasons, marginalised in public life in a secular culture? Be that as it may (and see, in contrast, the discussion in Chapter 11), my aim in this discussion is to present a way of thinking about these conditions of modern culture which can furnish a framework, at the individual and at the social or political level, for resisting the resultant degeneration of the quality of human life, hinted at in the above description of the changed conditions of our ordinary life. In contrast to my aim, Giddens (1990 4; 38) has argued that modernity means there *can be* no tradition in the sense of drawing on the citizen's sense of motivational identity. Ross Poole again, has claimed that

> Any process of *evaluating* these identities is liable to undermine them. For an individual to subject her or his identity (as wife/mother or breadwinner/head of

household) to such a scrutiny is to render that identity vulnerable... To ponder the identity in question is to render contingent what must be assumed as necessary and inescapable if it is to found an ethic of virtue (Poole, 1991:63).

This argument seems not to be convincing to scholars in one society presently undergoing rapid transition to a commerce-based culture, that is to say, China. On the contrary, there is amongst these thinkers a burgeoning interest in the virtue approach. And in fact, the occasion for my own formulation of the argument in this chapter was a conference (2012) at the Renmin (People's) University of China in Beijing directed towards the problem of how virtue ethics finds a place under the modern conditions of economic freedom. Xiao Qunzhong's conference paper, *Similarities and Differences between the School of Confucius Ethics and Modern Public Ethics*, has a similar description of modernity to the one developed here.

It is clear, for example, from a glance at the contents of recent issues of *Frontiers of Philosophy in China*, that Chinese scholars are taking up the task of re-presenting the virtue traditions, whether of the Confucian or the Aristotelian or Christian variety, for example, Yu Jiyuan (2008). Without this kind of philosophical bridging, modernity is likely, as argued above, to spin into a destructive downward spiral of liberals versus conservatives, in other words, to spawn Confucian traditionalists as it has Christian and other fundamentalists in other parts of the globe. The virtue tradition is being called upon by the central Chinese government to bolster the sense of ethics in the changing times, and for this reason, could be seen cynically as yet another attempt at centralised control (and is so seen, from my discussions with scholars in China). But this should not affect our analysis, simply make it that much harder to convince intelligent listeners.

Furthermore Marx - of particular relevance for rethinking virtue in the context of contemporary China - found no place for virtue in his view of 'human nature' and its flourishing. For Marx, the critique of "the conditions of production ... [has] shattered the basis of all morality, whether the morality of asceticism or of enjoyment" (*The German Ideology*, in Miller, 1984:32–33), allusions to Kantian ethics and Utilitarianism respectively. But he fails to see the need to offer a sustainable alternative: 'history' was going to accomplish what can only be brought about by human effort! His theory of a human being (derived in part from Hegel via Feuerbach and coming down to us through the 1844 Paris Manuscripts) included the idea of the human being as a 'species being', being able to think of themselves and their nature in a critical way and thus develop their ideas and put them into practice; expand the scope of their self-determination, for example (Marx, 1964). But, it omitted the crucial aspect of freedom of choice, the aspect of human transcendence that allows the possibility of ethics. Social transformation, one might suggest, takes conscious effort and virtue, without which the best ideals will be corrupted.

Possibilities for an ethic of virtue

I now want to introduce the framework of virtue ethics as a plausible way forward. It goes without saying that in the background I have in mind how the African ethical tradition may deliver its rightful contribution. The two crucial elements defining modern culture might be said to be: a) a greater degree of individual freedom of choice (which finds expression in democratic forms of government); and b) the critical scientific evidence-based method for arriving at the truth. Poole seems to think of these as a curse, in some sense. I want to argue that both these elements can be fully affirmed once we see them as constituent of our normative human nature, or human flourishing, and re-expressed to indicate this. More specifically, I am going to suggest that liberal modern culture has to be understood by means of its 'internal goods' (as explained earlier), and the mechanisms for being critical (for example, consensus democracy), understood as furthering those goods. The mistake would be to take the mechanisms as ultimate values in themselves.

Aristotle, untroubled by the modern paradigm of true knowledge as (deterministic) science, thinks of ethics as a perfectly legitimate and important practical enquiry conducted not neutrally by the scientific observer but by those already engaged in the quest for the best, the most worthwhile kind of human life to lead - but who are looking to *clarify* their goals, their hierarchies of preferences. "The end aimed at is not knowledge but action", he says (*Ethics*, 1095). Only in this way, can we properly understand the idea that "every art and every inquiry, and similarly every action and pursuit, is thought to aim at some good", as the opening sentence of his *Nicomachean Ethics* reads. It is an engaged attitude that he is pointing to. And we do not have to take his outline of the conditions for the good life (crucially involving virtues of character) as being challenged by modern empirical science, because the scientific attitude is precisely a self-consciously *disengaged* one.

Aristotle suggests using as guideline for this quest, the idea of human fulfilment, fulfilment of our human nature, of our most basic desires. These are, he thinks, the desires for rationality and for political participation. This is what MacIntyre and others refer to as the standard of 'human flourishing'. For 'us', however, (that is for the dominant global approach) this standard no longer operates, firstly because of the greater degree of individual freedom in deciding *which* version of human flourishing we want to adopt; and secondly, because any such version could not claim to be objective knowledge, because objective knowledge - according to the dominant default idea of knowledge properly speaking - is never normative; it is simply *the facts*, and no facts can lead to a value conclusion, as Hume famously showed. In countering the view of the dominant 'us', MacIntyre is useful - as indeed the presenters at the China conference to a large extent concurred, along with the ethics of Confucius and Aristotle.

Excellence in social practices: Skills and virtues

MacIntyre has argued that in the very ordinary notion of a social practice we can see that objective values do continue to operate in some parts of our modern, non-tradition-based culture. Objective value judgements, he says, are linked to these large-scale cooperative activities with internal goods in part constitutive of those activities or practices. Examples are the medical and legal professions, sports, and family life. In each case, there is an ideal of objective excellence which is not simply a matter of preference.

We might debate, as philosophy practitioners, about the merits of a particular philosophy essay, but we agree more or less on the criteria for what makes for a good one. These internal goods are transcendent of the agent; in other words, they are objective values, and they are shared. They make us more than ourselves: we become soccer players, or chess players, or ice-skaters, or philosophy journal referees, with objective skills, skills judged as true values for participants in that social practice, for people who appreciate that practice.

Are excellences and skills in the practice the same as moral virtues? Not exactly. You can be skilled at playing badminton but not particularly virtuous. However, there is a connection between the two. The reason is as follows. All practices, defined by their internal goods, need institutional supports; players often need to be rewarded; rules are required for allocating positions, for promotions and so on: medicine needs hospital administrators, and chess needs chess societies. The efficient execution of these supports is also of value, but not an internal value of the practice. Practices are threatened when players focus more on those external goods than the internal goods, when lawyers and doctors perform their jobs not in order to bring about justice, or health, but primarily for the money and prestige. When this happens, the practice is, in a technical sense, corrupt - even if the profession's ethical code has strictly speaking not been broken. The principle of resistance to corruption is the set of traditional virtues of character: those dispositions or habits of character that make one to be a certain kind of, not soccer player or lawyer, but person: qualities of good judgement, of courage in the face of disapproval, balance when the temptation to override the internal goods is strong, truthfulness when others are fudging the issues, a sense of justice when the easiest route is to give undue preference to some or other group. It is these precise qualities of character that are so needed in the current global situation characterised by Mary Clark as 'technologized megamachines'.

An example can illustrate why this is not so difficult or idealistic as it may seem: learning how to enjoy reading, an example I take from McCabe (2005a, Chapters 1-3). A child might read a novel because his teacher tells him to do so, and because he wants to please the teacher; but he really only becomes a reader of novels, properly speaking, when he discovers, one night while reading in his room until far past his usual bedtime, the pleasures of reading for its own sake. He now does it primarily because he appreciates the *internal* goods of the activity, the places one goes in one's imagination, the larger world one takes part in, the identification with the characters through which one learns so much about oneself. The *external* goods - praise from the teacher - while still appreciated, become secondary. Similarly, we can think of medicine or the teaching profession, which are called vocations because those who practice them can truly appreciate their internal goods, health and learning.

I want to argue, in other words, that the characteristic institutions of a liberal society, valuing individual freedom and equality above all, are only practically feasible when the culture as a whole sees itself in terms of a social practice with these virtues of character as internal goods. What is important then, as I shall now show, is for society framed in terms of liberal ideas to embrace a sense of communitarian values.

Abstract freedom and effective freedom: Liberal and communitarian values

Modern liberal society is characterised by the procedural values of fairness and individual autonomy. My argument in the last chapter was that the substantive value of growing participation is implicitly affirmed in the liberal approach. The communitarian approach, understood properly, can very well frame a liberal ethic. For a liberal, or modern outlook, making a normative issue out of participation seems a throw-back to a premodern culture defining persons in terms of their social roles rather than as individuals with choice. Participation is seen simply as a communitarian not a liberal value. My argument, based on MacIntyre's perceptive analysis, is that the procedural values are not true values at all, but emotively justified preferences of a dominant culture - *unless* they are relativised in the way suggested above, seen to be internal goods of a social practice, modernity. They are relativised by a notion of human flourishing, and its concomitant virtues of character.

The link can be seen, however, if one distinguishes the bare capacity for freedom or autonomy (essential freedom) from its realisation (effective freedom). The latter requires the development of virtues of character, openness of self-learning, an enabling milieu of good parenting, and so on - about which utilitarian and deontological ethics have little to say. In particular, it involves habits of good behaviour, both on the intellectual level - qualities of attentiveness, intelligence, good judgement - and on the level of practical decision-making - courage, temperance, justice and so on. The liberal culture, and the philosophical ethics associated with it, to that extent misunderstands itself and the conditions for its own sustainability. Its blind spot has to do with a normative idea of human nature: the bias of the human sciences is to see all such ideas as fully conditioned by the particular values of its own culture; for example, to do with how it frames its ideas about 'woman'. The default position is to abscond from any such framing; in other words, cut the bonds with nature at all. The human person is reduced to a choosing point or self. And this fits well with a culture in which the self largely manipulates its world, through technology. It does not fit well with the value of *participation* - which MacIntyre says is key to all ethical values, because we are by our nature social beings.

Moderating the commercial moral syndrome by virtues of character

What has happened in the change from premodern to modern is a shift in the kind of default social interaction. Whereas the premodern culture puts the focus on one's place or social role in the group, modern culture emphasises a greater degree of freedom. The duty of a parent and priest in the premodern period would be to oversee the adherence to the sets of rules governing the social behaviour of his children or subjects. The duty of the child or subject would be to affirm the authority of the parent or priest or king. Ethics would be essentially understood in terms of this kind of social grouping.

Is there any space in contemporary, modern, culture for the kind of ethics of virtue that seems more at home in the premodern world? Or are advocates of the virtue ethic approach going to be confined to a kind of 'ghetto' Aristotelianism, an Amish-like existence on the fringes of society? Jane Jacobs (1977 and 1994) has conducted a descriptive study of contemporary moral values in North American society that suggests otherwise. Her study found that our operative moral ideas form two quite distinct clusters of values, the guardian moral syndrome (premodern; key value: loyalty) and the commercial moral syndrome (modern; key values: equality and productivity). The latter cluster is currently the dominant one. But the former cluster, emphasising obedience but also, crucially, participation, gives identity, and it can be argued that it expresses a crucial element in any ethical framework. This is because an action is deemed morally good when the right thing is done for the right reason (and in the right way). If a person in passing bumps me painfully in the ribs with his elbow, I have to know, Was it an accident? Or did he have some grudge against me because of some past action of mine? Only when I know what was intended, or aimed at, by the action, can I judge it as morally neutral or else morally bad, or simply an immature and petty act of spite. It's the same action from the point of view of its consequences (my sore rib) but not in itself. The guardian moral ideas come into play when one sees oneself as a member, say, of a family or a nation or a religious organisation, identifying oneself - precisely as a member alongside other members - with common ideals or sets of intentions. The latter then provide the standard for the moral evaluation of one's own and others' actions - going beyond simply pragmatic considerations. From the point of view of consequences (the commercial moral syndrome aiming at productivity without regard for intention), one can say nothing strictly speaking of the *moral* quality of the act, neither morally praise nor morally blame the agent. It makes sense to say that the *ethical* foundation for a modern society lies, paradoxically, in the typically premodern ideas which respond to the need for bonding and for meaning, for *this* kind of participation.

Conclusion

Our normative model has offered us a way through the stresses brought about by the change that we call modernity. Given our framework modernity can be seen as a development of the customary society, a sophistication of this, rather than a break with it. The key value of modernity, the value of autonomy, can be seen as one value amongst others, the value of community or belonging, for example. It is misleading to ask if there are, in addition to individual rights, community rights. This is to frame an ethical question in terms of the 'modern' vision, namely, where autonomy (thus 'rights') is trump. The organisational measures needed to secure the values of human flourishing in community, the internal goods of human community, of being human in point of fact, these measures are necessary but not sufficient. They are the rules of procedure for arranging rewards, respecting each participant equally, and so on. The internal goods of the human community have, on the other hand, to do with virtues of character, trustfulness, generosity, self-knowledge, self-affirmation, personal growth. These come about through others, and if the transition to modernity is to be a success in human terms, society has to facilitate this interpersonal interaction. These are meanings which are shareable by all, without limit. One central character-virtue is precisely that of including others rather than simply getting one's own way. This is what we have understood as self-transcendence, and it is a normal everyday virtue. The unauthorised yet dominant procedures and assumptions of the megamachine have to be resisted by each individual in their own sphere of activity, through virtues, and at a social level by supporting the alternative structures - the traditional-religious central amongst these. These conclusions are not drawn by Clark, but it is of interest for public policy implications that she affirms the move (counter-cultural in the context of modernity), in the case of South Africa, of holding a Truth and Reconciliation Commission (Clark, 2002: Chapter 10).

I have argued that the shift from a customary, tradition-based society to a commercial and law-based one seems to preclude any ethic of virtue actually having motivational traction. But social inquiry of whatever kind (I avoid saying social *science* as this seems to prejudge the issue) neglects the ethical dimension at its peril. I have introduced the idea that the values associated with this modern society, in particular, individual autonomy, are the internal goods of a particular social practice, making the skilled or *virtuous* participation in such a practice a further (implicit) value. Making it *explicit* would, I have suggested, moderate the harmful aspects of modernity. And indeed, the effective realisation of our capacity for autonomy *requires* the development of virtues of character, openness of self-learning, habits of behaviour, and so on - about which an ethics of principles and 'rights' has little to say. A virtue-based ethic (associated in China with the philosophy of Confucius) can only succeed if the harmful aspects of a commercial, open society are identified, as for example, in Clark's *In Search of Human Nature*. Modern global culture, I suggest, has a blind spot about agency. For this reason, a foundation is lacking for the values of individual autonomy and equality - and for the virtues of character. A recent example of this, which has been shown to have crucial weaknesses, can be seen in attempts to re-think ethics and religion 'naturalistically'.

In conclusion, I can note, as matter for further research, that much impetus for inserting ethics in our conception of understanding the transition to modernity has come from a familiarity with the perspective offered by analyses sourced from underdeveloped parts of the globe, in particular, the idea of 'development ethics'. This approach has its origins in the studies of French scholar Louis-Joseph Lebret, O.P., and the group Économie et Humanisme in the 1940s and has been brought forward by Denis Goulet, *Development Ethics: A Guide to Theory and Practice* (1995) and more recently by the International Development Ethics Association (IDEA) (cf Des Gasper, 2006). The influence of liberation theology on this kind of analysis would also seem significant (cf Goulet, 1974; Dorr, 1992; Curnow, 2012). Again, the implications for translating African ethics into a contemporary key are evident.

Part Three

Applications

Chapter Eight

African Environmental Ethics: Beyond the Impasse

Introduction: The human animal in the eco-system

The first application of the Africa-friendly ethical framework developed so far, concerns environmental ethics. The argument here is that it is the supposed disunity of person and external world that is at the root of the global disrespect for the natural environment. The African philosophical tradition, in contrast, exhibits none of this disunity: the person is seen as part of nature. It can therefore supply the impetus to shift the unhelpful attitude to person and nature that is characteristic of modernity. In the more integrated view of person and world suggested in this chapter, it is the simple norm of 'being a person', or *muntu*, that could found a more helpful environmental ethics.

The background to any discussion along these lines would be the widespread critique of any approach to environmental ethics founded on the nature of persons. Only a 'non-anthropocentric' approach, it is sometimes argued, could be an adequate framework for an environmental ethics. I will argue that such an approach is not, however, ultimately coherent. In appealing precisely to human understanding and rational conscience, a 'non-anthropocentric' approach seems ultimately self-undermining.

My argument draws on an Aristotelian / Thomist metaphysics, congruent with the African traditional idea of 'vital force' running through natural and social reality. I argue that organisms - human or otherwise - are *not* functional elements in the eco-system but historically viable co-determinants thereof. The role of the human organism is that of co-determining through narrative and history. Human subjectivity is not, *pace* Nagel, confined to a species-perspective, but there is a supra-biological patterning of experience intending understanding and true value. However, the development of these powers of agency, and sympathy, are stultified by a picture of self-determination as the most absolute independence from the 'other'. In contrast, the African traditional value of *Ubuntu* posits a normative development of agency through others that can be unpacked to apply beyond simply social custom. The contribution this cultural tradition brings is enhanced if the metaphysics of 'force' or 'spirit' is interpreted non-dualistically and without appeal to a supernaturalism.

The Raskolnikov problem

A new mentality is required. In Dostoevsky's novel, *Crime and Punishment*, the central character, Raskolnikov, cannot see the point of another human being, his landlady, to whom he owes money, and, he calculates, is of less utility than himself, and he does away with her. His changed view, in prison for the murder, comes about through the influence of another, kind person. The question we are addressing is whether the African traditional ethics of *Ubuntu*, framed by a metaphysics of 'vital force' running through the social and natural world, can contribute to overcoming the dominant and unhelpful picture of the person as likewise disengaged from and indifferent to the natural world. I think it can, avoiding the idea of "humans understood to be just discrete entities", as Brian Henning (2017) at Gonzaga University puts it in his call for contributions to an anthology of non-anthropocentric approaches to climate change. Can it, at the same time, "reconceive subjectivity and agency" (as the call for contributions adds) so as to avoid the impasse pointed to in our opening paragraph above? I am going to put forward the interpretative framework of the Aristotelian / Thomist understanding of living beings, non-human and human, as both cognate with the African traditional picture and grounding just such a reconception of subjectivity and agency. The challenge is to reformulate the African traditional ethic and metaphysics so as to facilitate its reception in a culture of science. Empathy with other persons, central to the *Ubuntu* interpretation of being human, allows for a transformation of mentality that appreciates the value of our shared natural milieu. At least, this is what I shall argue.

The human organism and the eco-system: The role of sympathy

To resolve this predicament, we need then to show that placing living beings as functional elements in an eco-system misunderstands what it is to be a living organism. And in the Aristotelian tradition taken forward, as we have seen, by contemporary Thomists such as Lonergan, the identity of an organism is not properly explained in terms of its roles or functions within a whole, since it is itself a viable whole, what is called the organism's 'form' (see also Le Blanc's (1999) account of 'Eco-Thomism'). It is this approach that can, I will argue, answer to our problematic. This approach is, as much of philosophy, controversial. For a contrary view, see JM Coetzee (1999), who suggests the dichotomy reason / nature goes back through Descartes to Aquinas and Aristotle. He references Aquinas' idea that cruelty to animals is of no moral concern except insofar as it may accustom us to being cruel to humans (Coetzee, 1999:22). Aquinas' view is found in his *Summa Theologica* Ia IIae, Q.10 art. 6 and 8 (Aquinas, 1964).

Timothy McDermott (1989), one of the contemporary Thomists, argues the organism is not simply an organ *in* a system but co-determines the 'system' itself. The organism is an existing historically stable whole which cannot be fully explained in terms of mechanisms. The organism is favoured by nature, not because of its *function*, even the function of reproducing itself, for one could ask, What is the function of that? The attempt to fix the defining function is faced with an ever-receding horizon. We may ask what an eye is for, but it seems quirky to ask what a cow is for. Cows may be employed within a farm; of themselves; however, they are not parts of a production process but members of an eco-system. They do of course play roles in that eco-system, but, as McDermott adds, "they are not simply implementations of a function that the eco-system demands of them. Rather they are historical facts that have just proved to be viable in that eco-system, or rather in the eco-system as itself changed by their viability" (McDermott, 1989:xxviii).

The 'historical fact' that McDermott talks of is a synthesis of evolutionary biology and human history. The key to an environmental ethics that does not pit 'man' against 'nature' lies in this synthesis. Appreciating the 'historical fact' (some animals have been found to be domesticatable, others not) enables a responsible and creative further taking up of the planet's eco-system. The age of the Anthropocene is characterised by not only by evolving nature but historical narrative. We are inserted into nature. Darwin's impact on environmental thinking has been crucial, and has been extended to take into account the 'noosphere', Teilhard de Chardin's term for the sphere of consciousness and mind. Wilhelm Wundt, in the late nineteenth century, saw human consciousness as constituting "a decisive point in nature's course, a point at which the world becomes aware of itself" (cited in Menaud, 2001:269). This is an insight developed at length by Brian Swimme and Thomas Berry in *The Universe Story. From the Primordial Flaring Forth to the Ecozoic Era* (1994).

The task today is to self-consciously take up nature more and more into the human imagination and in this way, overcome the knee-jerk reaction to the realisation that nature will after all literally deliver the death blow to each individual person. This work on the human psyche is part and parcel of any environmental ethics that will have real purchase on our moral imagination and hence on our actions.

The novelist JM Coetzee (1999:35) understands this very well, pointing to our indifference to the suffering of animals, "we can do anything, it seems, and come away clean". As Mary Midgley puts it in a piece of analysis Coetzee (2003) later acknowledges as influential in his own approach, "criticism of the undeveloped heart is moral criticism" (Midgley, 1995:259). Environmental ethics calls for a maturing of our faculty of sympathy, and in particular, a greater integration of our ideas, especially about values, and our habitual decisions, and both of these with our feelings. The impotence resulting from such conflict within ourselves is well illustrated by Martin Prozesky (2009) in his phenomenology of our feelings about nature juxtaposed with feelings about those living on the margins of development whose struggle against poverty might further degrade the natural milieu. His examples are from rural KwaZulu-Natal, site of both nature reserves and of extreme poverty. What is crucial is, therefore, a process of growth towards a less conflictual set of choices. We will argue that this is achieved for any particular individual (as pointed to in African traditional ethics) only through the beneficial influence of other persons.

Objections

We turn now to deal with a major objection to this way of approaching environmental ethics, namely the contention that the project of developing a more consequential set of feeling-reactions to the lives of animals and the natural world in general, is nothing more than an expression of human hubris. Human subjectivity, the argument goes, is in fact enclosed within its species-perspective. This is the view of Thomas Nagel (1979a), who argues we cannot get to the value, to the 'how it is experienced as a value', of another species, to what it is like to for them to be themselves - his example is that of a bat. We can get no further, beyond our subjectivity, in finding some 'objective' description of the organism living its life.

> Facts about what it is like for the experiencing organism are accessible only from one point of view... It is unlikely that we will get closer to the real nature of the experience by leaving behind the particularity of its point of view and striving for a description in terms accessible to beings that could only imagine what it was like to be that organism (Nagel, 1979a:172-174).

These beings are us. Humans. But is Nagel right? Can we not, in response, point to a broader understanding of subjectivity. While it is true that we do experience a reality circumscribed by our sense-capacities unique to our species, still, it can be argued, this is just one *patterning* of experience amongst others. It cannot be *identified* with subjectivity since we can also have the subjective experience of coming to an objective understanding of things; for example, when we affirm our understanding of something as probably true (we are not saying it is probably true to us, but really so). I can explain this kind of experienced reality further.

It is common to refer to intentional actions as 'mental events', suggesting that they are simply there, as physical events are. This, however, is misleading in the case mentioned above; the experienced fact of sometimes actively 'standing by' certain standards of reasonableness as apt for the purposes of considering rival claims to truth. In taking responsibility for one's own contribution to the common growth of knowledge and understanding, one is becoming more present to oneself as being under certain normative demands - basically, to make something of one's powers of intelligence. Nagel's example of subjectivity is therefore a special case of conscious experience, not at all definitive of it.

The notion of patterns of experience comes from Bernard Lonergan and it enables us to account for the data brought forward by Nagel while avoiding the impression that this experience exists somehow 'alongside' the objective physical reality. What Nagel describes as the ineluctably subjective character of experience that Lonergan (1970:181–184) describes in terms of the idea of the biological patterning of experience which is characterised by knowing through sense and imagination, what he calls 'extroversion'. Such experience is non-objective, but *other* patternings of our experience are possible, according to how we are intentionally oriented. Experience is not uniform, all of one kind, but always patterned. A flock of birds passing overhead signifies for me, simply that, but my ornithologist hiking friend sees climate change. Same sensation, different perception. Lonergan points to the artificiality of speaking simply of pure sensation. Acts such as seeing, hearing, tasting never occur in isolation but always in some intentional framework.

When I would see with my eyes, I open them, turn my head, approach, focus my gaze... [But] besides the systematic links between senses and sense organs, there is, immanent in experience, a factor variously named conation, interest, attention, purpose (1970:181).

We can compare animal living with that of plants. *Conscious* living is only *part* of the animal's total living: vital processes go on willy-nilly. Consciousness is called forth to deal with the drive to sustain life, to respond to opportunities and dangers. The biological pattern of experience is concerned with these externalities within the full pattern of living.

Lonergan distinguishes a range of patterns of experience, biological, aesthetic, religious, intellectual, dramatic. (In the aesthetic pattern, for example, the biological drives are to some extent disregarded in favour of an interest in following a line which appeals primarily to one's imagination, evoking a wider range of emotions and desires). And this helps us to understand the confusion in Nagel's Cartesian construction of the dichotomy of the external and the internal (or subjective) points of view (Nagel, 1979b). This dichotomy pertains specifically to the biological patterning of experience, whose intentional object is aptly referred to as 'the already out there now real'. This refers to an object to which we are oriented already before taking thought - the table in front of me as I traverse the room after a power failure to get to the matches. I don't have echolocation, so I bump into the table - my sense organs are a limit, and the table has the immediate 'reality' of a being 'out there', external to me, of relevance to the biological success or failure of the organism (Lonergan, 1970:252).

But thinking of reality as what is external to me is not, however, of relevance to another patterning of experience, the intellectual, which aims at another kind of knowing, through experiencing, intelligent understanding and finally passing reflective judgement on the adequacy or otherwise of one's grasp of the object at hand. In the latter case, sensible, realistic concerns of the biological organism are put aside in favour of the exigencies of the enquiring mind. Objectivity now comes to mean the goal of dealing with (raising and answering) all the questions relevant to the question posed to the understanding. Thus, Thales trips into the well (failure in the operation of the biological organism) because he is contemplating the intelligible order in the movements of the planets.

The upshot is that our subjectivity is not something species-restricted, or not necessarily so. In giving my intelligence its scope, and my capacity for reasoned not rash judgement, I live more fully in the real world - of living things, for example. Nature is not something 'out there' *on which* I act either only to serve human needs (anthropocentricism) or not only as this (non-anthropocentricism). No, nature is equally *ourselves* as subjects and agents. The lives of animals are shared by being taken up in our understanding and being made part of our world and our history; not only domesticated animals but fynbos and game parks become treasured elements in our world. Truly, to do this is no easy task. There are problems with how detached one is about one's habitual horizon of *willingness* to follow through such inquiry. A transformation of one's feeling life, of one's psyche, is called for. The beast that is nature and that terrifies can be tamed by beasts in nature. Out of fear come projections of that fear, and in the ensuing hoarding of forces to fortify oneself against those enemies, it is the environment - sufficient for our needs but not our traumas - that suffers.

The problem of underdeveloped human agency

Our focus must therefore be on the problem of the underdevelopment of human agency. In an age of cultural relativism and consumer preference, agency is seen not in terms of how it is developed, but simply in terms of free will or choice. The normative element comes in only as a procedural regulation: all agents have *equal* sovereignty over their lives. This is a major reason why animal and environmental ethics is often discussed in terms of the extension of this norm of equality. But African traditional ethics takes a different line, as we saw in Chapter 2, thinking of persons in terms of a norm of development, and positing duties to the more developed members to exert influence over the less developed, in particular children. What needs unpacking is how this is to be conceived of in a way that does not posit a metaphysical hierarchy in terms of which that norm of being human is thought of as above nature, an essence that has a super-natural quality, the 'soul'.

In the Aristotelian / Thomist picture, we have a way through this dilemma: it lies in seeing non-human animal life in terms of voluntariness rather than mechanistically. The animal is not simply at our disposal, as we might think if we consider it as a tool, a machine, devoid of an inner life. The machine does not act purposively - the rear sensors of the SUV do not actually *see* the wall as we come too close to it, because the car does not 'have a world' in which certain objects play significant roles, as the bird does in the life of a spaniel. The dog chases the bird precisely because it sees it; it acts voluntarily. Making this behaviour intelligible to us (hence, appreciating it as *of value*) takes an effort of mind and of will, and we make an effort to consent to a range of appropriate feelings, inhibiting ones that would discount such purposefulness. We have to appreciate the voluntariness of the animal, its acting for a purpose, and see how its network of meanings make sense: an example would be when we are taken up in the singular intent of the lioness' hunt for the impala. This is more difficult but not impossible in the case of a bat. McCabe (2005a:96) argues that cruelty to animals is not so much a failure of justice (as would be the case if animal ethics was founded on 'rights') but of temperance, in other words of the virtue that responds to feelings of undue domination over or taking pleasure from the object.

The non-human animal reveals something undeniably true of the natural world: its directionality, its value, and this is revealed *in* the life of the animal. We do not have to take the implausible step to saying that animals have 'rights': the non-human animal does not share the space of meanings in which claims on other members make sense. Rather, the world of the cow is pre-defined by a set of meanings or responses that are biological in origin. McCabe argues that in the case of the human animal, the world is, in contrast, self-defined, invented, through tradition and history, and part of that self-understanding is 'rights' talk.

Has this, however, simply shifted the problem raised by Nagel from our (limited) structures of perception to the perspectival structures of our particular society and language? Would the idea that we are human agents by virtue of our social participation - the *Ubuntu* idea - imply our identity is simply that of 'the tribe' - the objection, mentioned in Chapter 3, of Stephen Theron (cited in Murove, 2009b:328)? And if the norms apply only to one society, simply custom, they have lost their compelling ethical force. In response, we can unpack the origin of action that we experience in ourselves. Shutte uses the term 'self-enacting' to describe the human kind of causality, not one thing causing another (my social determinants causing my attitudes) but I myself causing myself. As we saw in our discussion of personal growth in Chapter 2, this idea is central to understanding how the human person is self-transcending. In the act of choosing, the self that I choose and consent to (say, temperate rather than indulgent), I know is the same as the self that chooses and consents. I myself act on myself. I am able to take into consideration possible biases due to my particular social influences, my particular 'language'. Being self-moving in this radical way has been traditionally termed spirit, precisely to distinguish it from entities not thus constituted, not freely able to act in accordance with value, or an understanding of value, consented to.

Human spirituality but not a dualism

This might seem to have re-introduced a dualism of spirit and matter, human and nature. This is not so. In the African approach, the self-enactment is achieved, as already argued in our discussion of Shutte in Chapter 2, through relatedness to the other-than-self. The quality attaching to this acting on good reasons is something that is *developed*; its very coming into being in the neonate and child is arguably only possible through the intentions of the beneficial 'mother'. And the development happens through the quality of its relatedness to other-than-self. Self-determination grows in direct proportion (and not in indirect proportion) to a certain kind of *other*-determination: so far are we from the idea that freedom is *independence* from the other.

One thinks here of any person's dependence on the world around them, and in particular, other persons. In finding and appreciating value in the other person, one comes, through their influence, to a less conflictual self-affirmation. I affirm them affirming me as less conflictual (I respond to their initiative), and so overcome, in this way, my habitual self-image and orientation. My feelings are released to allow me to respond proportionately to nature (rather than disproportionately, for example to grizzly bears as does the central character in Werner Herzog's (2005) docu-film *Grizzly Man*). Nature becomes, bit by bit, our common home, where we can be 'at home'. By showing how my self-enactment is achieved precisely through the other person, African traditional philosophical thought heads off any idea that the self is over and against the world 'out there', and this undercuts the basis for environmental neglect.

African traditional thought I: Not a supernaturalism

Finally, we need to say something specific about the core African idea of *seriti / isithunzi*, or *force vitale*, and about *Ubuntu*. The first should not be understood supernaturalistically. B Bujo, for example, agrees there is a moral order over and above the social nexus. He argues African traditional ethics is not simply anthropocentric, but that there is an other-worldly reality to which reference must be made. And he adds that God, as creator, "has to intervene in the moral order if the human person does not follow the laws set by him" and, furthermore, punish crimes (Bujo, 2009:114). Here we have one reason why sensible folk might be suspicious of the African traditional framework of thought: the God intervening - perforce breaking one of the four fundamental forces of the universe, say, gravitational - would undermine, first, the causality of human agency, sketched above; secondly, the integrity of the scientific enterprise (including the science of climate change); and finally the universe itself. Whereas a reference to a value-pervasive natural reality such as *seriti* lends itself to seeing the human person as becoming fully human through a dependence on the natural and social milieu, the supernaturalistic interpretation of this once again downgrades the natural world, *pace* Bujo the only world there is. African traditional thought has to come to terms with a shift away from a dual worldview, heaven and earth (which at any rate, never was a reified dualism, as it was in some European versions thereof), one that detracts from responsibility for the planet. The oversights of the European Enlightenment, which we have stressed, should not encourage us to discard its very liberating achievements in secularising human consciousness.

African traditional thought II: Not a moralism

Secondly, the *Ubuntu* idea. I am looking to this to ground the shift in mind-set that we have tasked ourselves with. I take *Ubuntu* as an attitudinal ideal - not a metaphysical essence or nature. I am not advocating an environmental 'moralism', something imposed which does not particularly resonate with people: to the claim that this or that is the human telos or essence or the moral status of animals, the reply could be, So what? Rather, I am doing 'transformational philosophy', addressing the problem of a lack of development, and moving it along. In the face of our disengaged Raskolnikov character, we offer the idea of a growing self-enactment (more intensely engaged) as one moves from sensing (seeing the bat fly in the dark) to making sense of how it does this (echolocation). Does one not value such understanding, or rather oneself as understanding? Of course one does. Again, not rushing into a claim for the truth of one's interpretation but reflecting on its possible inaccuracy. Oneself as being reasonable (not unreasonable), at least with respect to this object at hand, is something to celebrate. Similarly, with oneself consenting to a desire because it is all things considered worthwhile - it corresponds to the value of the animal living its life, say - and inhibiting other desires because they are shallower (the desire to kill the bat). Again, this human phenomenon, oneself as responsible, is, it goes without saying, of value. The awakening to these subject-enhancing moments as of value fashions the kind of mentality we are seeking, engaged rather than disengaged. Raskolnikov appreciates his new transformed self.

The engine of this self-development, in the *Ubuntu* approach, is the other person. For, in ethics we are concerned not simply with successful action (say, the effective culling of elephants), where the *means* taken might be irrelevant, but also with the *intention* behind the action. Is the chain around the dog's neck for its own protection or an instance of cruelty? This concern presupposes a 'you' that 'gets' the intention, amongst a range of possible intentions. If I am doing ethics in a cross-cultural context (such as the present one) I make my point carefully so as to bring clarity to my interlocutor in terms that can be seen by them as possible intentions. The only foundation possible for ethics is not something already determined ('nature'), of which I must convince others, but rather the *reasonable attitude* of commitment to achieving some viable community with others rather than getting one's own way. The interlocutor and I must necessarily share a common life, in which a range of intentions make sense. I correctly interpret the Bulgarian official at the gate to be indicating 'yes' (because he is smiling) to my request to enter even though he is shaking his head rather than nodding, which would be the more common gesture for indicating assent. To the extent that environmental *ethics* (rather than an environmental pressure group!) has actual purchase, it will be hand in hand with a commitment to the achievement of a community of engaged persons.

Conclusion

How far have we succeeded in responding to the Raskolnikov problematic? Peter Singer is not convinced of our approach. Responding to Coetzee's idea of sympathy, he argues that "we can't take our *feelings* as moral data, immune from rational criticism" (Singer, 1999:89). Any unit of life, he says, is basically equivalent in value to any other unit; there is no place for basing values on how we *feel* about any living being. Your feeling of loss at the killing of an animal (or the animal's own loss of certain lived experience) is simply *subjective* data, not of any significant account in a moral calculus. There is no moral harm if such killing is painless: another equally valuable life can furnish a replacement. This seems close to Raskolnikov before his change of heart. Singer's challenge reinforces the importance of overturning, as we have tried to do, this truncated and unhelpful view of 'subjectivity'.

I have argued, in response to the impasse of a non-anthropocentric conception of environmental ethics, that animals – human, non-human – are misrepresented as equal functional elements in an eco-system. Organisms co-define the system, and are historically viable facts. The human organism takes up the evolving cosmos into a self-conscious narrative, doing this either well or badly. Human subjectivity is not, *pace* Nagel, imprisoned in one perspective – this perspectival attitude corresponds only to the biological patterning of experience, pitting ourselves over and against the world 'out there'. But there is the problem of an underdeveloped human intelligence, integrity of will, and feeling. To the extent that human self-determination is thought of in terms of the most absolute *independence* from the 'other,' there will be a neglect of the need to address the conflicted and undeveloped core of personal agency. The African traditional concept of agency as developmental and normative is a counter to this, and can be unpacked so as to avoid any notion of such a norm being restricted to social custom. The framing metaphysics of 'force' or 'spirit' needs, I have argued, to be developed so as to avoid any dualism of 'man' / world, and also any supernaturalism. So far as distrust of the other leads to the kind of hoarding that has detrimental effects on the environment, the *Ubuntu* idea is a useful weapon in dialogues on the ecology. And the current politics of the USA does indeed suggest a link between such distrust, finding expression in the unbridled competitiveness of the free market, and environmental disregard.

Chapter Nine

Tradition, Modernity and the Virtues in Music Professionals: The Example of *Amakwaya*

with Markus Detterbeck

Introduction

Our second venture in applying our ethical framework uses MacIntyre's notion of a social practice to think through the challenges of traditional music groups in an age of commerce. MacIntyre's understanding of the 'internal goods' of any practice highlights the appropriation of those goods, moving from ideals to actual skills and virtues. In this case, we consider the place, if any, of virtues of character in any adequate understanding of one particular group of African music professionals, in the context of a shift from a traditional to a modern commerce-driven economy. The empirical details, historical and contemporary, of these groups of South African choral singers which I draw on for my understanding of the tradition, and which make up the large part of this chapter, are based on the Ph.D. thesis at the University of KwaZulu-Natal of Markus Detterbeck (2003), and because of this overall indebtedness, no further detailed page references to that document will be made here. The journal article on which the chapter is based was, however, written jointly by him and myself. I am grateful to him for allowing me to use this material in the somewhat different context of this book.

The conclusion drawn from my interpretation of the evidence is that character does make a difference, if the authentic practice - and the values associated with it - is to be able to carry forward, in different circumstances, what has been of great value to society. The relevance for ethics in the context of African traditional culture is crystal clear. The contrary view

- we will term this the modernity thesis - is that modern social developments entail a radical discontinuity in history and break with tradition and its accompanying ideal of the participants motivated, to a significant degree, by reasons of virtues of character. Representative of this view, already drawn on above, in our research on professionalism in general, is Anthony Giddens. In his book, *The Consequences of Modernity* (1990), Giddens writes that "the modes of life brought into being by modernity have swept us away from *all* traditional types of social order, in quite unprecedented fashion" (1990:4). The radical reflexivity which is the mark of the modern, means one can no longer appeal to tradition. Or rather, if one does justify tradition, this is 'only in the light of knowledge which is not itself authenticated by tradition.' And such justified tradition is "tradition in sham clothing" (1990:38).

I want to present what I think is a counter example to this thesis, namely the South African black choral tradition, *amakwaya*. This chapter then focuses in on the details of one specific social practice over a number of years in a crucial time of changing social circumstances. In order to understand the contemporary practice, we will need to go into some historical detail.

The picture drawn by the modernity thesis is that of a social system in which individuals are subject to, or subject themselves to, a system of rewards which disengages persons from their traditions with their internally generated criteria of excellence, isolates and individualises them, emasculating their specific motivational parameters or frameworks. With this counter-example, I want to show the tenuous nature of the thesis that this is *inevitable*, a necessity of social and economic development. I suggest that it can be reasonably hoped that the *amakwaya* tradition will continue to synthesise elements from other cultures without fully losing its continuity with past tradition. The way, for example, in which dress codes were adopted, and also the way in which ideas of 'progress', 'education', and so on were assimilated, points not to a capitulation to modernity (represented by the colonial powers and missionary ideas) but rather to a negotiated identity, embracing various elements and not essentially in opposition to the 'other'. This negotiation, entailing an intelligent refusal of immediate rewards of a commercial kind, draws on virtues of character embodied in the music tradition and its internal goods.

The term *amakwaya* is used to distinguish the choral practice of the mixed black choirs that emerged from the mission stations in the nineteenth century, from other South African vocal and choral traditions, such as *isicathamiya* or Gospel. In the first part, it is argued that the development of this *amakwaya* tradition has had an integral connection with questions of cultural identity and that this formation of identity can be seen to mature from one of imitation to one characterised by negotiation. The hybrid musical form of *amakwaya* symbolised, in restrictive political circumstances, the general political and social aspirations of black people, as is evidenced in the lyrics and performance practice, as well as in the comments of the choristers themselves. The tradition somehow gave meaning and sense to people's lives, and had a not insignificant role in the emergence of a national culture. The identity being constructed, while for the most part, an open one with the potential to inspire a more embracing cultural unity, was however mixed with elements of a class stratification and exclusivity, pitting the educated middle-class and 'progress', against rural and uneducated 'traditional' folk.

In the second part of the discussion, I argue that this aspect of exclusiveness has been reinforced more recently by commercialisation, and competitiveness, even simply monetary gain, has increasingly played a distorting role in the choral practice. The evidence indicates that the African cultural practice here in question is able to resist - through assimilation - those seemingly overwhelming detraditionalising forces. An appreciation of the hybrid character of the genius of *amakwaya* tradition, along with its role in giving meaning, would encourage participants and leaders to be aware of and take measures to counteract potentially undermining elements in the present situation.

Choral singing and identity: From imitation to negotiation

We can begin with a brief vignette illustrating the impact of the missions on choral singing. Ray Phillips, an American Board missionary, recorded the following experience he had around 1918, when he attended a rural wedding:

> We discovered on our arrival that both Christians and heathen had been invited to attend the joyous occasion. On one side of the collection of huts were assembled the heathen; on the other the Christian folk. On the heathen side the wedding dances were being put on by a long line of sparsely dressed men, young and old. They stamped and shouted and sang, looking up into heaven with staring eyes. They were evidently invoking the blessings of the spirits of the departed on the newly-wedded pair. When the dancers lagged there were the women to encourage them by their steady hand-clapping. There also were the equally encouraging pots of home-brew beer containing a powerful 'kick.'
>
> The side of the kraal occupied by the Christians, however, was quiet and dignified. Here in his black frock-coat was the preacher, vigilant to guard his flock. All were attired, as nearly as possible, like the white people they had seen. And they were seated on European chairs. (Their heathen brethren squatted on the ground). What could the Christians do to contribute to the joy of the wedding? The pastor solemnly stood up and selected a hymn; they turned to the places, stood up together, and in good harmony sang one of the great hymns of the Church: 'Holy, Holy, Holy'. Then they resumed their seats. But all the time, on the opposite side of the kraal, the heathen commotion continued without check, the noise rising and falling - stamp, stamp! grunt, grunt! the bursting into song, the waving of the shields, and the vicious jabbing of the spears (Phillips, 1930:93-94).

This report gives us an idea of the alienation of black mission communities from their past. It reveals how far the mission-educated Africans had departed from their ancestral roots, being almost completely prevented from participating in their own past culture.

This development of a new class of Westernised and educated Africans was a process marked by ambiguity. The *amakholwa* (from Zulu: *kholwa* - to believe), as this middle-class came to be known, could, however, be understood in two distinctly different ways. The first is that of a scorned minority that was left out both of the black traditional communities and the white communities. Norman Etherington (1978:67) speaks of the 'flotsam and jetsam' of black society washed up on the mission stations, their motivation to convert and settle on mission land being primarily nurtured by the fact that they had no other place to go. The second interpretation depicts the mission-educated elite as new emergent urbanised leaders - for example, Houle (1998), and Marks (1986). Scholars point to the influential personalities who rose to positions of authority within the wider Zulu society, playing a crucial role in forming political parties. Names such as Rev Canon Calata, ZK Matthews, Chief Luthuli and Dr Zuma come to mind (cf Wilson, 1986:194).

A closer look shows that these two contradictory perceptions belong to successive periods in the history of the black middle-class, with the turning point around 1900. What led to this remarkable transformation? Leaving the rural community meant leaving the protective community of shared values and ideas, the secure position of traditional identity. The separation from traditional society had a traumatic effect on those who arrived at the mission station. Imbued by the missionaries with Western ideas, they gradually came to perceive imitation and assimilation of Western identity as a possible escape route from the exploitative situation created by the colonists. Under the influence of the missionaries, the majority of black Christians were successfully weaned from traditional beliefs and practices. The rejected now became the rejecters. All the aspects of African social, religious, political or cultural life that were condemned by the missionaries as being 'primitive' or 'heathen' - traditional customs, beliefs, dress, music - were now regarded contemptuously.

The mission stations became, as David Coplan (1985:26-27) puts it, "islands of acculturation in a traditional sea" that led to the polarisation of the traditionalists (*amabhinca*) and *amakholwa*. But the unyielding opposition to the black Christians on the part of white people led, in turn, to a re-evaluation of this turning away from tradition.

Daniel Msimango, a resident of Edendale station, expressed his confusion and disappointment over this situation in an article published as early as 1863:

> We are in the light and yet in the darkness. We are in the immediate neighborhood of the white man, and yet we are far removed... Which road are we to take to the right hand or to the left? Are we retreating instead of advancing in civilisation?" (*Natal Witness*, March 27, 1863).

The situation provided *amakwaya* with the necessary energy to form a new social stratum with a distinct identity. In *amakwaya* groups, a decisive shift from uncritical imitation of Western influences to an informed negotiation between Western and ethnic values is evident in the last decade of the nineteenth century. The first signs occurred in the late 1880s when many mission-school Africans were beginning to wonder whether they had been wise to trade "the birthright of [their] cultural heritage for a Western pottage of unattainable goals and unkept promises" (Coplan, 1985:30). A strong sense developed that a satisfying self-image could not be built entirely on adopted European models. The aspect of the new identity bound up with the musical aspirations is well illustrated through Skota's *The African Yearly Register. Being an Illustrated National Biographical Dictionary (Who's Who) of Black Folk in Africa* (Skota, 1930). This is a sourcebook documenting the change of the middle-class towards an identity described as 'New Africans'. This register is both an appeal for recognition by the white rulers and a directory of black ideas and ideals. Many of those whom Skota mentions in his *Register* are the 'New Africans' categorised by Herbert Dhlomo as "progressive thinking African intellectuals and leaders." At the same time, these individuals had a growing consciousness of their ancestral heritage. "The New African knows where he belongs and what belongs to him; where he is going and how; what he wants and the methods to obtain it" (Dhlomo, in Couzens, 1985:33). Their attitude to members of the lower classes was distinctly different from that of the first-generation converts. They no longer rejected their traditional heritage, but attempted to incorporate it into their conception of a new African national culture. They saw themselves as providing leadership for those previously left behind in a 'savage state'. And the prominent *amakwaya* personalities feature in the Register, as does the category 'lover of music'. The development of a syncretic African choral tradition was one weapon that could be used in order to define and express a distinctively African concept of modern civilisation.

Aspects of negotiation in the choral repertoire

We turn now to another aspect throwing light on how Western and African influences were negotiated: the threefold sectionalised repertoire of *amakwaya* practice itself. This repertoire consists of neo-traditional songs (modernised versions of songs taken from African folk repertoire), Western art music (of mainly European origin), and African eclectic compositions (by mainly mission-trained composers). As Zakhele Fakazi, Secretary of Imvunge Choral Society, puts it, "you do Western pieces, and then you do African pieces, and then you start dancing. That is standard... When they have movements, then it's wedding songs" (Personal communication to Markus Detterbeck, Mariannhill, November 5, 1999. All interviews referred to in this chapter were conducted by Detterbeck, and took place between 1999 and 2001). The point that we want to emphasise is that almost all performances of *amakwaya* groups are based on this structure, and, with the distinct function and meaning of its various parts, this distinguishes them from other choral practices. The choice of repertoire, ranging from simple borrowing in the case of neo-traditional wedding songs, to the wholesale imitation of Western aesthetic and performance practice, reveals to what extent *amakwaya* mediate foreign influences. That this cultural negotiation still continues today is evident in the inclusion of neo-traditional wedding songs, as a sign of their desire to remain true to their ancestral roots, just as the inclusion of Western compositions is a sign of their continued aspirations towards a 'modern' way of life. The section of African-composed eclectic choral works may be viewed as a distinct attempt to reconcile these two cultural elements.

The styles of African composers allow a rough categorisation, which is determined mainly by the degree to which Western or African musical aspects and traditions are used. Their growing awareness of their African roots, which culminated in the black consciousness movement and later in the idea of the African Renaissance, had a formative influence on *amakwaya* composers and the stylistic development of their compositions. Starting with an almost exclusive imitation of Western musical structures and ideas, by the end of the nineteenth century, composers increasingly were looking for ways to find their own style. They never gave up Western elements completely, and all periods reveal a clinging to European ideas.

The development of African-composed compositions can further illustrate this point. Various periods can be distinguished, with Ntsikana Gaba, born around 1780, as an influential precursor, with his 'Great Hymn' and other compositions being transmitted orally for half a century. But the works of the first group of composers, who emerged from the mission stations almost fifty years later, show that many of the features of Ntsikana's compositions, which are today regarded as embodying a genuine African aesthetic, had been lost. African vernacular words were the only African element, and what we find is mere imitation of the melodic and harmonic structures of hymns taught to them by the missionaries. Examples of this are John Knox Bokwe's *Vuka Deborah!* (early 1880s) and Enoch Sontonga's *Nkosi Sikelel' iAfrika* (1897). A decisive change set in towards the beginning of the twentieth century. Initially the recourse to African musical elements that coincided with the emerging nationalism concerned only rhythm. Composers started to replace Western hymnic square rhythms by introducing polyrhythm, multiple downbeats, syncopated rhythms, interlocking and interrhythm, into their composition. To understand the difference to the standard Western rhythm, one can think of the regular (say, four-beat) metre of any church hymn: what polyrhythm (or cross rhythm) does is juxtapose that with a three-beat metre to create a new and more complex rhythmic grouping. Examples are PJ Mohapeloa's *Mokhotlong* and RT Caluza's *Silusapho Lwaze Afrika*, or *iLand Act* (1912), the political content of which is evident. It was only towards the middle of the twentieth century that composers began to explore what Mzilikazi Khumalo, one of the foremost *amakwaya* composers, calls a 'distinctively African style' of choral composition. In the late 1980s he created, with *uShaka Kasenzangakhona*, a large-scale work that is based on the European form of oratorio, but which uses many African elements. His most recent development is the composition of an African opera, *Princess Magogo*, which premiered in Durban in 2002.

The link drawn here between music and identity is not fanciful. In traditional African culture, music and choral singing were never simply entertainment. Amongst southern African Nguni, music is regarded not only as an expression of one's creativity, but also as a powerful means of communication with the ancestral world and the natural environment. Music creates a strong feeling of community. Men, women, and children join in spontaneously, no matter what their status or function in the society, and "any individual who has the urge to make his voice heard is given the liberty to do so" (Pewa, 1984:27). And it was possible for a singer to sing a message that would have been unacceptable in direct speech, and even figures of authority could be challenged, for example, the king or the chief. These customs were recently alluded to by Mangosuthu Buthelezi, then Minister of Home Affairs, at the preview of the *Birth of an African Opera* at the Playhouse in Durban, April 18, 2001:

> Music and song play an important function in our nation. They express how chorally we perceive and experience life, and mark joy and sorrow, love and war, and each of the recurring seasons. They manifest the ethos and pathos of our nation. Other nations have consigned the expression of their culture to writing or buildings while, since time immemorial, the Zulu nation has consigned it to music,

dances and rituals. For this reason, music is one of our most important cultural expressions.

Today, choral music has become the most popular form of musical endeavour amongst black communities in South Africa. With hundreds of choral groups rehearsing on a regular basis and receiving financial sponsorship from the private sector for big choral events like the annual National Choir Festival (NCF), these mixed choirs have arguably become the most important musical group in South Africa. The value attached to choral singing goes back a long way: "If there is an assurance of civilised advancement," wrote a correspondent in 1911, "it can be found in beautiful singing, especially in concerted singing" (*Ilanga* June 23, 1911). Singing, and in particular, choral music, we want to argue, played its role in the process of the formation of black middle-class identity. In an arguably parallel context of subaltern groups in Peru, Thomas Turino concludes that music plays a crucial role in group identification. People "adapt, alter, combine, and create cultural resources in unique ways, and for very specific reasons, the search for security, feelings of self-worth, and some kind of liveable space not least among them" (Turino, 1993:3-4) In our own case, this importance was recognised during the socially restrictive years of the 1960s, as the following extract shows.

> The deeper and more realistic purpose of our music is the positive building of our nation on the cultural plain [sic]. If the magnitude of this campaign has reached unprecedented heights it is only because music is the only talent we can develop to the international level without any restrictions... It can be nothing else at the moment. (*Journal of the Transvaal United African Teachers Association, TUATA*, June 1962:4)

This perception, as the writer continues, was partly responsible for the increasing focus of these choral groups on competitions, by means of which they hoped to "produce [not only] singers but musicians - composers of world standard." In music and singing, the possibility was seen of achieving the goal of drawing level with and even excelling the white communities. The ambiguous nature of this development, and its link to the elitist identity-formation associated with *amakwaya*, is what we now turn to in the second part of this discussion. Again, our purpose is to interrogate the possible role played in these developments of virtues of character, habits of acting that embody intelligent responses to possible ways forward, grounded in a vision of true human flourishing together with others.

Competitions, tradition and modernity

The new music was creating meaning for the choristers and their audience. At the same time the identity being forged was one, as we said before, that was to some extent a self-consciously elitist one; in other words, positioning a certain group as privileged over other groups. One manifestation of this privileging is the competitive dimension to be seen in *amakwaya* performance, issuing in the present-day National Choir Festival and all it entails for choristers today. Before the National Choir Festival, there is an undignified scramble to ascertain the judges' opinions on the material they will judge. And this would run counter to the tradition in which external criteria of what counts as 'good' in choral singing - for example, the European approach - were always, after the initial period of imitation, sifted through by a process of negotiation, producing something truly original.

Thus, the very success of the choral music - signifying triumph over adversity - ushered in a new danger, that of betraying the aesthetical values of the art form in favour of success in a simple competitive sense. And this development would seem, to some extent, to support the modernity thesis: no longer does the choral practice of itself bear the same meaning-giving force for the choristers and audiences. We will suggest, however, that this does not at all indicate that the ideals of the tradition will inevitably be lost, as long as appropriate and realistic steps are taken to counter such tendencies. It is argued, against the modernity thesis, that the goal of an authentic identity in a tradition is a well-founded one and needs to moderate the future planning and direction of choral music. Jean and John Comaroff make a similar point in their Introduction to the collection, *Modernity and its Malcontents: Ritual and Power in Postcolonial*

Africa (1993); namely, that the very term 'modernity' highjacks the issue, by suggesting that there is no alternative to 'progress', understood in its European and American paradigms. And Turino, in his more recent research (2000:6), adds in agreement with this, that modernity "is a continuation of evolutionary discourse that posits European and American post-Enlightenment ethics and economics as the apex of universal development through the rhetorical hijacking of contemporary time..."

What is it about the intensity of the choral competitions that strikes the observer as so surprising? Here, we have to take into account the subaltern status, during the apartheid years and before, of the black choristers in South Africa, in their places of residence and also their school or work situation. Winning at the competitions began to symbolise achievement in general, measured against world standards, a way of 'beating the system' which was all the time, with apartheid, closing in on and marginalising black people. Where the efforts of *amakholwa* to achieve a sense of identity and self-worth by imitating Western culture had largely failed, success at competitions could now succeed. It would convey the message to the outside world that here, as an NCF chairman puts it, we have men and women of true worth, at 'world-class levels' (George Mxadana, *Newsletter of the Old Mutual / Telkom National Choir Festival*, 2000, nr 2:1). "No man or woman who has a heart beating in his breast can afford to stay out of competition today," remarked IE Zwane in 1965 (cited in Detterbeck, 2003:237). While at first glance, the competitive side of music performance might seem to be of secondary importance, this is in fact not at all the case, and again stresses the link between the singing tradition and the formation of identity.

With such aspirations governing these events, demonstration is everything. "Here we are showing our culture, values and norms," one competitor remarks (Xolani Cele, Imizwilili Choral Society, questionnaire, 2000). It is felt that one can even overpower the other groups by the sheer volume of sound one's choir produces: in this way, one 'makes oneself heard', in a land in which one's voice has, in other spheres, been silenced. You need power, various commentators repeat. "First of all you got to have power. Because without power, you are nothing.

In someway you got to be supported by singing. And if you don't have power, really, you cannot survive" (Thulani Maqungo, Tsakane Adult Choir, questionnaire, 2000). And winning, being number one, is everything. No doubt, this is the case with any competitive event, but here this seems to take on added meaning, which can only be understood by taking into account the broader social context of the singing. "There is only one winner - and this winner takes it all," confirms Sidwell Mhlongo, conductor of the Gauteng Choristers, voicing his disappointment on achieving second position at the NCF in Cape Town in December 2000. Participation in a choral contest is a matter of testing yourself. As Ray Kantuli, an *amakwaya* veteran, puts it, "if you see somebody doing something good, and you have got a constructive jealousy, you want to be above that person." The day of the contest is the "moment of truth," adds Thembelihle Dladla of the Pietermaritzburg Choral Society (questionnaire, 2001), it is the opportunity to "put ourselves on the stage to see where we are." Here again, we can perceive the social background of the participants as one of disruption and alienation. Being on centre stage is important, and the audience then has the role of affirming their approval.

This focus on identity, part of the history of the tradition, seems to continue today: even after apartheid, social structures for many do not offer a sense of security, and the choir becomes 'a family affair', "something fairly permanent in a situation where there is little permanence" (Thanduxolo Zulu). This sense of belonging is attested to by other choristers. "I can't be without singing," says Falithenjwa Mkhize, "I can't be without the choir - without the choir it's like being hungry." But it is, finally, a fragile affair: a good 'choir family' is one that wins. Thabane Sello, who sings with the Lesotho-based Maseru Vocal, stresses the importance of joining a choir - "a winning choir," he adds, "because I don't think anyone likes to be associated with losers" (questionnaire, 2000). And Thokozani Ndolomba, a chorister of the Pietermaritzburg Choral Society, argues that "if you join a choir that is not successful, you waste your time... you want to be successful, you want to be recognised and known."

The culmination of these expectations is for many the Finals of the National Choir Festival. Preparations begin early in the year, and one cannot help feeling that the thrill of challenging other choral groups dominates the atmosphere at the venues for the preliminaries, selected according to rotation so as to reach as wide an audience as possible. But this narrow focus - for the entire year! - on a few competition pieces, as interpreted by those particular judges - constricts the sustained growth of the choirs and their repertoires. The motivation is there, but its negative side is, amongst other things, the competitiveness as manifested in: secrecy, lack of cooperation, and in an attempt to outguess the judges by working out exactly what aspect of the winning choir in the previous year had swayed the results, and then imitating that. Already in 1967, it seems the conflicts between choristers and adjudicators could turn the events into fairly grim affairs. In a letter to *The World* newspaper (quoted in *TUATA*, September 1967:32), a reader complains that the annual Reef Eisteddfod has begun to be dominated by threats to choirs and conductors, and that one of the best choirs, from "consideration for the safety of its members" has been forced to stay away. Various commentators have judged the event not capable of bearing the weight of such aspirations and hopes, and the Johannesburg conductor Richard Cock will have nothing to do with the choral competitions. He comments that they are taken too seriously, "ranging from death threats to physical attacks of adjudicators after the competition." At times, they may degenerate into near chaos, as is evident from the following account given by Douglas Reid of one regional preliminary held in the Jameson Hall at the University of Cape Town:

> It was raining outside. They had packed people into this venue, so that you couldn't even breathe. They were right on top of each other. And then three adjudicators at the table, myself being one. In order to cope, we needed a secretary, who would table up the results and all the rest of it. And what happened unfortunately was... the choir that came third, in fact came fourth. In looking at all the numbers - everything was under pressure - we had mixed up the third and the fourth position. A mistake by

the secretary and of course by the adjudicators that were there. We should have been checking through things. But at the end of a competition everybody wants to know the results before you can even think. And after the results were announced, there was a whole to-do at the back - so we were rushed out, even Peter Morake and the secretary. And while we were waiting, I looked at the results and I discovered that three and four were the wrong way around. It was one point difference. So Peter went in and announced that straightaway - Gosh! People stormed, they took the typewriter, they threw the typewriter across the floor and they were all upset. So what we had to do, a public apology was made immediately. And it was decided - because money was involved as well - that in fact an award should be made to both choirs. And the one choir that had got third place now said that they were ruined because they were now fourth and they had been told they were third. The choir that was fourth said that *they* were ruined because they should have been third and they were announced fourth. A press conference was called... and it went out on the air, a public apology was made, that the wrong result was announced and that an award would be made to both choirs. And that they both had been good choirs and there was just a single point difference. I tell you, you'd have thought the world had come to an end.

This account speaks for itself. The vision - of harmony, community, emancipation - previously animating the choral practice, is in danger of dumbing down to an undifferentiated goal of power in one form or another.

In order to sustain the authentic tradition, the choristers would have to see the aesthetic values of this kind of music as part and parcel of their normal motivational framework, bound up with - not of course coextensive with - their sense of their general identity as persons and members of society. And the evidence is that, in spite of the examples given above, this way of seeing things does indeed largely hold. The continuing but fragile tradition includes good music - however complex and culture-specific this notion is – as part and parcel of what it means to be a successful human being, a model for others: ideas of pleasing the audience, of giving meaning and identity, of offering a technical challenge to the choristers, and so on. Our notion of an authentic music tradition within the framework of an authentic national culture presupposes this idea. For Giddens, on the other hand, a reconstituted tradition is a sham, without intrinsic drawing power, although one might join in with others (sharing the mock-tradition) because of extrinsic benefits in status, or hegemony, or because tourists demand it, and so on.

The choral tradition seems to have been a way of giving meaning, under stringent and potentially destructive social conditions. The question that arises, under present radically altered social conditions, concerns whether an adequate account of society can be given without reference to any such elements to do with meaning. In his study of the exigencies circumscribing contemporary South Africa, Daryll Glaser (2001:216-220) discusses with equanimity the (to us incommensurable) possible factors of social cohesion, the English language, Christianity, consumerism, and sport! The approach seems to proscribe any discussion of strongly valued goods of the kind which promote an identity and counter disintegrative tendencies, such as consumerist attitudes, which would override, for purposes of gratification, the cooperation and commitments made in the name of the communal project. But the *amakwaya* tradition seems to suggest a way of seeing persons as, importantly, 'participants in meaning', and this perhaps points to a difference of outlook between the traditional African and the modern Western picture, in Charles Taylor's phrase, of the 'unencumbered self' (Taylor, 1989, Chapter 2). Our point is that there might be many aspects in which one might think of a renaissance of a cultural tradition as 'sham' – we can point to purist approaches to African choral music – but the project itself is not *necessarily* correctly judged sham as a whole.

Questioning the modernity thesis

The modernity thesis would have it that factors to do with virtues of character have little or no place to play in our understanding of social development. Some aspects of this approach have already been unpacked above, in our discussion of a 'post-traditional society' (Chapter 7). What is thought to be at stake in the alternatives, tradition or modernity, is well explained, as we saw, by Ross Poole (1991). According to Poole, market conditions associated with contemporary society break down the sense in which the individual is first and foremost a *participant,* rather than an isolated individual. He illustrates the problem by the example of the family as a social practice, and the kind of normative constraints that govern members of a family (analogous to the way in which choristers, through natural and learned talents, slot into certain roles in the choir). In pre-modern society, the individual is first and foremost a participant, and one's behaviour patterns are governed by particular relationships to one's child, or colleague, or husband, and so on. The tradition gathers individuals through their shared beliefs about common meanings and values. Because of the way one identifies oneself, the dyad egoism / altruism does not apply, but rather as a father in a family, or a chorister in a choir, for example, one achieves one's own good through the achievement of the good of others too. But later, so goes the modernity thesis, the role-defined identity that is part and parcel of a pre-modern society, gives way to the self-concerned critical and socially unencumbered individual. In dissenting from this view, however, we are not proposing as basic drive in persons unselfishness rather than self-centredness. It is not that the mother, for example, is altruistic rather than egocentric, at least in the sense in which these are constituted in modernity, i.e. as practically as well as conceptually opposed: if I give more time to you, I give less time to myself. Rather, modernity's conception of instrumental reasoning is being thrown into question (Poole, 1991:54). Applying these ideas to our own problematic we can say that modernity has constructed an identity which is incompatible with our proposed guiding standard of an authentic identity, authentic participation, in the choral tradition, which symbolises and gives meaning to one's life as a whole.

Once the identity of the individual is conceived in abstraction from his relations with others, the assumption of pervasive self-interest becomes almost inescapable...

> The identity required by the market is that of an individual who is not tied to particular activities and responsibilities. (Poole, 1991:7 and 61)

And this means that the countervailing tendencies to do with winning at all costs will have much more of a foothold on the motivations of the choristers and others in the choral scene. External goods of reward and so on, increasingly dominate the internal goods intrinsic to the tradition, to do with the aesthetic qualities of the music.

For Poole, the greater options available in modern societies break down the drawing power of traditional identities. Is this an accurate view of the matter? Clearly, the modern period has ushered in the conditions for a greater degree of individual freedom of choice. But this has led to the assumption that participation in the (past) tradition is *defined* by its uncritical attitude towards the status-quo allocating roles in the cooperative social project. The dichotomy traditional / modern seems, in our secularised culture, part and parcel of the received wisdom of how history is moving forward: 'those people then,' we think, were for the most part less critical, narrower, less aware, more prejudiced, than we are now. Only if the traditional identity or sense of self, so the argument goes, is thought of as an inescapable destiny, not social and contingent but natural and necessary, will it have drawing power (Poole, 1991:62). One could think of the affirmation of the choristers of their roles, and the discipline required of these, in the creating of the music. In other words, and to repeat in this context what has been drawn on in our previous discussions above, Poole is implicitly arguing that there can be no *critical* adoption of the role-based social participation. "Any process of evaluating these identities is liable to undermine them," he argues (1991:63). To scrutinise these identities is to make them vulnerable. But only as invulnerable and necessary can such identities found an ethic of virtue.

But a critical (and negotiated) approach to identity seems to be, on the contrary, a very characteristic of the choral tradition we have been studying: all new influences are creatively sieved through before incorporation. Poole assumes, rather than argues for, the inevitable hegemony of the picture of persons as isolated individuals freely choosing from an otherwise value-neutral range of aims and behaviour patterns - over against the picture of the individual as participant. (A view somewhat moderated in his later *Nation and Identity*, 1999, Chapter 2). In contrast to this, other studies argue that the expression of meaning supplying an internal link between individual and group, perhaps through religion, or cooperative community projects, or traditions such as *amakwaya*, is an enduring need which, if denied, results in all kinds of social dysfunctions, and indeed constitutes 'a threat to our society's fundamental democratic values'. This at least, is the conclusion of a research into attitudes amongst young people in Brussels during the years 1996 to 2000, testing the hypothesis that questions of *meaning* in a detraditionalised society might be either trivial or of a transitory nature, an attitude that would seem implicit in Glaser's analysis of South African society. It was found that on the contrary, such questions are important from the point of view of people's well-being and society's health too (Elchardus and Siongers, 2001:197).

The institutional aspect, as has been repeated throughout this book, can always corrupt the practice. The institution - here for instance the setup of choral competitions - is structured by means of a set of rough-and-ready public rules for the allocation of external goods of power, status and financial rewards. If the internal goods are achieved, all benefit, but in the matter of external goods, one individual is in competition with others - only one can achieve first place, the others must be content to be second. The ethos of any practice - its promotion, for example, of loyal ways of behaving - is designed to guard against being overtaken by the desire for those external rewards, money and position. In a particular kind of commercialised society, traditions and their sustaining 'visions' will only be maintained with difficulty. Iris Murdoch, in her study of art and Plato, insists that 'a sense of beauty diminishes greed' in pointing us "in the direction of the real and the good." It has a certain authority that overcomes egoism "in its protean forms of fantasy and illusion" (cited in Kerr, 1997:88). This contention seems to be borne out by our study of the choral tradition, expressive of and forging a fragile identity beyond the self-interested isolations of the past.

Conclusion

It is our contention in this discussion that if the choral tradition is to flourish under present conditions, the dangers of the detraditionalising forces of the global market, coupled with the fact that the institutional goods of any social practice may be a disintegrating force, need to be taken into account and realistically dealt with. But if one has followed the description above tracing the maturing tradition, it will be clear that the tradition has its internal resources. There are many voices within the tradition, critical of the current emphasis on competitions. And the same time the competitions have always been tempered by an encompassing meaning-giving vision, an aspect which is uncharacteristic of what is understood by 'modernity'. We hear of choristers overcoming obstacles of time, money, and marginalisation, to attend regular voice classes at the university in order to learn "how to care for our voice, what exercises to do, how to project." And they re-affirm the negotiated nature of the choral tradition, inclusive of African music, of wedding songs (included in order to please the audience), and of the challenging 'advanced Western music'. "It is the love of music that gives us the energy," they enthuse. This attitude is in accord with our findings in the area of ethics in an age of commerce in general, namely the importance of an orientation towards the actual value of the particular product as part and parcel of an encompassing vision of what makes for human 'living well together'.

Chapter Ten

Character and Professionalism in the Context of Developing Countries – a Debate about Mercenaries

The professions in the context of development

In the previous chapter, the tension was highlighted between any normative tradition and the demands of modernity. This tension is most evident in the area of professionalism and professional ethics. Africa the continent is rich in such normative traditions, linking the individual to the community, both living and dead, past, present and future, through ideals of character and behaviour. But it is often thought that particular traditions, stressing perhaps personal relations to family and clan, should be put aside. Such traditions must take a back seat in the age of the modern state and professionalism. The idea that the demands of the professions do not coincide with our normal ethical outlook, is discussed in, for example, Jacobs (2005). The starting point for discussions on this topic is taken as Thomas Nagel's essay, *Ruthlessness in Public Life*, in which this kind of moral division of labour is put forward.

The case of South Africa's immediate history is illustrative in this regard. An example from a few years ago shows some ethical confusion. During a protest against proposed legislation to ban 'virgin testing' amongst Zulu people, the following arguments were put forward:

- virgin testing goes against the individual rights of women and should be banned;
- virgin testing is part of traditional Zulu culture, and the state is obliged to respect different cultures;
- those participating are doing so freely, and their individual rights to do this should be protected;

- anything that helps to roll back the increase in HIV/AIDS infections should be encouraged, and virgin testing is one such measure, as it helps prevent premarital sex;
- in the traditional prayer for rain, the virgin group, forming the head of the procession, is indispensable.

How are we to make sense of this seemingly incommensurable mix of ethical approaches? We have here arguments based variously on cultural pluralism, on utilitarian grounds, on individual rights, and on religious belief (Leclerc-Madlala, 2001).

Some clarification can be gained through considering how the country has emerged out of a period in which one particular 'grand narrative' was imposed on all citizens through laws and also the education system. The social order during apartheid was identified as 'Christian' of a particular Calvinist kind, and 'national' of a particular racial and 'European' kind. Post-apartheid South Africa has emphasised the plural nature of good society, where no one has a monopoly on the truth in matters of how we should live; every cultural perspective being given due recognition. At the same time, however, the new government sees as its mandate, the facilitation of a reconciled community based on a sense of commonly held standards of acceptable behaviour, highlighted by the Truth and Reconciliation Commission (TRC). On the one hand, the bottom line is set by individual 'rights'; on the other, it is set by nation-building and the conditions for good community. The TRC tries to tell a story that shows that we are all taken up in the same drama to try to live out ideals through adhering to decent action in favour of those ideals.

The attitude of the Commission (2002) to its own report is best summed up in its Conclusion (TRC, Vol 5, Ch 6, 162):

The findings outlined above, to a greater or lesser extent, touch all the major role-players who were party to the conflict that enveloped South Africa during its mandate period. No major role-player emerges unscathed although, as already stated, a distinction must be made between those who fought for and those who fought against apartheid. There are many who will reject these findings and argue that they fail to understand the complexities and historical realities of the time, and of the motives and perspectives of those who perpetrated gross violations of human rights. In this regard it needs to be firmly stated that, while the Commission has attempted to convey some of these complexities and has grappled with the motives and perspectives of perpetrators in other sections of this Report, it is not the Commission's task to write the history of this country. Rather, it is the Commission's function to expose the violations of all parties in an attempt to lay the basis for a culture in which human rights are respected and not violated.

Example after example from the Final Report show that some common idea of the common good, the good not just for one individual or one group but for all, has a general acceptance, there is a tradition, and that tradition entails certain ideas about the virtuous or decent way to act. The standard for the act is set by the overall ethical vision of the agent, or the group, but what is interesting is that all parties to the conflict seemed to agree that not *everything* could be justified by the (good) end intended: there must be some kind of proportionality. A common ethical community seems to be entailed by anyone deliberating on the level of moral value.

This particular example of the ethics of a state in transition bears out the views of various writers dissatisfied with the hitherto dominant liberalist approach emphasising universal and formal principles attaching to the abstract individual, and prescinding from any notion of 'the good life'. The acceptance by all parties in the conflict of the encompassing grand narrative points to a prima facie argument against those who claim that there *can* be no such framework in contemporary plural society. Various contributors to the International Development Ethics Conference (Kampala, Uganda, July 2006), where the ideas put forward in this chapter were first presented, make similar points. In their own paper at this conference, Helena Cobban and Coralie Bryant (2006) point, with reference to Cobban's book, *Amnesty After Atrocity? Healing Nations after Genocide and War Crimes* (published in 2007), to the financial impracticability of proceeding, in transitional state procedures, along formal legal lines, comparing the Truth and Reconciliation Commission approaches of South Africa and Mozambique favourably with the option in Rwanda of prosecuting individual perpetrators. Not only is the latter course prohibitively expensive, but the evidence in Cobban's case studies points to the need, in societies in transitions of this kind, for healing narratives, if the former conflictual attitudes are to be turned around. Be that as it may, another speaker at the conference drew our attention to the misgivings of many World Bank fieldworkers about at least one 'grand narrative' of huge importance in Africa, at least from an institutional point of view, namely the Christian and Islamic religions (Marshall, 2006). Negative aspects of such religions, from the point of view of development, included a certain divisiveness as each sought their own converts, as well as opposition to World Bank priority programmes such as the expansion of 'reproductive rights', and finally, assumptions about knowledge which appear not to be evidence-based, thus hampering rational discussion with development organisations.

The controversial thesis of Alasdair MacIntyre, well canvassed in Part Two, is to the effect that the erosion of Europe's concrete moral narrative issued in an ungrounded and unmotivating ethics of principles. Onora O'Neill (1996:200ff) argues that even from a Kantian perspective of general obligations not attached to any particular tradition, there is an obligation not to be indifferent to human need. One cannot, as she puts it, universalise indifference, and mentions with approval Simone Weil's *The Need for Roots*. The most systematically developed argument that a persons' engagement in moral discussion, entails an implicit commitment to the achievement of a common ethical community is given, in my own judgement, in the little-known article by Robert Johann (1975).

This is useful for our discussion of professionalism, because whatever one is doing, has to be seen in the broader context of values: the soldier must, eventually, live in peace next door to the country with which he is engaged in battle; the teams that compete in professional soccer must talk together afterwards; and so on. We need to see others always as potential co-citizens, fellow inhabitants of our space, neighbours. Under pressure of increased commercialisation, these broader goals might be forgotten: the business becomes unethical. We can invoke here, as promised in our introductory account of this book, MacIntyre's perhaps overused concept of a social practice, with internal goods partly constitutive of that practice, as good scholarship is constitutive of the university. I can repeat here the summary of this idea: any work has its own particular skills aiming at its own particular goods; for example, in medicine, it is health. But apart from these goods internal to the practice, there are the auxiliary goods to do with the institutionalisation of the practice; for example, doctors aim not only at the provision of healthcare, but also at promotion and salaries for themselves. These latter goods are goods of competition. The institution becomes corrupt when those goods take over as the prime *motivating* forces. Increasing commercialisation of society could foster corruption, in this sense, and lower the moral status of the professions. This leads us to our next point.

The context of development

The contemporary global structural setup aggravates the situation. Donal Dorr (1984), some years ago, spoke of pyramids of power, whether in the area of money and banking, or of what he calls 'idea power' (educational institutions and media), or politics or religion. At the top are the very few benefiting from the skewed allocation of power; at the bottom, the masses suffering most under the structure but more or less powerless. In the middle are the 'service people', the professionals perhaps, doctors, teachers, military, and so on, who have the power to do something about the injustice of the status-quo but who are also offered the possibility of moving up to the top of the pyramid to join the elite.

In the local cultures and ethical traditions, we have perhaps some possible resistance to such pressures. An ally to these pyramids of power is to be found, on the other hand, in the promotion by the popular press of a 'celebrity culture', where more traditional conceptions of 'Great men and women' (exemplars of the cultural tradition, of African humanism for example) are subverted. The elite in this case, is defined purely commercially, in terms of power and prestige, rather than ethically. In times of change, too, the overall goods are less motivating; no one identifies any longer in an immediate and spontaneous way with the 'nation'; there is a loss of 'roots'; sections of the population are disaffiliated; the individual is left free-floating, ready to drop into the hands of the system. While socialism may have been discredited some years back, the market forces, it is widely admitted today, should not be allowed to operate in a social vacuum. The International Labour Organization (ILO) has written of the global need for the promotion of what they term 'decent work', which means not separating the economy from society. This idea "brings the economy back into the context of the life of the community, of society". The Director of the ILO Juan Somavía notes that it is essential:

> the world becomes aware of the importance of values and of spiritual references in politics, human rights, and religion in the world. The significance of spiritual traditions and religions in the world, and their focus on the identity of each individual person, goes without saying. Hence the importance of the linkage between the world of politics and the international system on the one hand, and what the different spiritual traditions represent in terms of the values and aspirations of society and of every human being, on the other hand... (cited in Wilson, 2004:15).

The aims of the ILO need to include not only full employment and workers' rights, it is argued, but social protection and social dialogue too.

In the case of South Africa, the late economist, Francis Wilson, notes on the negative side, after more than a decade of democracy, factors such as widening inequality and a spirit of greed, unemployment, poverty, collapsing hospitals and dysfunctional schools, crime and threats to personal safety, and uncalled-for armaments expenditure. This is not just pessimism: the progress in having a Constitution enshrining human rights, in achieving a negotiated transition, in getting rid of capital punishment are all acknowledged, as also the TRC process and the relatively well-managed macro-economy. The point is simply that more focus is needed on the overarching narratives in the cultural traditions, from which policies could draw their standards.

Moral narrative framing the discussion

The approach being suggested here is that standards of excellence in the professions need to be moderated in terms of an overarching moral narrative to do with the flourishing of individuals and of society. There are two kinds of objections to this idea. The first maintains that this is, under conditions of modernity, simply not possible. In the previous chapter, we drew on the argument of Anthony Giddens (1990), to the effect that, under modern social conditions, all traditional types of social order are undermined, subject to radical questioning and thus rendered inoperative. Similarly, for Poole (1991), market conditions associated with contemporary society break down the sense in which the individual is first and foremost a *participant,* governed by the requirements attaching to their various social roles, head of household, elder brother, citizen and soldier, and so on. Because of the identity-conferring tradition or narrative, there is no perceived essential conflict between one's own good and the good of others. But the market forces require individuals unattached to such constraining roles.

Such analyses, while intriguing, would seem from a common-sense point of view, too extreme to be judged completely true of present global conditions. A second objection, however, claims that our suggestion even if workable, is not *desirable.* Kwame Anthony Appiah (2005) takes the value of individual autonomy as trumping other values, such as membership of a community or tradition. He acknowledges that, in fact, people are members of communities, and repudiates the idea that belonging dutifully to a community rules out being a fully autonomous individual (2005:43) and cites with approval Charles Taylor's idea the self exists only in 'webs of interlocution' and that stepping outside such horizons would risk one's personal integrity. Appiah also admits that individuals do not subject their membership to continual questioning, as would seem to be demanded, famously, by Kant, for anyone claiming to be 'enlightened'. On the other hand, he does not feel that in order to make sense of one's life one needs to have an overarching narrative or unity to it, in which all the different aspects find their place. In other words, there is no necessary character ideal needed for an adequate ethical framework.

Charles Taylor (1989) argues to the contrary. In the course of a historically detailed study of how identities have been variously shaped by ethical ideas from the Greek times to contemporary European society, he at the same time identifies the root of the contemporary unwillingness to accept this evidence. Once the idea took hold of a disengaged individual with a merely instrumental stance towards the world, rather than a participative one, the idea that 'reality' is essentially, or in itself, without values became the default position, what he terms 'naturalism'. The world is seen as disenchanted, *enzaubert*. This view of things is supported by the pre-eminence of the sciences as avenues of true knowledge, and by the overwhelming impact technology has had on individuals' sense of control over an environment-out-there, at least on the (over-)developed world. And that means that our 'meanings', the meanings we live by, are simply superstructural appendages to what is really going on. The world, society, is fully explained without these. Taylor, on the contrary, tries to show how such meanings, the constitutive- or hyper-goods, the ineluctably higher, the framework of values, operate in all modern European thought-traditions, including that of liberal individualism, with its valuing of autonomy and individual choice as supreme. These are kind of existential or religious determinants for people.

How would Appiah respond to this? He does grant the peculiarity of holding at once the idea that individuals are essentially determined by their social environment, but at the same time holding as prime value that of autonomy, the capacity to act in a way that goes *beyond* the forces of that environment. He 'resolves' this only by calling on Kant's idea that from one aspect we can view ourselves as determined, but from another, as free (2005:58). There is no space to treat the complex philosophical issues involved here, even in a summary way. Appiah's suggestion, however, does nothing to show what motivates the universal ethical principles of good professionalism. In the Kantian jargon, we would describe taking a bribe, for example, 'as if' this was something one should treat as of moral importance even if from the broader perspective whether or not one held to these values had no ultimately determining effect on the social outcome. The latter, on this reading, would be fully explained without recourse to such parallel or epiphenomenal events such as one's *reasons* for action.

Appiah's approach is unhelpful because our concern lies precisely in the *relative* roles in behaviour, in motivation, of, on the one hand, formal moral principles attaching to the abstract autonomous individual, and on the other hand, of overarching identity-giving narratives. I will therefore assume that the project of seeking how to integrate professionalism in traditional African culture is indeed a worthwhile one and turn to seeing how our approach could affect how we see one particular aspect of contemporary African scene so far as concerns nations and development, and that is the question of mercenaries.

Mercenaries in a utilitarian moral climate

Why should anyone raise the question of mercenaries? Surely, we know they are not encouraged by governments and are indeed illegal in most countries. On the other hand, it is true that organisations styling themselves 'private military companies' do in fact exist and have been used by various governments around the world. In the 2002 Green Paper on private military companies submitted to the British parliament, reference is made to the cases of Angola, of Sierra Leone - involving 'Executive Outcomes' - and of the American government in the Balkans. In some cases, to be sure, there have been mercenaries involved in actions that clearly are not justifiable. But this is also the case for many operations by conventional forces, so this is not an argument for or against. A colleague of mine has recently suggested that from a utilitarian point of view, it would make good sense for governments to employ mercenaries rather than regular conscripts in military operations, for two reasons: often they might be simply more efficient; and secondly, any military engagement threatens the lives of those engaged and it is the duty of the state precisely to *protect* the lives of citizens (Baker, 2005).

What are we to say about this idea? We have been suggesting the importance in development ethics of sustaining overarching moral traditions; in this, the state has a primary role to play, as a natural ethical unit inspired by those traditions. It is tasked with ensuring the flourishing of citizens but also in the context of those outside its borders, who have a place in the ethical story. The unwillingness of citizens to participate in a particular military conflict (or, as suggested above in the context of a utilitarian moral climate, in *any* war), shows a disaffiliation from the moral narrative, the loss of a sense in which the state is more than simply a 'gang' for the benefit of its members, even, to use St Augustine's term for the Roman Empire in its decadent phase, a *magna latrociniae*, a great band of robbers. War is such a grave matter that utmost caution has to be taken that it is ethically justified, and the unwillingness of citizens to take part in the conflict themselves would seem to indicate a gap between authorities and people that throws into doubt the legitimacy of the declaration of hostilities. Furthermore, in the context of development and of a globally skewed structural distribution of power, it is seriously misleading to limit ethics to utilitarian benefits to individuals abstracted from their embeddedness in cultural traditions and values.

Be that as it may, there might cf course be *other* reasons for deeming that private military companies should be made legal; just as in many countries (and this is my colleague's point), what was previously thought should be illegal, the practice of prostitution, is now legalised and brought under the rubric of 'legitimate commercial activity' (the term used for practitioners is 'sex-workers'), whatever we might think about the morality of gaining money from this kind of work. The question can be raised as to whether there is something *wrong* with being a mercenary: this would be of direct relevance to our topic, because we have suggested that remaining rooted in the cultural and ethical traditions is of vital importance to a country's development. Is the condemnation of this kind of activity simply outdated, just as trade and commerce were previously considered not quite respectable activities, in view of the fact that one was treating others not at all in terms of their role in relation to one's relevant social whole but simply as potential consumers.

So, is there something wrong with being a mercenary? We have been talking, in the context of development, about the need for a growing sense of the common good. This refers to a good which is good for me as well as for you; what one might call internal goods of society rather than goods of competition in which, if I benefit, you lose out. Now to put it at its most bland, we could say simply being a decent human being is one of those goods, leaving it open to how one fills in the term, 'decent'. Clearly, this would mean that the person's intentions were just in nature, and that their aim, likewise, could be judged reasonable, and that they acted habitually in this way. In other words, we are calling on an Aristotelian-type analysis to help us here, and this is partly because Aristotle, of course, thinks of the individual as a *zoon politikon*, a political animal.

A second reason for invoking this kind of theoretical framework is the fact that it was out of this philosophical tradition that there came the method of analysing the ethics of engaging in military action in the form that has come down to us, namely the Just War theory (cf Ethics Centre, 2016). Could a mercenary be considered justified within the Just War tradition? This is the second question we will ask. And thirdly, we will ask whether there is something about this particular area of life (soldiering) that entails certain normative constraints which would rule out mercenaries. Just as in the case of prostitution, one *could* argue there is a normative connection between the activity of sex and, say, friendship or family; here, we can ask whether there is some such connection between *soldiering* and *being a citizen*. Is the notion of membership of a *social practice* the appropriate framework for considering this issue? To take the South African case, is the mercenary part and parcel of the new vision of an efficient and professional African culture, or should he or she be confined to the historical past along with the perpetrators of racist violence? The background to this question is first, the increasing use by the government, in the last years of apartheid, of semi-legal and covert military forces; and secondly, the integration, after the 1994 elections, of the *uMkhonto weSizwe* (literally, Spear of the Nation) liberation forces with the former SA Defence Force (now the SANDF). These factors led to the formation of private military companies after the demise of apartheid, the most well-known of which was 'Executive Outcomes'.

I am concerned to elucidate the question *whether virtue actually matters* in this area of life, namely soldiering. The larger question has to do with what categories one uses to theorise about development in general. Is virtue somehow an *internal* aim of good soldiering? Do we need to rethink our notion of good professionalism in this way? I am not concerned with throwing stones at mercenaries - if all that matters is getting the job done, then it is hypocritical to blame those who have to do the dirty work while leaving untouched, at least if they are successful, those who *make use* of these services. (Similarly, to use the analogy with prostitution, there would be no whores if there were no johns and no pimps - or are the latter 'just doing their job'?)

Defining the term 'mercenary'

But first, a note about terminology. The definition of a mercenary as someone who engages in military combat for money or 'private gain' - as defined by the Further Protocol of the Geneva Convention (UN, 1977) - misses the point, for two reasons: first, other soldiers are also paid; and secondly, the definition seems to make assumptions about the mercenary's *motives*. A better description would refer to:

> soldiering not out of obligations incurred through citizenship, but because of professional contractual obligations of a private nature.

I want to take the best possible case of mercenary, in other words, we make no reference at this stage to his motives; it is not assumed that he is necessarily only interested in money, a 'lucrepath,' in Baker's term (Baker, 2005). We can restrict the discussion to what may be termed 'private warriors', meaning specifically, a mercenary who is in some sense a *professional* soldier, i.e. abides by the rules of engagement in war (the *jus in bello* principles - no intentional or direct harming of civilians, acceptance of the normal signs of surrender and just treatment of prisoners, and so on). This would exclude 'terrorists', for example, since they do not abide by these rules, even if they were fighting for a just (but 'private') cause, and persons employed as hitmen by syndicated crime gangs and mafias, whether national or international. It would also exclude any privately contracted security employees within the state, such as car guards so prevalent in South Africa today, security company personnel, and so on, operating within the law. The latter groups are not engaged in soldiering, i.e. representing a state or putative state or government; there is no *general assumption* that other forms of achieving the ends of social order or justice (whether intra-state or inter-state) have broken down; there is no enemy. In South African law, to take one example, such security personnel have to justify each use of firearms against another person, according to the law that applies to all. If a purported criminal is shot by a security guard, an attempted murder or murder docket is opened.

One is not speaking here of evaluating the moral worth of any particular person's particular actions, and further, everything said here is ceteris paribus, or as Aristotle says, 'for the most part'. In an infinitely complex world, anything is logically and psychologically possible. Blanket condemnation of women who stray from the norm (particularly in a corrupt and hypocritical society) is very critically seen by Jacobean playwright John Ford. In *'Tis Pity She's a Whore* (1629-1633), it is the incest prohibition which is transgressed, but the point being made is more general, and the title brings to mind the final remark of Shakespeare's memorable character, Othello, who at the end of that play, remarks, "But Iago the pity of it, Iago, the pity of it." *Here*, the context is of course, the unjust condemnation of Desdemona. In any *particular* case, knowing the circumstances is everything. We don't want to suggest the nightmare of a 'moral police' enforcing blanket application of moral laws (intended as abstract expressions) and leading to a condemnation of anyone supposed to deviate from the 'true path'. Rather, we are intending to build up a picture of what kind of social institutions would best facilitate people flourishing as free human individuals.

Skills and virtues: Aristotelian distinctions

In Aristotle's analysis - in Books 1 and 2 of his *Politics* - of properly praiseworthy acts, he argues that an act is meritorious to the extent that it embodies deliberate choice of that act, which avoids both the impulse to excess and the impulse to deficiency. Such impulses - say, towards fight or flight, or to indulgence or insensitivity - are part and parcel of the human make-up, but so is our capacity to think about what we are doing (at least if we have had a measure of childhood training in good habits). Employing the latter capacity is employing prudence (practical wisdom, *sophrusone*), and prudence is always understood within the context of a good, flourishing human life, exemplified in the fulfilled man. Courage is a mean between extremes, and so is temperance, but of some things, such as adultery, there is no mean; one is not supposed to be adulterous with neither too many women, nor too few, and instead just the correct number. No, ethics cannot be completely cut off from the excellences attached to our roles as human beings, as men, women, citizens, soldiers, householders, parents, and, in general, various ways of relating to others in different kinds of social practices (kinds of 'friendship' in Aristotle's terminology). Flourishing and 'friendship' go hand in hand. The job of political leaders is to facilitate these social practices, not simply to suppress crime. And these social interactions are 'by nature': no one would choose to live without friends. We are social animals and have natural drives or tendencies (involving our basic needs) towards forms of society. We are 'attracted' or drawn towards forming sexual friendship as well as towards the citizen-and-state kind of relationship (for 'state' gives us the chance to be self-sufficient and hence to a large extent self-determining, a central component of flourishing as a human person).

In the classical Greek tradition, the idea of virtue was close to the idea of a skill, and at first (say, in Homer) attached to various social roles, warrior, household manager, etc. At issue between Socrates and the Sophists was whether one could learn a skill (for example, rhetoric or the art of politics), apart from learning to appreciate the proper good that use of the skill achieves. Aristotle agrees with Socrates that the first without the second could not possibly be worthy of praise or admiration in any way. In certain human activities, what matters is only the product, and hypothetically a person without meaning to but seated at the piano could hit the right notes by accident, to produce the music which we enjoy. We would still praise the music. What we praise in the case of a virtue, however, as distinct from a skill or art, is not the product alone but also the intention. What is crucial is whether or not the agent chooses the act for its own sake, rather than, say, for the sake of vainglory (*Nichomacean Ethics*, 1105a - 1105b). It is not enough simply that they achieve the end. The private soldier achieving victory 'within the rules of engagement' *would be a necessary but not sufficient condition to make the act ethical or an act of virtue.* Thus, the issue in question in our case, could be phrased, 'Should the mercenary (*skilled* in the art of war) also be thought of as a warrior (possessing the *virtues* called for in war, particularly courage) and thus a valued member of society?' And this raises the question as to the motive of the agent, a question brought to the fore in the Just War theory.

Applying the Just War theory

The Just War theory is a virtue ethic. Aquinas' formulation of the principle of a just war is to be found in *Summa Theologica*, IIa IIae, Q.64, art.7, dealing specifically with the question of whether killing is permissible in self-defence. The act of self-defence, he says, has two effects, "one is the saving of one's life, the other is slaying of the aggressor." However, the act would be wrong if it were out of proportion to the end - in this example, using more force than was necessary; and also if it were done out of "private animosity." The Just War theory flows from this (IIa IIae, Q.40, art.1).

In this ethical framework, the focus is not so much on the end to be achieved, nor on the principle of the act, but on the nature of the act itself: for example, is it an act of cowardice, rashness, or courage? The principle of double effect lies at the heart of this approach to military action: the virtuous soldier does not directly intend the killing of the enemy but, instead, intends justice (last resort proviso). What is of concern is that the act be proportional and not disproportional to the (just) end intended. The kind of end it is supplies also the standard for judging the act.

But killing is not proportional to the private ends of contractual warriors, whatever these might be - say, supporting a middle-class family: this end is not grave enough to justify killing. Killing is only a proportionally appropriate act when military action for the just cause (restoring justice and peace) has been embarked upon by the proper authority, as a last resort, with a reasonable chance of success.

Let us describe the state as a social practice with internal goods constitutive of that practice (this would entail some normative idea of a nation or regional culture at least as an imagined ideal), then the professional or conscripted soldier acts in a way that is judged by these precise standards, i.e. he or she acts as a citizen. The latter category somehow *makes sense* to her, in her action. Could the private military company constitute a similar social practice? Not really. If the Just War theory is to make sense, in the case of the citizen soldier, the enemy has to be seen as people that in the future I will have to share a world with, my country and their country, my culture and their culture. That idea moderates my possible action to secure victory. (I am not saying that this normative framework is typically fostered by military chiefs; on the contrary, the enemy is often and unjustly demonised). In the case of the employee of the military company, there is a disengagement from all this. This may be exacerbated by the fact that the mercenary is typically engaged in combats far removed from their own home territory. Even if there is a commitment to the rules of war, rules always have to be applied, and in order to apply them well, virtues are required. It is as if one were aiming at the good of friendship, but one only knew the rules (say, no deception) in an external kind of way. Or one was aiming at good scholarship but had no intuition about how the rule forbidding plagiarism made sense: one simply knew the rule was there, perceived as obstructing one's smooth path to good scholarship,; yet another hurdle to jump! An act of killing which aimed *directly* at achieving the technical goal of military success abstracted from the good of citizen-in-state-amongst-other-states would therefore not be an act of virtue but of vice. It is a disordered act, even if not that of a 'lucrepath'.

A further point is the fact that the appropriate authority who initiated the military action and called in mercenaries de-legitimises the cause, as it de-legitimises the claim of this group to represent a nation of citizens, to 'speak for them' in the matter of a cause of injustice serious enough to elicit the response of the citizens to take up arms, and/or to enforce the conscription obligation. (This is not the case for states that see themselves as part of a supranational entity, to whom they have delegated their duty to citizens to defend them militarily, if necessary).

Since a person acquires virtue through *acts* of virtue and no other way; the typical mercenary would, other things being equal, not be virtuous, a 'decent' human being and valued member of society, living in accordance with the traditions critically appropriated in present-day circumstances.

Overvaluing the skilled professional

This argument is going to stand or fall to some extent with a whole approach to 'professionalism'. Could the mercenary properly be considered a good 'professional', rightly praised for getting the job done well, valued in our society, as in a previous age the warrior was valued for their particular skill or virtue, namely courage, exemplified in soldiering? The question is posed to contemporary opinion in the film *Lord of War* (dir. Niccol, 2005), where the central protagonist is a gunrunner (played by Nicholas Cage). The gunrunner is blind to the harm he is doing, and when asked why he continues, simply says, "Because I'm good at it." There is no concern here for the protagonist having a real appreciation of the overall moral vision framing the action. In Aristotle's treatment of this issue, he remarks that such persons (in our case, the gunrunner) would have a *kind* of virtue (a kind of courage); and indeed, from the point of getting the job done, they would not seem to be hobbled by the necessity of ensuring that one's action was strictly proportional to one's goal, namely just peace.

> It is quite possible that the best soldiers may not be men of this sort [i.e. completely virtuous] but those who are less brave and have no other good: for these are ready to face danger, and they sell their life for trifling gains (*Nicomachean Ethics*, 1117b).

In other words, the 'best' professional (meaning here the most effective in terms of a narrowed set of performance criteria) may be someone who lowers their (moral) sights. Persons of moderate rather than complete virtue, it could be argued, do meet the criterion of courage, the mean between rashness and cowardice, zealously pursuing goals for which the virtuous can't muster enthusiasm. But they fail, as we have seen, in their appreciation of the ends. In a parallel case, one could ask whether the 'best' lawyer is the one who disregards the ends of justice but uses their skills solely so as to achieve the lesser goal of the successful defence of their client, whether actually guilty or not. I discuss the case of the lawyer in my article, *Does Character Matter? Guardian Values in an Age of Commerce* (Giddy, 2007).

For Aristotle, then, one can speak about a mercenary being 'good' in some sense, or exhibiting 'courage' but this is like speaking of courageous burglars or (his favoured example) adulterers who "undertake many risks for the sake of their sensual desire" (*Ethics*, 1116b). As Aquinas makes clear in his commentary on this text, Aristotle is referring to mercenaries, "who are prepared for danger not by reason of any good of virtue" but for money and the hope of booty (*Commentary*, para. 593). True virtue is to be found not in these soldiers who calculate the odds and flee when "the danger exceeds their skill." "They are the first to run away, while those possessing the fortitude of the citizen, refusing to leave, give up their lives" (*Ethics*, 1116b). They think it disgraceful to flee in these circumstances. Their self-understanding as citizens alerts them to the need to uphold the common good (in this case overriding the good of the individual who is risking his life). There is no virtue without the virtue of practical reason, and that is only acquired through being oriented towards the more adequate moral vision, as citizens, but not mercenaries (qua mercenaries), are.

Professionalism and the ethical traditions

We conclude then that reference to an orienting ethical narrative and its accompanying vision of human flourishing is always important in applied and professional ethics, and should be taken into account in any number of contentious issues about whether or not a certain action is permissible. Ethics has to do not simply with human rights, nor simply with what can be done in the spaces still left open after political calculations have been done, but finally with what makes for the flourishing of good persons. This is at least the legacy of African traditional cultures, where such personal flourishing entails a self-transcending and an intrinsic community dimension. And it is probable, as Hans Kung (1997) suggests, that this can be reasonably affirmed of all great ethical traditions, and hence for an emergent global ethic.

In Ross Leckie's scholarly fictionalisation of the life of Hannibal, he has the Carthaginian, who had been schooled from childhood to see Rome as the ultimate enemy, about to embark upon his winter crossing of the Alps, hesitate for a moment as a passage from the *Nicomachean Ethics* comes to mind:

> 'We call an object pursued for its own sake more final than one pursued because of something else...and happiness more than anything else is thought to be just such an end... something perfect and self-sufficient.' I remember feeling of it as of many passages [in Aristotle] that there was some great truth there, but one I could not comprehend (Leckie, 1995:123).

His inability to think in terms of ordering goods in the Aristotelian sense in favour of the truly worthwhile and praiseworthy, is perhaps the mark of a man of action - not a fully rounded person, and a danger to himself as well as to others. Maybe he is a skilled professional, an effective fighter, but he has lost all sense of what it is all for. And that is the point of this discussion: the need for professionalism in Africa should be understood in such a way as to preserve the best in the tradition, a critical idea of what constitutes the good life, the flourishing of individuals together.

Chapter Eleven

Secular Public Policy and the African Ecclesial Response

In this chapter, I turn my attention to the way democratic states deal with religion and, in particular, to the question of decolonising the current practice. In the background is, on the one hand, MacIntyre's critique of the excesses of liberal ethics and Lonergan's decoupling of the value of individual freedom from an ethical relativism and, on the other hand, the African traditional ethics of *Ubuntu*. The default secular public policy of liberal democratic states, also in Africa, have been largely determined by the standard ethics of modernity critiqued by MacIntyre and Lonergan. They could well learn from this Africa-friendly critique.

The colonial legacy in sub-Saharan Africa, has, I argue, issued in secular public policy, in two versions: the Anglo-Saxon focus on tolerance for different worldviews (with its remote origins in Protestant resistance to a religious absolute) and centred on each individual's choice of life direction, and the Francophone focus on human creativity or *liberté* (with its remote origins in the Catholic idea of grace perfecting nature) which is blocked by religion's heteronomous approach. Both versions, I will suggest, elide what is the foundation of African culture, the basic human need for a commitment to solidarity. To decolonise would be to reverse this: (a) for the African Protestant church to situate the individual's 'yes' or 'no' to God in a philosophical anthropology of personal growth; (b) for the African Catholic church to decouple objective normativity from a premodern cosmological hierarchy.

Introduction: Two versions of secular policy

While I was teaching at the University of Lesotho in the 1990s, I realised that the two main political parties, the Basotho Congress Party (BCP) and the Basotho National Party (BNP), had emerged out of the two religious traditions that had had such an impact on the population, the French Evangelical missionaries on the one hand, and the Catholic Oblate missionaries from Ottawa, on the other, both, as it happened, French-speaking (cf Breytenbach, 1976: 92). But, as I came to understand it, these origins in the religious past were, to my surprise, very largely unknown to present-day citizens of Lesotho. Conflicts attached to the ambivalent emergence of modernity in the developed world were to some extent determining the political landscape of an African country whose culture predates these movements. Clearly, the impact of colonisation on the local culture is multifaceted. For a general perspective on how the Protestant missionaries affected the consciousness of black South Africans, Jean and John Comaroff's *Of Revelation and Revolution Vol 1. Christianity, Colonialism and Consciousness in South Africa* (1991) is enlightening. You can't turn back the clock, but the way forward should be informed. The bureaucratic power should not be 'anti-politics', in James Ferguson's term in his 1994 study of how this is precisely the case in contemporary Lesotho. A country's development depends on overcoming blind spots such as this one. I want to suggest a similar situation pertains in contemporary democratic African countries in respect of the secular character of the governments. These secular approaches - the Anglo-Saxon on the one hand, and the Francophone on the other - follow the two versions of the Christian religion out of which they emerged: roughly, the Protestant and the Catholic. It is important to see these links if one is to motivate the project of a decolonised ecclesiology. Very briefly, and to anticipate, the focus in the Anglo-Saxon version is on tolerance for different worldviews (with its remote origins in Protestant resistance to a religious absolute) and centred on each individual's choice of life direction. In the Francophone version, the focus is on human creativity or *liberté* (with its remote origins in the Catholic idea of grace perfecting nature), which is blocked by religion's heteronomous approach. Both versions, I will argue, elide what is the foundation of African culture, the basic human need for a commitment to solidarity.

A decolonialising process must begin with tracing how the movement that began with Jesus' radical modification of the Jewish religion became enculturated in these two different ways. This will lead us to ask critical questions about the further inculturation of the faith in the African context and to suggest how an understanding of the negative aspects of those moves could help in the invention of an African church rooted in, rather than side-lining, the reality of the African lifeworld.

The version of the religion out of which Anglo-Saxon secularity emerged, sees God intervening to lift persons out of the state of sin, on the condition each individual responds with a 'yes' to this gratuitous offer; the hierarchy of the organised church centred in Rome fudges this challenge. Once you subtract the religious dimension, individuals are seen as blocked from reaching objective truth and society must allow each to form their own way forward - and protect the rights of religion too.

The other version posits a transcendent god securing a cosmic and moral order; natural human potential flourishes by divine grace, symbolised in hierarchies of power tracking the god's overall position. Once you subtract the religious dimension, there remains in this Francophone version of secularity the natural human capacity to determine one's own life; religion, because of its heteronomous point of view, is excluded as obstructing this free self-determination. Jansen (2006) contrasts the French policy of secularity or *laicité* with the Anglo-Saxon model; the latter stressing tolerance, while the emphasis in the former is on free creativity, breaking with the 'belonging,' seen as hierarchical, and which is committed to a pedagogy "to institutionalize a culture of Republicanism" (Jansen, 2006:477).

In these characterisations, we are dealing, it goes without saying, in 'ideal types'. Protestantism can be described as uttering a "No to a Church in whose self-understanding the essential notion of tension between the spiritual essence and the empirical form has been eliminated" (Meinhold, 1975:1294). This attitude of the Roman Catholic Church, described as thinking of itself as 'franchised', hence unquestionable (Mackey, 2006:20), remains an obstacle. The classic point of difference - from the other side now - is whether grace is 'imputed' (Protestant) or 'imparted' (Catholic); the latter holding to "the non-total destruction of the freedom of man by original sin" (Alfaro, 1975:1034). EL Mascall (1946:80) points to Protestant theologians arguing that "in spite of his guilt and worthlessness, he is, if he has faith in Christ, treated *as if* he were innocent, by the imputation to him of the merits of Christ..." (italics added).

Both versions elide what is the foundation of African culture: the basic human need for a commitment to solidarity (Carrabregu, 2016). The most salient expression of the value of solidarity in African culture is perhaps the idea of *indaba*, rule through discussion and consensus (Kiyala, 2022). It is important to be aware of this, because what we have in secular public policy is an ethical move - and thus open to scrutiny on the matter of the most basic human values. The secular public policy is founded on the values of running the country on democratic consensus rather than some other, say, traditional way. It arises from the appreciation of greater individual freedom and an enlarged critical space in European and then colonial culture.

That is our first brief account of the two kinds of secular public policy and their shortcomings. We now turn to unpack the nature of the two inculturations of the religion, leading in turn to the secular policies with which we are familiar.

Pulling it apart: Two inculturations of the Christian faith...

The first inculturation of the religion, moving out of its Jewish cultural background, was in response to the classical Greek and Roman world. Inculturation, argues Haight (2004:249) "involves reformulating Christological doctrine in a way that addresses the questions of the culture and uses the language of the culture in response." These responses will not be in the language of their source, scripture. According to Tillich (1962), what was happening here was the reception of the Christian religion by a culture marked by the 'anxiety of fate'. This was provoked by the uncertainties attaching to a life in which political and natural (and supernatural and demonic) forces dominated and controlled the lives of everyday people. The fully transcendent God of the new religion relegated such forces - the sun and the moon are good examples - to mere accessories of a well-run household; the one to light the day, the other the night. In the framing normative order now newly established, the natural human potential to flourish is actualised by divine grace, working through normal human capacities. The power to do so comes from above, and the church hierarchy embodies that ladder of power, from bishop down to ordinary faithful. This does, of course, reflect a feudal system of social organisation.

The second inculturation took place at the start of the modern period, in response to the rise of the middle-class and the greater degree of individual freedom and the value of equality that characterised the new commercial ethos – well-explained by Linda Woodhead in Chapter 4, 'The Reformation in Context', of her *An Introduction to Christianity* (2004). The anxiety to which the religion responded was now not of the cosmic order as such but of any person's particular place in that order of salvation: are they matching up to what is demanded of them? The old hierarchical order - securing everyone in their God-given place - is seen as a block to this kind of critical self-awareness, a "lack of faith in the power of God to save" (Woodhead, 2004:159). It is an anxiety of guilt and condemnation. A central element is the fact of human fault, but God is the power that reverses this through the believer's reorientation, made possible by God's gratuitous gift of Christ. Justification comes exclusively through the conscious reception of this gift, by faith alone. As Woodhead (2004:170) explains, "the righteousness of God" so feared by Luther would not condemn him but save him. "Not that he makes them righteous, but that he ascribes or imputes righteousness to them." This is a justification through faith in God alone. The idea of rising to holiness through greater participation in the legalistic hierarchical church and society is seen as a block to true faith.

And their secular legacies...

The two versions of secular policy come about by subtracting the religious dimension from these general views of the world. In the case more familiar to the anglophone world (we can call it Version B, since the religious culture associated with it came later), the key idea is that of a scepticism about any purported claim to absolute truth. Human beings are essentially blocked in the exercise of their intellect and of their power of willing, hampered in what they can know and in the scope of their willingness. There is a default scepticism about 'grand narratives'. Each person has the right to put forward their version, and so do the religions. The underlying principle is that of the equality of all such claims. Ethics is a matter of the principles of fairness. Kant formulated this view of ethics through the idea that no one should treat another person in a way they would not themselves like to be treated. As MacIntyre (1966:193) puts it, for Kant, "the test of a genuine moral imperative is that I can universalise it." This is the attitude that Kant thought was the ground of the dignity of the human person: they should never be treated as a mere means to someone's goal. The approach of the Enlightenment, central to Kant's thinking, is summed up by the idea that each person should stand on their own feet: *sapere aude*, dare to be wise, said Kant. No religious authority can override this individual dignity of thinking for yourself. At the same time, the state has no jurisdiction over what the religion holds to be true. Faith is not reached through reason. The secular policy can be phrased as, Leave them alone.

The second version, Version A secular policy, is more typical of Francophone countries and is known as *laïcité*. If you elide the religious dimension of the grace-filled natural order, you have a focus on the idea of human potential for free self-determination and hence on the free formation of conscience in order to actualise this potential. This is the duty of the state and for this reason religion is set aside as obstructing this through its heteronomous point of view and its hierarchical forms of social arrangements. Growth in human self-understanding and in a more whole-hearted orientation towards true flourishing seem to be blocked by the hierarchical expressions of God's role and of the cosmology, which infantilise. The slogan of this version of secular policy could be, Leave us alone. Democratic citizenship is seen as a form of resistance to heteronomy, as Nancy (2006) argues, and heteronomy is associated with religion. But the educative role of the state must be balanced by citizens' free choice of symbols in the public space outside of the organs of the state: veil, soutane, turban, saffron robe, religious habit, or for that matter, blue jeans torn at the knee (Miaille, 2016:76-77).

With their shortcomings

What is missing in the Anglo-Saxon version of secularity has to do with the problem of motivation. Without the cosmological or theological framing of the kind religion used to offer, what motivation is there to follow principles of rational fairness if one can flout them with impunity? As MacIntyre (1981:45) argues, Kant gives us no good reason to follow this principle. In the religion version accompanying this approach, God may be seen as securing, in his perfectly just overview, an ultimate foundation for such motivation. But this in turn throws up the problem of natural disasters such as plagues or earthquakes, by the nature of things causing much undeserved, unjust, suffering. This is termed 'the problem of evil', in other words how such unjust suffering squares with the idea of God as fair, and the discipline of theodicy is the result. In his lengthy exposition, *A Secular Age* (2007), Charles Taylor links this to the Deist movement, a movement which "reshaped our understanding of Providence" (2007:221). For an extended discussion of this, see my article (Giddy, 2020). The failure of theodicy would throw the whole religion into doubt.

For Tillich, from whose writings I have sketched the two versions of the Christian faith, neither of these has purchase in contemporary culture. "The contents of the tradition, however excellent, however praised, however loved once, lose their power to give content today" (Tillich, 1962:55). But he points in particular, to the Version B religion as problematic in putting to one side a philosophical anthropology that could ground a new expression of the tradition. The upshot of this (he is speaking of some Protestant theologians) is that "the doctrinal concepts of the biblical message were preached as objective truth without any attempt to mediate the message to man in his psychosomatic and psycho-social existence" (1962:131-132). The choice of a 'yes' or 'no' to God is too abstracted from the actual intersubjective conditions of human growth.

The oversight is shared by the culture *and* the version of the religion associated with it. The take-away point here is then to see how, within these frames of thinking, one could integrate the 'yay' or 'nay'; the basic orientation, in a philosophical anthropology.

What is missing from the Francophone version of secularity has to do with the problem of the idea of a normative human nature. Clearly, secular self-determination is a normative idea. Yet any norm for human persons prescribed to them seems very close to what is being *resisted* in democracy; namely, an ideal imposed from above. Does this not imply the framing of a cosmic hierarchy? The blind spot of this ethical approach has to do not with motivation as such, but with the *quality* of such motivation: without the proper symbolisation of the capacity for self-determination, for transcendence, the culture will become shallow, the most marketable products tend to swallow up all the rest. Shrove Tuesday morphs into the Rio Carnival. (The recent pantheonisation of Josephine Baker, symbol of universalism and equality, is an attempt to reverse that trend). For this reason, one can expect a drift into the extremes of a transhumanism and, in reaction, a shift of citizens to the political right. Vergely's (2019) discussion of the 'illusion' of transhumanism is indicative. It leads also to philosophical theological critiques of modernity and the secular state as such; for example, that of Brague (2018) and, earlier, MacIntyre (1981). In the absence of a normative human nature, argues MacIntyre, we cannot know "which of our desires are to be acknowledged as legitimate guides to action, and which on the other hand are to be inhibited, frustrated or e-educated..." (1981:46). Brague observes that modernity wants no external authority determining its norm. "The relationship between man and the divine takes on the form of 'it's either him or me'. Humanism must thus tend to become an atheism" (2018:4). The irony is, of course, that this view is shared (from the opposite court) by writers such as Pinker (2012) and Dennett (2017). The take-away point here, to be discussed in detail below, is *not to see normativity as inevitably linked to a pre-modern cosmology and theology.* The personalist frame of thinking found in the African traditional ethical approach is key to the project and we turn now to this.

Putting it together: The ethics of *Ubuntu* and the ontology of 'living force'

Any account of decolonising the churches will have to refer to the foundational elements in African traditional thought. It might also be that these could make an important contribution to world Christianity.

Our discussion in Chapters 2 and 3 have laid the groundwork for this. Two basic concepts can sum up the African traditional approach: the idea of a person becoming a person through others (captured in the concept of *Ubuntu*); and the idea of a transcendent 'living force' running through all living beings in different degrees and sourced always in the god. The key value is that of solidarity. A commitment to solidarity is arguably at the foundation of any social arrangements that work through ethics, discussion, and consensus; right rather than might. It has a religious foundation. It is the transcendent living force that is the source of anyone's generous recognition of the other person. This religious dimension does not, however, entail a dualism of the ordinary world and the spiritual. The supernaturalism that pertains to any premodern culture can be seen as a more incidental part of the religion, and unhelpful in the case of a religion in the context of science and democratic pluralism. It is the supposed conflict with the ordinary self-determining lives of people, the supposed truth (known by the few) that trumps all that, that forces democratic society to put religion to one side.

The secular humanist assumptions of democratic society sit uneasily with African traditional culture. Some of what we have already described in Part One of this book can be summarised. For Bujo (2009:114), as we have mentioned above, there can be no morality in the African frame of thinking without God. A hierarchy of power is taken for granted, as the only possible way of how the already-achieved power of elders or ancestors and finally of God, could be donated and received by those not yet developed. But that hierarchy is within the context of an inclusivity which is of equal or greater import in the culture. This whole exchange of influences amongst hierarchically ordered persons and powers, a matter of giving and receiving, gives meaning to the centrality in the culture of respect. The focus is not on individual conscience and guilt, but on respect and shame, and on social categories attached to the roles of father, elder brother, wife, mother, and so on. Morality does not highlight equality but rather the value of including everyone.

The starting point is not the individual but the community. But this is not an ethic of 'the tribe'. This is because there is a universality in the intention behind the ethic, which is underpinned by the idea of an order constituted by the fundamental power or 'vital force'. Life is an exchange of influences amongst hierarchically ordered persons and powers. The affirmation of this hierarchy is therefore of great importance, hence the centrality of the attitude of respect.

The key point is that 'spirit' here is not opposed to materiality. Rather, its embeddedness with what is other than itself enables its actualisation. It is enacted through its relationality to the other. This is the key idea of *Ubuntu*, humanness. Seeing persons in the frame of the cosmic order does not imply they are determined by the physical and social environment. 'Living force' is ultimately not material and deterministic but spiritual. For this reason, there is a critical element in the idea of the person seen in terms of *Ubuntu*, I can distance myself from and take into account my positionality, my 'tribe'.

Envisioning decolonising

In African traditional thought, you become who you are; the idea of *Ubuntu* is a normative one. And it is precisely through solidarity that such personal growth is enacted. To decolonise, so far as concerns Version B secularity, is to see how the emphasis on solidarity in the African traditional understanding of ethics can modify the secular ethics to bring in the social conditions for virtuous behaviour and so make following the principles of ethics more plausible. It can also modify the church's self-conception away from the supernaturalism that is a reaction to the gap in the secular ethics and away from an understanding of salvation abstracted from those social conditions for human flourishing.

The African traditional understanding of the shared spiritual force running through all living beings does not see human freedom as in conflict with normativity: growth in one's powers of self-enactment is only possible through other-determination, through specific normative intersubjective transactions. To decolonise, so far as concerns Version A secularity, is to reject the dichotomy suggested above between liberty and the idea of a normative human nature. At the same time, this move will modify the church's self-conception as based on hierarchical structures disallowing the freedom that is the animating value of modernity.

It is a big ask to suggest moving away from these paradigms. There are advantages of social power and also money in emphasising a supernaturalism that cannot be accessed by ordinary citizens in a democratic frame of thinking and, in the other version, a sacral hierarchy of authorities. But we have a good model in the largely felicitous Truth and Reconciliation Commission (TRC) of South Africa, which operated as a sacral element in a secular context, in the words of one commentator (Szablowinski, 2020; cf Gade, 2013). The much-needed transition was brought about not through contestation and the urge to get one's own way, but through prioritising the community of dialogue, through solidarity and the attitude of forgiveness that re-establishes that solidarity.

There is, on the other hand, and linked to the influences from the colonial inheritance, a tendency to import a dualism into the articulation of African thought: the religious dimension is seen as juxtaposed to the world, as 'supernatural'. For example, as we saw earlier in our discussion (Chapter 8), Bujo (2009:114) sees God as punishing wrongdoing, and intervening to do so; while Oluwole (1995) argues for the supernatural element as integral to the African approach, expressed in the reality of witches. So, throwing off the dualism from the colonial past is not a simple path. On the other hand, there is the example of the 2015 beatification of South African Benedict Daswa, bludgeoned to death in 1990 for his opposition to witchcraft, refusing – for reasons to do with his Catholic faith – to go along with the idea that rain will be forthcoming through the agency of a witch. One could envisage a future good secular government, being consistent with its secularism, celebrating this example of religious faith embracing science. But such consistency is rare, giving way to pragmatic and popularist versions of democracy and its attitude to religion and unable to counter religious charlatans.

The religious foundation of secular culture

The African approach allows one to see how religious traditions might be incorrectly positioned in the modern democratic state. It can be argued not just that religion is not opposed to a secular, democratic and scientific culture, but that this culture, in fact, arose out of religion. We can argue this while admitting the conjunction of the two is not perfect and while pointing to shortcomings in the secular policy.

One writer who has developed this idea is Gauchet (1997). He builds on Max Weber's (1905 and 1992) thesis linking the rise of Protestantism with secularisation, but does not see religion as therefore falling away; rather, it takes on a new form, or new forms. Secularisation is, therefore, not seen as hostile to religion. Furthermore, Gauchet builds on the idea of the move of the major world religions, through their internal impetus, towards more humane versions of themselves, bringing the religion down to earth, as it were. This move, first identified by Karl Jaspers, has been tracked by various scholars, in the first place by Voegelin (1956-74) and later by Armstrong (2006) and by Bellah (2011). The crucial time of this development is seen as the period 800-200 BCE, known as the Axial Age. Examples are the post-exilic prophets in the Hebrew tradition, the move of Buddha to simplify the Hindu tradition, and the well-known breakthrough towards an open philosophical frame of thinking found in the classic Greek culture (Socrates was executed for being seen as an atheist – but it is crucial to note what kind of god-belief he was dissenting from). It is religion that overturns the need for supernaturalism and sacred hierarchies: "thanks to religion, a society with no further need for religion arises" (Gauchet, 1997:15).

Given this thesis, it raises a question about the reasonableness of either of the two versions of secular public policy. It is, of course, also true that the religions do not by and large present themselves in this secular and humane way. The secular policy was made easier by the way the churches held onto their self-understanding which presented itself as opposed to democratic values and often to science as well. It is this problem that we have to confront in any ecclesiastical decolonising project.

Solidarity: The experience of God

We have been suggesting that, through the influence of traditional African thought, in particular in a fruitful dialogue with aspects of European philosophical tradition, secular society can be seen in terms of a spirituality, and an affirmation of faith in God as the source of the democratic way forward. The African churches remain 'colonised' to the extent that the religion is seen as opposed to such spirituality and stays with a supernaturalism that has become articulated in terms borrowed from the history of religious struggles in the metropole. We have suggested that the Christian religion was enculturated, first, in the thought-world of the Greco-Roman culture - giving expression to the classic Christian dogmas not sheltered from the influence of the feudal model of society, and secondly, in the modern world that was shaped by science, technology, commerce, greater individualism and democratic forms of governance. It can therefore be expected to be again enculturated differently in a different culture. And the suggestion is that dropping the supernaturalism is appropriate for a Christianity that is, through the beneficial traditional African frame of thinking, open to the secular, humane, culture.

We have introduced the problem, in the current models of secularity, of an oversight of the foundational value of solidarity. Eagleton (2022) remarks that in a liberal civilisation "everyone may believe more or less what they want - but only because they don't matter much in any case, and because the idea of human solidarity has withered at the root." It is important to see what is at stake here. The neglect of this key value leads to an ethical frame of thinking that is that of contestation. In neglecting recognition of the other, what is spawned is an unhelpful politics of identity, a phenomenon well-described by Taylor (1994). As mentioned above, a counter-example would be the South African TRC. But it is often overlooked that making commitment to solidarity, the central element in the ethos of the culture, introduces a specific religious element. The recognition of the other, and the attitude of forgiveness that can restart the solidarity, points to a predicament: each person, themselves in need of recognition by the other, cannot by virtue of that all-consuming need, give it. Yet, as we know, authentic recognition is given and received, evidenced by persons' growth in integrity of will and in overcoming self-deception. That gives good grounds for a reasonable trust in a power transcendent of normal human capacities blocked by the impasse referred to here. To be dependent in this way that all persons are, is a mark of finitude. But amidst finitude, we have evidence here of the operation of non-finite power - just as intuited in African traditional thought.

Beyond a colonised church: Re-expressing Christian faith in a new key

Unpacked in this frame of philosophical psychology, we have discerned at the heart of the secular society, a religious dimension. The issue, then, is whether the dominant formulations of ecclesial identity are not, in fact, a hindrance to the project of decolonising the churches. Supernaturalism puts the religion at a distance from the culture; similarly, hierarchical ways of symbolising (and legislating) the religious dimension block the recognition of how 'normal' the religious element is in any person's struggle to make something of their lives. In fact, one could see, in the narratives of the life of Jesus that highlight his embodiment of the messiah or Christ symbol, an expression of the transformative intersubjective transactions referred to in the account of solidarity given above.

How does this fit in with the traditional ways of formulating the Christian faith? Our argument can be described, very roughly, as theology from below. This phrase captures a shift that can be understood by means of Lonergan's analysis of a succession of 'realms of meaning' over the ages - an idea drawn on in Chapter 4 (Lonergan, 1972:85-100). The common-sense realm of meaning of the biblical storytelling can be contrasted with the theoretical realm of meaning that was introduced so memorably in the classical Greek philosophical period. Even as the evangelical narratives were being composed in the language of story and metaphor, a more theoretical interest was at hand, concerned to formulate the nature or essence of the matter at hand - Plato looks to define 'justice', for example, in *The Republic*. Socrates looks for internal coherence in the views of his interlocuters - continuously showing up contradictions in their common-sense views.

The inculturation issued in the theoretical formulation of the basic beliefs, moving away from the articulation of the religion in story and metaphor. Was Jesus man, god, or demi-god? The councils of Nicaea and Chalcedon are the outcome of this move. Roger Haight (1999, Chapter 9) gives an example of someone who, in Lonergan-type categories, is operating in the theoretical realm of meaning is Irenaeus. Christ's nature must be divine, he argues, because otherwise it would not be the actual presence and power of God we are talking about in the cause of Jesus; and Christ's nature must be human, to sum up our human flesh and blood life. What is interesting for our discussion, is that present-day believers overwhelmingly turn to the narratives of Jesus largely within the common-sense and not the theoretical frame of thinking. This leads us to the point that today, one has to deal with a self-consciousness about this fairly radical difference in approaching one's faith: one has to face in oneself the two approaches.

This awareness, so far as it constitutes a third approach, signals the arrival of the realm of interiority. This can be clarified by noting how the meaning of 'science' has shifted. In the earlier, classical, version, scientific theory was supposed to be descriptive of the world as it really is. But we can note how such description is distanced from how the world is actually experienced: science talks about mass rather than heaviness, temperature rather than how hot or cold it feels (metal feels colder than wood at the same temperature). So one has to ask, for example, which is the real table, the hard surface I touch, or the atoms and molecules, electrons and protons that are described in physics? One lives in two worlds, and my mind now becomes the site of a differentiated rather than compact consciousness. Interiority refers to my relation to my own cognitional operations. In the final analysis, I have to judge with my powers of reason how far to take the theory, how to apply it in different situations, and so on. 'Theology from below' draws on the data from the experience of one's subjectivity.

Very little of this realm of interiority is recognised in the way churches position Christian doctrine. The starting point of 'theology from above' is one or other doctrinal proposition, say the Trinity, or the two natures of Christ. But these propositions – or their purported authoritative nature – seem to people today to invalidate, or sidestep, their experience of themselves, an experience that draws on a familiarity, from the narratives of countless novels, with how persons grow in resolving clashing or contradictory beliefs, and possible self-delusions. The propositions, it is said, must be accepted on authority – in other words, bypassing our normal powers of intelligence. But we are only too aware of how good people can deceive themselves – the pastor in Barbara Kingsolver's novel, *The Poisonwood Bible* (2005), is one recent example from fiction. We are aware of how in well-intentioned communities there can be psychological abuse – the more recent Roman Catholic bodies such as the Neo-catechumenate, exposed earlier by Urquhart (1966), now being investigated by the Vatican, is a good example (*National Catholic Reporter*, August 6, 2021). That persons are expected to rise to the level of authenticity is part and parcel of living in this realm of meaning. Recitation of the classical doctrinal statements would seem to be more or less peripheral to someone's lifeworld today.

In conclusion, the Christian religion can be enculturated differently, given the present cultural environment of Africa. Decolonising will mean (a) for the African Protestant church to situate the individual's 'yes' or 'no' to God in a philosophical anthropology of personal growth; (b) for the African Catholic church to decouple objective normativity from a premodern cosmological hierarchy.

With religion at the heart of the ordinary culture of democratic participation, neither the Anglo-Saxon secular policy of 'Leave them alone' nor the Francophone secular policy of 'Leave us alone' seem appropriate. These are now exposed as imported versions of shifts in ecclesiastical approaches not at all reflecting the particular genius of African traditional culture. Decolonising the African churches will imply, finally, decolonising secular public policy.

Part Four

The University Curriculum

Chapter Twelve

The African University and the Social Sciences

This final Part Four of the discussion applies the philosophical framework developed in Parts One and Two to the question of the university curriculum. In this first chapter, the ideas of Lonergan are expanded; in the other chapters, much of what has been developed already is now applied directly to the question of the university. Since the aim is that these chapters can stand alone, brief summaries are given of some of the material already canvassed above.

The African university, it goes without saying, must needs build upon the cultures in which it is situated. Traditional African cultures, so far as moral thinking is concerned, are objectivistic. A boy or a girl is initiated into and encouraged to grow towards an objective ideal of what it is to be, for example, a Zulu or Mosotho, man or woman. The very notion of being a human person admits of degrees: one becomes a person, through participation in the community.

But such objectivistic ethics finds little resonance in modern Western culture, a culture associated with the development of the African university. On the contrary, once the empirical method began to be systematically applied not only to physical reality but also to human behaviour, moral values came to be seen as fully intelligible in terms of their social genesis. Value systems are thought to be relative to one particular society or other. Our era, argued Samir Amin (1989), is characterised by a cultural relativism which in the West is expressed by praise for provincialism and in the developing nations by a wave of fundamentalisms. "All aspirations for universalism are rejected in favour of a 'right to difference'" (1989:116) and all cultures have their "individual, incommensurable histories" (1989:135).

The view that any person has the right - and even power - to judge others is replaced by attention to the relativity of those judgements. Without a doubt, such judgements can be erroneous, superficial, hasty or relative. No case is ever definitively closed; debate always continues. But that is precisely the point. It is necessary to pursue debate and not to avoid it on the grounds that the views that anyone forms about others are and always will be false: that the French will never understand the Chinese (and vice versa), that men will never understand women, etc.; or in other words, that there is no human species, but only 'people.' (Amin, 1989:146-147)

Making a similar point, Mary Midgley mocks the extreme individualism associated with ethical relativism. The current moral obsession of Western society, she writes (1989:174), is that of "a self-righteous preoccupation with putting down self-righteousness;" no one, it is supposed in a quite self-contradictory fashion, is justified in censuring anyone else.

I want to argue here that this apparent conflict between, on the one hand, the standards of empirical method and the aims of the university, and on the other hand, the outlook associated with traditional African cultures, is resolvable. The solution lies in understanding the history of the rise of the social sciences as academic disciplines, and the challenge this presented to the classical Western philosophical view of morality. For such classical morality was, like traditional African ethics, objectivistic. As in the African case, there arises, with the challenge in particular of the social sciences, a need for the reformulation of such ethics.

Moral objectivity and the social sciences

From the perspective of the dominant modern culture, the classical tradition in ethics could be judged to be uncritical, since it seems to presuppose a certain theory of human psychology, often implicitly dualist. Our rationality, it had been supposed, functions autonomously of the influences, biological and social, operating on us. A certain set of ends is said to pertain to human behaviour universally, regardless of circumstances.

The modern period is characterised by the loss of the sense of a predetermined place in the cosmos; by an awareness of cultures other than that of Europe; by the awareness of historical change within a single society; by the imperative, thrust upon us by the availability of the appropriate technology, to choose our lifestyle, to remake our environment. The upshot of these changes has been the emergence of a heightened sense of 'subjectivity.' All that we do today, the little and the great events, is photographed or otherwise recorded, for our self-scrutiny, our further consideration. The centrality of an abstract concept of human nature is gradually replaced by a historical awareness of how human beings see themselves in different periods; what they value, how they create meaning. Human responsibility is oriented towards our participation in forming history, modifying and transcending to some extent all conditioning social influences.

To this mentality, Aristotle's argument – in his *Ethics* (1097b) – that an understanding of the 'function' of human life will determine the normative notion of happiness, seems antediluvian. The classical view sees human nature as the same everywhere and always, contrasting the abstract and universal truths with the concrete and particular instantiations. Casuistry is the application of the universal truths about human nature (metaphysical and moral) to particular cases. But the particular is inexplicable except by the stipulation of a chance occurrence, the way things happen to fall, and what is a chance occurrence is not subject to scientific explanation. This, at least, is how things were thought of. The laws of human nature remain unmodified by circumstances and context.

What is clear today is that this way of looking at things reveals a bias towards the formulation of an idea of human nature in terms appropriate to one culture only. There is an oversight of the cultural (and historical) *variation* in the pattern of particulars characteristic of human behaviour. A good example is the way in which the place that sex occupies on the moral map has, in classical ethics, been taken to be a constant. The writings of Foucault have served to disabuse us of that notion: modern conceptions differ radically from those of ancient Greece, Foucault

(1985:187ff) shows, according to which heterosexuality was less of a moral issue than was the attitudes of control and submission.

The moral objectivity associated with the classical tradition was later formulated in terms of natural law, or the law of human nature. From the contemporary perspective, this approach seems to discount the particular individual's subjective experience of those variable and changing circumstances which confront one in the course of one's moral deliberations. The imperative of self-determination has replaced the centrality of the imperative for one's desires to submit to the rule of the rational side of our nature. The norms that do exist, it is now said, are constructed, not discovered in nature. The principle of universalisability; for example, expresses the implicitly agreed conditions for social living (contractarian ethics), while according to utilitarianism ethics, is based on the principle of maximising human happiness in the sense of counting votes, with no predetermined character assigned to the content of such happiness.

In his tone-setting *The Phenomenology of Mind* of 1806, Hegel introduced a contrary theme into Western philosophy: that to be a subject is to be in self-conscious relation to others. "Self-consciousness exists in itself and for itself, in that, and by the fact that it exists for another self-consciousness, that is to say, it *is* only by being acknowledged or 'recognised'" (Hegel, 1967:229). It is, he argued, the existence and appropriation of such personal influences as these that makes us what we are. In this way, Hegel turned the critical searchlight of modern scientific method towards the human subject itself, a move that was rapidly developed (without the baggage of Hegel's philosophical idealism) into the distinct disciplines of the various social sciences. Much of Hegel's insight fits in with the traditional African concept of *Ubuntu*, humanness: to be a person is to be in relation to other persons, to become oneself through others. But the question remains as to how one is to take the social sciences - in particular, perhaps, for the African academic enterprise, where this idea of humanness still has purchase as a moral imperative.

Typically, the social scientist correlates sets of data and interprets these through grasping statistical trends apparent in them. But what is the status of such statistical trends? Does the understanding of the social forces operative in our lives replace a previous interpretive schema in terms of moral values, and so on? In other words, is it suggested that our notion of human freedom and responsibility - the foundation for attributing praise and blame to human actions - is shown up as naive by the social sciences? Is human behaviour determined? Where does that leave the doctrine of basic human rights? Or the conviction, for example, that the struggle against apartheid and its legacy is objectively just? Is there an objective moral basis for the legal system? Is there any ultimate reason to be moral? If not, how is one to justify traditional moral laws at all? What is it to live a happy and fulfilled life? How is one to evaluate the traditional African ideas and values associated with marriage? Unless provision is made for the organised discussion of such questions at the university, rationality as such is bound eventually to fall into disrepute, and a rule-of-thumb moral relativism takes over in the student's mind. An easy prey will be found for individualism and materialism, for the needs of the industrial machine to dominate and gradually undermine the needs of local cultures. What is likely is an inverse Eurocentrism (Amin, 1989:146) and an unreflective parochialism.

Standard empiricism and its critique

In addressing these questions, we are faced with the weight of a scientific tradition which has defined itself largely in opposition to pre-critical notions of a normative human nature. In the classical conception, reality is ordered by a rational principle which can be observed in the regularity of the planetary movements. The laws of the universe are thus the laws of thought, and they are described by the science of logic. Human behaviour, too, must be brought into harmony with these metaphysical truths. Moral science is concerned with the correct reasoning from laws revealed in tradition. Such laws are generally known, and the problem is to apply them to particular cases.

The modern period is characterised by a reaction, beginning with Francis Bacon's *Novum Organum* in 1620, against these metaphysical certainties of the medieval era (Bacon, 1905). The objectivity associated with scientific knowledge is contrasted with human subjective reality, the realm of goals and values. Human knowing is thought of either in terms simply of sensing, as in empiricism, or else in terms of the conceptual or interpretive schemes understood to be underlying the phenomenal manifold, as in rationalism. In either case, in order to know, one places oneself outside of the reality one is investigating, eliminating, as far as possible, subjective elements. There is the problem – unpacked in Chapter 4 in our discussion of a possible way forward for an African philosophy of mind – of the duality of objective and subjective perspectives, of reality as verified and public, and, on the other hand, as experienced and private.

In modern social science, it is our experienced reality that is documented and the data correlated. Case studies seem to give insights into psychological or social realities. Equally clearly, they do not fit Plato's criterion for true knowledge, namely knowledge valid at all times and all places. There would therefore have seemed good reason to drop the whole edifice of classical metaphysics and ethics. It is the inability of the classical view of knowledge to incorporate the facts of our diverse experience, as well as the obvious successes of modern, experience-based and experimentally confirmed science, that has led to the rejection of theories of ethics based on so-called 'human nature.' And this has meant that there is a foundational problem at the heart of contemporary moral philosophy.

This situation constitutes a dilemma in terms of the aim of the African university to embody the scientific spirit without destroying traditional culture. But, of late, the dominant view of science has come under a radical critique, amongst others by postmodernists. One of the most impressive of such critiques is that given by Nicholas Maxwell (1987), a scientist-turned-philosopher. Maxwell argues that the dominant view of scientific inquiry, which he calls 'standard empiricism', undermines any attempt to grow in one's understanding of what values, what projects, merit advocating. For, such understanding is of a quite different nature from scientific knowledge thus conceived. In standard empiricism, he argues, the former kind of knowledge is deemed to have no place in rational inquiry. While scientific understanding is agreed to be objective, impersonal, factual, rational, predictive, testable, and scientific, any genuine example of the appreciation of goals of action - 'person-to person' understanding - would, it is thought, lack all the above features. The latter would, on the contrary, be subjective, personal, emotional and evaluative (and thus non-factual), intuitive (and thus non-rational), nonpredictive, untestable, and unscientific (Maxwell, 1987:181-184).

And this, Maxwell argues, has disastrous practical consequences, for thereby such person-to-person understanding is downgraded. But in order to promote the understanding and achievement of what is of value, the person-to-person understanding must be considered - from an 'objective' point of view - as prior: we need to "enter imaginatively into the other person's life-problems and possible solutions." The Enlightenment aim of promoting individual happiness cannot be achieved "if individual people cannot empathetically understand those different from themselves."

> The great danger is that in a vast, complex and diverse world people, instead of being enriched by diversity, will merely come to feel threatened and isolated by it, and will as a result hunger for some form of collectivism or nationalism (of the left or right) which banishes individual liberty and diversity. (Maxwell, 1987:186)

Maxwell's critique of modern epistemology is shared by postmodernism. Postmodernism concludes to a radical scepticism about the capacity of language to make transparent the proposition. Maxwell simply points out that the notion that scholarship and science have a pure dimension; a value for their own sake, makes sense only if these are understood as part of contributing to people realising what is of real value. And this can only happen if primary recognition is given to people articulating their personal problems of knowledge and understanding and proposing solutions.

> All this is sabotaged when scholarly and scientific research is sharply dissociated from personal problem-solving in life as demanded by the philosophy of knowledge... Scholarship

and science tend to become esoteric, formal, scholastic and decadent, remote from the interests and concerns of non-academic life, pursued for the sake of academic career and status rather than for the sake of shared personal understanding. (Maxwell, 1987:59)

Lonergan has a similar critique. He compares the current situation to one prevailing in a primitive society: that of the Trobriand islanders observed by Malinowski. Malinowski pointed out that while in matters of practical living the islanders exercise their rational faculties (taking, for example, the law of cause-and-effect in its proper way), beyond that realm, intelligence yields to myth and magic. No human emancipation here of the kind associated with the Enlightenment. But what about contemporary society? Lonergan (1990:101) comments that the tendency is to be content

merely to make more cultivated and more civilized the intelligent and rational part of Trobriand living, while maintaining a surrounding no man's land which used to be inhabited by myth and magic but which is now empty – we do not admit, Here be strange beasts; we simply do not bother about it. The real problem of human development is the problem of occupying this territory, this blank, with intelligence and reasonableness, just as we have occupied the territory that can be controlled by sensible consequences.

Either this area is brought within the compass of rational inquiry (that is, the questions there are assumed to make sense), or irrationality on a large scale will move in to occupy the vacuum.

Maxwell's analysis is all the more telling for the purposes of our discussion because he identifies himself with the Enlightenment tradition rather than any form of classical ethical naturalism. But it does not address the specific problems raised for the university in the context of traditional African culture and moral values. I refer to the problem of integrating, building on, and developing the deposit of wisdom about the moral life, which comes to us from traditional culture, whether African or Western.

For, such wisdom has classically been expressed in terms of a normative conception of human nature. And in the modern period, 'nature' has come to designate the pre-human dimension of reality, and is contrasted with the social and historical. To quote Lonergan (1972:81):

> History, then, differs radically from nature. Nature unfolds in accord with law. But the shape and form of human knowledge, work, social organisation, cultural achievement, communication, community, personal development, are involved in meaning So it is that man stands outside the rest of nature, that he is a historical being, that each man shapes his own life but does so only in interaction with the traditions of the communities in which he happens to have been born and, in turn, these traditions themselves are but the deposit left him by the lives of his predecessors.

The question that arises from the above remarks is as follows: Does our historical conditioning preclude the operation of free will and the applicability of traditional categories of moral responsibility? Or is it rather - as Lonergan suggests above - that such conditioning enables us to appropriate our lives through the lives of others and the influences of the social structures?

On the dominant view in the social sciences, the first alternative must be true. Science in the modern age has been conceived as inquiry into and knowledge of non-statistical causal laws determinative of actual events. Lonergan terms this the 'classical' concept of science. On such a conception the social forces can only be understood as operating deterministically. Social scientists are faced with the prospect that their contribution to our understanding of how we should live will be largely neglected. Further, the integrity of the discipline is sometimes taken to conflict with any belief in the existence of objective moral values, which are seen as epiphenomenal (an exception being made for the cases when the social science itself is directed to the ends of social development, justice, and so on - moral ends). This is a methodological point about what constitutes true knowledge in general. The notion that science provides the only knowledge worthy of the name, is the central philosophical myth that has accompanied the rise of modern Western culture. It finds expression, for example, in the programme to map what are called - for example, in Smith and Jones' *The Philosophy of Mind* (1986) - 'folk-psychological intuitions' about our powers of self-determination to what are supposed to be the scientifically established truths of the matter (in one version, meaning brain activity). Moral values are understood in the same philosophical tradition to be established by contracted agreements amongst individuals performing utilitarian calculations. It is true that knowledge that can be put to practical use in technology (as scientific knowledge can) does have an undeniable reality or importance. So do the outcomes of individuals' utilitarian calculations (which will determine what can be produced and marketed to them at a fair profit). But a philosophy whose greatest influences are notions such as these could not adequately fulfil the project of re-expressing traditional African belief-systems and values. One thinks, in particular, of the fundamental convictions that, as Shutte puts it (1993:9), "human persons transcend the realm of the merely material, and also that in order to develop as persons we need to be empowered by others." There is, therefore, a need for a framework of discussion which allows for a critical appropriation of such ideas.

In the following section, it will be argued that such a framework is indeed provided by Lonergan's understanding of scientific method. On Lonergan's understanding, knowledge given in science does not undermine our ideas about the possibility of self-determination. Indeed, scientific knowledge presupposes the further, strictly philosophical understanding of the norm of critical knowing. That this is the case is perhaps most clearly seen when one analyses the nature of statistical method.

The theory of knowing, in Bernard Lonergan

Lonergan's theory of human knowing has been a foundational element in much of what has been discussed in this book. However, it is important here to spell this out somewhat more systematically. The standard empiricist view of knowing posits a notion of scientific objectivity achieved through the elimination of subjective elements. Lonergan presents an alternative view of knowing which does not presuppose the dualism of subject and object but entails a heightening of the presence to self. Objectivity is seen as the fruit of fidelity to the norms intrinsic to the process of coming to know anything at all, of authentic subjectivity.

Empiricism stresses the role of sense-experience in the constitution of knowledge, and rationalism the role of ideas. Little attention has been paid to the role of that further questioning by means of which the inquirer considers his or her own grasp of the nature of the object. This is the role of judgement. Judgement considers not the possible intelligibility to be found in the object of enquiry (its nature or form), but the extent to which it actually applies. More so than perception or understanding, judgement is clearly a matter of a certain quality of performance, a norm to be attained in an ever-deeper way. To a question of this latter type - expressed not as What is it? but Is it so? - one can always answer that the evidence is not yet sufficient to form a judgement. That, itself, is a judgement. In such a case, and when one does judge that the understanding is indeed true, probably so or certainly, one commits oneself.

> The variety of possible answers... closes the door on possible excuses for mistakes. A judgement is the responsibility of the one that judges. It is a personal commitment. (Lonergan, 1970:272; 1990:297)

And this leads to a consideration of what the content of such responsibility could be, of a possible norm or standard and its necessary elements. When one judges, one is questioning the extent to which one's understanding covers the data. At the heart of knowing is the act of understanding the insight that grasps the intelligibility in what is presented to the senses. But intelligence is not enough; for, without attentiveness to the full range of data, the theory will be biased. Furthermore, to pass judgement on what one does not understand, is arrogant; while to understand but not to subject that understanding to critical judgement is, as Lonergan says and as discussed in Chapter 4, in the analysis of an appropriate African-influenced approach to the philosophy of mind, "quite literally silly"; only through such judgement does the distinction emerge between philosophy and myth, astronomy and astrology, and so on (1988b:206-207). Human knowing consists, then, in the threefold process of experiencing, understanding and judging. Insofar as one follows the norm of attentiveness, intelligence and reasonableness, one is knowing. The implications of this are that any form of determinism is refuted: all the statements of the social sciences, for example, presuppose this normative structure, and implicitly affirm it to be true. Lonergan's term for the latter is 'self-transcendence,' and it has a cognitive and a moral dimension.

A proper understanding of statistical knowledge will afford a deeper insight into the nature of this fundamental norm of human living. Indeed, given the existence and obvious success of statistical methods - in particular in the social sciences - in giving us new and more profound insights into the influences operating in our lives, an understanding of its nature must be an integral part of any account of human freedom and responsibility. It is not enough simply to restate, along with the classical tradition, that human beings by the law of their nature, are rational and free. For, this could be taken to exclude from consideration all the questions that arise when one considers the truths about human development, or the lack of it, found in the theories of Marx, Freud, and others.

In our discussion of how MacIntyre reworks the virtue ethics tradition (Chapter 6), we drew on Meynell's distinction, amongst social scientists, between those giving a 'strong' interpretation, or else a 'weak' one, to the opinions of, for example, Marx and Freud. In the strong interpretation, our powers of intelligence and reason are seen as a mere reflex of economic and social factors (Meynell, 1981:64). In the 'weak' interpretation, on the other hand, such human powers are seen as not fully determined by those environmental factors. And, clearly, it is this latter interpretation that could accommodate objective moral values in the overall picture of human behaviour.

Furthermore, the strong interpretation involves what can be termed a performative contradiction. Meynell argues that "[a] ny account of human beings, from which it can be inferred that they are incapable of cognitive and moral self-transcendence, of getting to know what is true independently of their material and social milieu and acting in accordance with that knowledge, is self-destructive." On the strong interpretation "no-one, including Freud or Marx, thinks or writes as he does because there is good reason for him to do so." There would thus be no reason for a serious consideration of their writings.

The technical term for this argument from internal contradiction is 'retorsion' (see Meynell, 1981:12–15). It plays a central role in Lonergan's philosophy (for example 1970:329; 1972:18). It justifies the special role in the university of the kind of systematic self-reflection found in philosophy.

This difference between the two kinds of interpretation in the social sciences is of crucial importance for the programme of the African university, and for its ability to contribute to the quality of our lives in general. On the strong interpretation of Marxian theory (for example), truth and morality would be seen as entirely relative to class interests. There results that unreasonably constrained conception of standards of excellence in academic scholarship, the standard empiricist view argued by Maxwell to be detrimental to the interests of the university. On the weak interpretation, however, group bias due to economic and social class is seen not to determine but significantly to condition what people believe and value. In this case, a different view of academic excellence is implied. What is held as the standard is in the first place a self-understanding which results from a critical appropriation of one's inherited ideology. And encompassed within the same one standard is the norm of willingness to put into effect, as one can, those actions which are judged to be objectively the most worthwhile ones, which take into account the well-being not only of oneself and one's group but of people in general. The university can formulate its policy in a way which gives recognition to the goal of traditional African moral teaching, namely the objective development of the person. We can now turn to a more general framework for understanding the social sciences, consequent on the above analysis of human knowing, which will develop the views on the African university expressed above.

A higher-level viewpoint: Positioning ethics in the humanities

The upshot of Lonergan's understanding of scientific explanation is that there can, in the nature of things, be real development; an emergence which is creative in the sense that it could not be predicted in advance from causal laws alone. And this gives an overriding vision to the scientific enterprise and to the academic culture in general. Lonergan's term for this vision of the process operative in the natural and human world is 'emergent probability.' Besides the laws which can be discovered in nature and social affairs, there is the statistical residue which is not simply left to be thought of as 'chance circumstances,' but is subject to probability analysis. But what is probable, sooner or later, occurs, given large enough numbers and sufficiently long time-periods. A higher-level viewpoint can systematise what, on the lower level, remains only random. And this can be observed in nature: the higher cycle of animal life, for example, can only emerge if the lower cycles (plant life and chemical processes) are already operative. And to the extent that the laws explaining the lower levels are not fully determinative of what occurs, there is, at that lower level, real potential (determined by the probability fractions) for further development. As Lonergan writes:

> There can be autonomous sciences of physics, chemistry, biology, and psychology, because on each earlier level of systematisation there are statistical residues that constitute the merely coincidental manifolds to be systematised on the next level. It follows that higher laws and higher schemes of recurrence cannot be deduced from lower laws and lower schemes of recurrence, for the higher is engaged in regulating what the lower leaves as merely coincidental. Moreover, since there are statistical residues on every level, it follows that events on any given level cannot be deduced in systematic fashion from the combination of all the laws and all the schemes of recurrence of that and of all prior levels (1970:608; 1990:631).

It is commonplace that the laws empirically established in the social sciences do not apply without remainder to human behaviour. Much behaviour seems to slip through the net of the conceptual apparatus built up by the social scientists. This would indicate that the data relevant to human behaviour are intrinsically open to fuller, higher systematisations of the kind indicated in the quotation above. Human freedom and moral agency should not therefore be considered as epiphenomenal. At the same time, the terms and relations posited on this higher level are not detached from the facts arrived at by social scientists.

However, as indicated by Meynell, these conclusions about the status of the findings of the social scientists are by no means universally accepted. For the contemporary mindset, there are two distinct but related obstacles to an easy affirmation of the resolution suggested in Lonergan. First, there is the question of how we are to take the findings of the human sciences, the laws of human behaviour. Are they implausibly supposed to apply only to the body, leaving the mind free to take up the moral attitude? And an answer to this question is given in our admittedly very brief summary of Lonergan's understanding of how statistical science serves to complement the classical scientific method. Probability ratios identified at the level of psychology, for example, indicate a real potential for self-transcendence, the understanding of which is given through a higher systematisation. Thus, Freud identifies in the patient, statistically significant correlations between conditions of human development (the need for some degree of awareness of one's own impulses, for example) and such things as sudden slips in speech and action, symptoms of physical disease, and so on. At the same time, the analyst can bring into play what are properly speaking exigencies of a higher level; those pertaining to self-understanding and self-determination, and so get the patient to appropriate themself more fully. The correlations reveal a non-random falling-short in the development of the person.

The second obstacle is that created by the myth of the exclusive status to knowledge, truly speaking, that is claimed for the specific sciences. Metaphysical entities such as that of the 'person' are dismissed as epiphenomenal. But, as the argument from retorsion showed, to deny the reality of cognitive and moral self-transcendence is to fall into a performative contradiction. There is therefore good reason to accept the weak rather than the strong interpretation of the findings of the social sciences. These latter factors, although not determinative of human behaviour, are nevertheless either integrated into our understanding of ourselves or else operate in a seemingly random fashion to upset our well-laid plans.

This is the key to the insight into an understanding of our human reality and its constraints, and so of moral pronouncements, that is given in the development of statistical method and knowledge. For the human person can be understood by a variety of sciences, physical, chemical, biological, psychological. The essence of any living organism is development. And development proceeds not according to causal laws only, for causal laws interpret only one static stage of development; nor is the development in accordance with statistical law, for the changes that occur are not random but with a direction. Lonergan thus postulates a third method; genetic, appropriate to the study of living things.

In the case of human behaviour, this has important implications. The various sciences which each contribute to the understanding of the human person on one or other level, chemical, biological, psychological, can all be integrated into an understanding of the necessary structures of understanding and of self-determining. These structures, as we saw, are presupposed in any pronouncement of any scientist, or any claim to knowledge. They are also assumed by everyone when they make moral judgements; when they judge someone to be treating them unfairly, for example. But how is such integration of empirical data and moral norm to be achieved? This question would seem to warrant detailed philosophical attention. To begin with, one might consider how ethics was seen under the fascination of classical science alone: the human will operating autonomously of the deterministic laws of physical nature, and the intellect – supposed to be unaffected by those laws – guiding the will. But questions abound: How does the intellect effect a change in the will? How do these two faculties interact? And is not the notion of the will arbitrarily choosing between good and evil, implausible?

A contemporary restatement of the classical view has it that

> what one wills is a consequence of what one thinks about
> the good... Thoughts about what is good or desirable,
> while genuinely matters of belief and cognition, have
> also a necessary effect on attitudes or volitions (Simpson,
> 1988:43; 49).

Simpson argues that the good is the proper object of the will,
as the visible is the natural object of the eye. But this begs the
question raised by empirical analyses of widespread discrepancies
between ideology and behaviour, given certain constant
environmental factors. Moral relativism can be overcome only by
providing a way of integrating such findings into a framework of
critically justified values. In classical culture, the standard of truth
and goodness was thought to be a universal given, exemplified
in the best man in society, for example in Athens. But modern
culture, to repeat, is characterised by a plurality of value systems.
The notion of 'being human,' can no longer be assumed in its
normative sense. For the cluster of shared goods of society that
are entailed by such a notion would have to be properly justified.
It is just this that is missing from restatements such as that of
Simpson (1988). In this respect, they can be faulted in ways that
would apply also to theories that knowledge of the absoluteness of
the moral imperative can be given in a 'moral intuition.' Simpson
speaks of a 'sense of the noble' as providing the necessary link
between the reason and the will (1988).

Is this a plausible answer? The general foundational
problem in modern moral philosophy is addressed by Alasdair
MacIntyre, as we saw in Chapter 6. MacIntyre illustrates
the problem for the case of the philosopher Hutcheson. The
inadequacies of the latter's notion of a foundational 'moral sense'
which is, argues Hutcheson, "prior to all reasoning" (quoted in
MacIntyre, 1988:272), can also be applied to Simpson (1988).
In contrast, argues MacIntyre, in the Aristotelian tradition the
ends desired were seen as rational, and justified by reference
to the existing polity (with its consensus of ends) and to human
nature. *Phronesis* referred to the basic human capacity to decide on

practical matters by deliberating within the framework of these reasonable ends.

But in Hutcheson *phronesis* turns into 'prudence,' a faculty of non-moral calculating - "a cautious habit of consideration and forethought, discerning what may be advantageous or hurtful in life" (cited in MacIntyre, 1988:276), which to be moral must be informed by "a high sense of moral excellence." This amounts simply to the bald pronouncement that moral objectivity exists. As in Simpson (1988), the ethics is implicitly dualist: 'caution' is always over against spontaneity of desire. There is no framework for the integration of new data about how we grow in self-understanding and in the quality of our self-affirmation (and thus no real understanding of a virtue such as *prudentia*, according to MacIntyre). Against theories such as this, social scientists are bound to protest, as for example does Karen Horney (1950:13-16).

The guiding idea in this critique of any restatement of the classic ethical approach is that the whole idea of our capacity for moral objectivity needs to be spelled out and given proper philosophical justification in terms of the powers of cognitive and moral self-transcendence. In this way the results of empirical studies of the social formation of our self-understanding and of our commitments can amplify how we understand the good.

In Lonergan's account the will is seen simply as the human capacity, not to choose a course of action in a causal vacuum, but to relate oneself to oneself, and in this way to integrate the various influences, on the various levels - physical, biological, economic - co-determining one's condition. Such integration constitutes the essence of the appropriation of one's freedom. The moral imperative is understood, not in terms of conforming to the moral law as opposed to following one's inclinations, but of self-knowledge and self-affirmation, and this is achieved through one's relation to others, as Hegel saw, and as in affirmed in traditional African thought, and, finally, as is confirmed in multiple ways in the findings of the social sciences.

What is random (or rather 'chance'), from the point of view of classical science can, in modern science, be seen to be subject to a norm from which particular events will not diverge systematically. This enables the scientist to predict a certain verified trend to the subject investigated. Such methods therefore affirm a dynamic structure to reality and so can encompass our human, self-developing, reality too. Indeed, they are an expression of our ability to grasp the nature of things and so re-act on the world, thus altering the conditions for our further development. The genius of statistical science lies in its ability to give an account of regularities which pertain to our experienced reality. It is thus able to capture the nature of the social forces which come into play in the subject's decision process, whether consciously or not. In this way, our knowledge of human flourishing, traditionally grounding judgements of moral value, may be amplified in important ways.

Further elaboration of this point is in order. One's development may be initiated on the organic level, as with the transition from baby to toddler to child, and as biological needs call for the construction of housing and systems of food production; or the psychic, as when one is stimulated to reconsider one's urban lifestyle after the experience of the quiet of a week in the country; or the intellectual, when one conceives first of a problem in present modes of living and employs one's intelligence to find a solution. Whatever the case, unless there is a corresponding adjustment on the other levels, one's attempt to strike out anew is bound to remain merely a flash in the pan. For example, to the pressure of material necessity, one may make adjustments in one's behaviour, at best, as Lonergan says, tolerated by the inner subject. Again, the demands of the organism are registered by neural signals, "but the signals need an interpreter and the interpreter an intelligent and willing pupil." (Lonergan, 1970:472; 1992:497) Finally, an excellent resolution can be frustrated because one's imagination is full of schemes of living that allow scant place for such an ideal and one lives then not a new but only a dual life.

To the problem of human development there is no facile solution in the intellectual level integrating the psychic, and the psychic the organic. For one cannot say the pure spirit of enquiry, the ineradicable and pure desire to understand that is the clue to the whole thesis of Lonergan's *Insight*, is the true 'I', while the sensitive psyche is an 'It', on which one may operate as an object. "Both are I and neither is merely It. If my intelligence is mine, so is my sexuality. If my reasonableness is mine, so are my dreams" (Lonergan, 1970:474; 1992:499). There arises then "the necessity of avoiding conflict between the unconscious and the conscious components of a development." This necessity can be formulated by means of the term, genuineness. To adopt genuineness as a norm is to acknowledge in one's development the tension between transcendence and the limitations of that transcendence due to the existence of relatively autonomous schemes of recurrence compounding the human self. To fail to acknowledge this tension is to block any further sustainable development.

Each autonomous science helps in our understanding of the constraints of human development. Our experience of particular times and situations contributes, in a way that was neglected in the classical approach, to our knowledge of human nature. But the empirical sciences need to be coordinated. And Lonergan's analysis, through its critique of the naive and popular – but mistaken – view of objectivity, achieves this. Objectivity is reached not through eliminating as far as possible our subjective interpretation but through the thorough employment of our attentiveness, understanding, and judgement. As we learn more about the various factors - not rigid laws but real trends – operating in our own lives and the lives of others, we deepen our understanding of the biases, or likely biases, obstructing the free operation of our spontaneous drive to understand and know, and undermining our native willingness to do what we understand to be the right thing. In an interesting research paper, psychotherapist Peter Galloway (1995) uncovered the gap between the urge to idealism amongst seminarians and their reality. In an African view of things, integral to higher education would be the provision of space for a systematic treatment of these issues.

Chapter Thirteen

Traditional-Religious Knowledge in Humanising Education

Introduction

We can distinguish the problem from its context. The problem is the current focus of educational systems on the means for achieving our aims, through science and technology, while neglecting to subject those aims themselves to rational scrutiny (Maxwell, 1987). The project of humanising higher education would make these aims and purposes central to teaching and learning.

The context of the problem is our global multicultural society which has elements both of scientific method, framing education systems, and of traditional-religious ways of understanding. In secular liberal democracies there is a hands-off approach to these religious traditions, but there is evidence of a link between this policy and the formation of cultural ghettos (Carrabregu, 2016; Elchardus and Siongers, 2001). A more fruitful way forward sees liberal humanism as arising out of religion (Gauchet, 1997). Traditional-religious understandings speak to the problem of personal development, potentially providing the corrective to what is neglected in the science and technology approach to higher education. What is needed is a method for introducing these traditions into the heart of public debate and, working alongside other disciplines in the humanities, in the framework of higher education.

Marcel Gauchet has argued that the humanisation of our contemporary society has its roots in the traditional-religious worldviews, seeing these as providing the impetus for the overturning of religious (or any) social hierarchies and heteronomous ways of thinking: "thanks to religion, a society with no further need for religion arises" (1997:15). Gauchet is drawing on the theory that the major world religions have been through a process of internal transformation towards a more humanistic version of themselves, the so-called Axial Age transition (Bellah, 2011; Taylor, 2012). But religions today seem by and large to be stuck in pre-Axial hierarchies and in a heteronomous, other-worldly orientation. It would seem incumbent on institutes of higher education, operating in a democratic and science-based culture, to counter this impasse. If our democratic and humanist way of thinking arises out of religion, then it would seem desirable to have a continuing dialogue with our religious past.

However, Gauchet - inconsistently, to my mind - sees what remains of religion today as inevitably super-naturalistic, other-worldly, displacing human freedom and responsibility to the god, or gods, above. One reason for this is that his historical account lacks a critical foundation in the normative structures of human agency presupposed to any empirical inquiry such as his own. In other words, secularism cannot plausibly be viewed as a simple historical fact. The normative agency operative in bringing about democratic social arrangements continues to offer, through citizens, a challenge to religions and their reformulation. It is not necessarily the case that religions stand or fall with a heteronomous and super-naturalistic way of thinking and its consequent hierarchical authority structure (Johnston, 2009; Moingt, 2010). It could be that what falls away, insofar as the religions understand themselves properly, is rather the super-naturalist frame of thinking and the hierarchical structure of the ecclesial community (Mackey, 2006).

A critical philosophy of human agency is needed. But amongst the English-speaking reading public there would seem to be an absence of trust in philosophy as an effective resource in the project of humanising our broader culture. Former French Minister of Education, Luc Ferry's attempt at making philosophy practical, *Apprendre à vivre* (Learning how to live) is, for this reason, given the English title, *A Brief History of Thought* (2011), that situates it properly in the Philosophy, rather than the Self-help, section of the bookshops. This is because philosophy can only be of help in our humanisation if there is a subject and agent to call upon in this project - and this has by and large vanished from philosophical discourse - in particular in the anglophone Analytic tradition. 'Self-help', therefore, would seem void of any critical foundation, a matter of popular intuition.

This gap in how philosophy frames itself is linked to a society geared towards technology and commercialism, where the focus is on what we have control over. In academic thought the dominant approach is that of scientism, as well pointed out by Robinson (2010), in her aptly titled book, *Absence of Mind. The Dispelling of Inwardness from the Modern Myth of the Self*, neglecting the knowledge about our capacity to *do* science, to set ourselves the aims and standards that are presupposed to any science.

In this chapter, I will revisit our earlier discussion (Chapter 4) on how the standard questions in philosophy should be revised, on the grounds of a critically based understanding of human agency and with the aim of its proper appropriation. Second, I will outline the dialectic at the heart of any personal development that is the proper domain of theology (working alongside other disciplines in the humanities) and that calls for the integration of the latter discipline in secular universities. This will also enable traditional-religious approaches to human life to be taken into the heart of the public debate and avert the formation of cultural ghettos that is often the outcome of a liberal hands-off policy whether phrased in terms of 'leave them alone' or, as in the French *laïcité* approach of complete exclusion of religion from public life, 'leave us alone' (cf Miaille, 2016).

Secularisation

Before that, however, I need to outline how religions became excluded from the space of public discourse, and hence from any fruitful role in a humanised education system: the process of secularisation. The more common view of the matter contrasts the 'ignorant', pre-modern tradition with the humanist approach. Grayling comments that it is not possible for religious people to be humanist "without inconsistency or at least oddity" (2007:26). But Gauchet sees secularisation, as already mentioned, as arising out of religion, in particular the Christian religion in Western Europe. It is this more interesting view that I will discuss, albeit very briefly. The central value in the new secular outlook is the power of human agency itself. This entails democratic governance but also future orientation, scientific method, and the productive use of nature (Gauchet, 1997). The secular approach stems from an option to refuse any transference of human agency to any supposed other, 'higher', power. And this refusal is something learned over the long history of religion.

Gauchet situates his interpretation of the Christian religion within the Axial Age shift - around 800 to 200 BCE - towards a more humanist understanding of the religion that, as mentioned above, scholars have seen in all the major religious traditions. But in contemporary thought-culture the critical appropriation of the traditions lacks a starting point. There is, as will be argued for in the following section, no objective norm of being a (critical) subject. In the popular view of science, subjectivity is opposed to the objectivity associated with evidence-based theory; our subjectivity is the alien element in a universe of matter, giving rise to the so-called hard problem of consciousness (Solms, 2019).

If objectivity is seen as detaching oneself from one's subjectivity, the idea follows that all religions are parochial, stuck in the attachment that blocks any objectivity. For this reason, theology is not a proper subject of higher education, and, furthermore, religious bodies and their self-understandings have no place in the common discourse of the res publica. Gauchet's idea is that this common discourse has its origins in religions. But because religions continue to *express* themselves in the language of (uncritical) heteronomy, in those unquestioned hierarchical frames of thinking, they are confined to the past and, as long as they are still operative in contemporary culture, to the private sphere.

However, any account of the genesis of our democracy and our humanism, such as that of Gauchet, cannot counter what is presupposed to any science, namely human agency. The agency now operative in democratic social arrangements continues to challenge religions to be more consequential in their own humanising processes. The upshot of this is that the democratic government - or citizens insofar as they are committed to the set of values associated with democracy - implicitly critiques the fundamentalist view of religious faith (which side-lines our normal powers of rationality) and, on the other hand, the reductionist view. A reductionist account of religion sees modernity as essentially conflicting with religious traditions, while a fundamentalist account sees no norm of rationality and responsibility in our common human life, i.e. one that would operate equally in religions as in democracy itself.

Gauchet's explanation of the genesis of secularism focuses on three factors (I am summarising my discussion in Giddy, 2019). First, the rise of the state. With power now residing in the earthly despot rather than in the heavens, people can now see it as potentially within their grasp; hierarchies (the original word itself carries the meaning of 'sacred') are, henceforth, doomed. Second, the idea of the god's complete transcendence of the world. The incommensurability of the god with any intramundane forces allows us to see human freedom, and responsibility, not as alongside, or under, a higher power, but as established in their own right. Third, there is a changed attitude to nature. In the pre-modern culture, Nature was seen as defining our 'place' in the universe, and whose norms we defy at our peril, as testified to in the countless narratives documented in Sagar's *Literature and the Crime Against Nature* (2005). Now, in contrast, nature is seen not as normative but simply as material to be creatively transformed and humanised; the basis for a commercial exploitation of the material world.

Gauchet's historical interpretation is powerful. The second factor, pointing to the incommensurability of god and universe, is argued for in contemporary scholarship by Mascall (1943) and McCabe (2005b). The third factor has its remote origins in Max Weber's thesis linking the capitalist ethic with the rise of Protestantism (Weber, 1905 and 1992). There is, however, an obvious flaw in the first of these explanatory factors, insofar as the original despot's seizure of power is itself left unexplained; we ourselves can realise our opportunity for free agency by seeing the despot's seizure of power, but how did the first despot come to this realisation? This problem is linked to the more general one of not accounting for the powers of human agency - of coming to the truth and acting more or less responsibly - presupposed to Gauchet's own empirical study. Gauchet's own oversight has to do with a Sartre-type truncated understanding of human agency based on a dualism of 'in-itself' (nature) and 'for-itself' (freedom) that disallows the normal transcendence associated with human agency. And this oversight is exactly what I have in mind in the project of humanising higher education. It manifests itself most clearly in the dominant approach to philosophy in the English-speaking world.

Revision of the philosophical agenda

I have been suggesting that what is needed in order to humanise higher education is a foundational focus on self-knowledge, on the appropriation of our subjectivity and agency. In contrast, the dominant approach in the English-speaking philosophical world starts with the epistemological problem addressed from the point of view of scepticism (often phrased as 'Is it all a dream?') and moves through to the 'intractable' problem of free will (Salazar, 2019; Pinchin, 2005). In all this there is, as I will argue, an oversight of self-knowledge, a point already made in the discussion in Chapter 4 of a metaphysics that has learned from African traditional ways of thought. The foundation is missing for the dialogue with traditional-religious worldviews that we are seeking.

A very brief sketch of the historical background is needed to understand the emergence of the Cartesian set of philosophical problems with which I am taking issue. The key factor here is the shift in the post-Copernican period from what one might term a common-sense culture to one in which meaning is 'controlled' not by sheer volumes of additive experience (the sage) but by theory and science. As an example of this shift, we can take the classic case of Newton's dissent from the common-sense idea that bodies have a natural tendency to fall down. Newton disagreed: all change - whether from a stationary position to movement or from uniform motion in a straight line to something else - must be explained by the intervention of outside forces. The key idea is that of inertia. Treat all physical reality, he suggests, as nothing like our experience of intentionally aiming at something (the stone 'wants' to reach stability) but as inert. The upshot of this new approach is the contemporary conventional wisdom that sees the universe in terms of a dualism of the purposive, end-directed, reality of free personal subjects choosing for themselves and the non-purposive causally determined reality of objects that is the proper domain of science.

Such major cultural shifts can lead to widespread scepticism about truth and value objectivity. Common sense is discredited in favour of the real, scientific facts of the case. But even science is seen as socially constructed (Boghassian, 2006), and by this is meant, not objectively true, but relative to some person's viewpoint.

Newton proposed to explain the shift from a common-sense paradigm of knowledge in terms of the distinction between relative and absolute motion (see Prosch, 1966). If one imagines a spinning bucket filled with water, with one observer standing on the edge of the bucket and the other away from the bucket, two different observations will be recorded. As the bucket begins to spin, the water will, at first, remain still - but for the first observer on the turning edge of the bucket, it will appear to be moving; as the water catches up with the bucket, the first observer will see it, now, as stationary. Naturally, the observer outside the bucket now sees the water as moving. But whose perspective is the correct one?

Newton could invoke some absolute time and space to explain the difference in perspective, but this is unnecessary. For, there is further evidence to resolve the dispute; namely, the fact that, after a while the water on the surface of the bucket takes on a concave shape. The water has begun to climb the wall of the bucket as the force of the walls, through friction, drags the water into motion. This further evidence can lead both observers to the conclusion that the water is really now moving, even though this contradicts the common-sense evidence in front of the eyes of observer number one. Common-sense relates things to us, from our perspective, while theory relates things to one another. In a sense, the latter can be termed, in the title of Nagel's book, *The View from Nowhere* (Nagel, 1989). But it is not really a view at all. Relativism can be refuted without recourse to some absolute time-space viewpoint. Objectivity is reached by asking further questions until the evidence is accounted for and a reasonable judgement can be attained. That means that we can, through our reason, to some extent transcend our perspective on things.

It is this notion of transcendence that challenges the dominant picture of our subjective reality, as ineluctably determined by and reflecting outside forces, thus restricted to one or other perspective. The influence of Newtonian science on philosophy was to see human agency simply as another item in the closed network of causal forces.

If we turn to contemporary philosophy, help seems to be at hand in the existentialist approach. This philosophical movement highlights the need to speak about agency and subjectivity as much more than an item in a system of causes and effects. Philosophy, existentialist thinkers point out, needs to say something about what it means to be a self-conscious subject faced with the need to make something of oneself (see Romano, 2019). No objective account of the person can replace the existential awareness of one's open choice to determine one's life. Consciousness, we can say, is not something alongside my body, but simply my being more or less present to myself, the awareness that accompanies my feelings and my ideas. I am never simply 'angry', because being aware of this feeling I can - with effort! - take up an attitude to it. Self-knowledge is acquired by heightening my presence to myself.

Having this kind of consciousness or awareness of ourselves, implies an ineluctable tendency to ask questions. This posing of questions, an openness to my reality, is emphasised by existentialists. And this implies that there is a transcendent normative framework that makes me me. When I judge some understanding as probably true, it is I myself taking hold of myself; similarly, a considered action marks me as the one who chooses that kind of action, as responsible. The conditions for rising up to this set of standards that mark what we are, furnish the foundations for an ethic.

A revision of the introductory standard questions in philosophy is called for. These standardised questions miss the vital element in any critical philosophical framework, an element that could open the ethical potential in modernity and in the project of higher education. Nagel's (1987) classic introductory philosophy textbook, referred to earlier in a number of contexts, poses the following topics: how do we know anything; other minds; free will; right and wrong; justice; death; the meaning of life. This approach is framed by scepticism about knowing how things really are, getting from 'inside' my mind to the outside world. As a consequence, no growth in intellectual virtues is envisaged. Similarly, an objective account of human behaviour invokes the idea that every event has a cause, so eliminating the notion of free will, and with it, the chance for an ethic that envisages growth in moral virtues.

Nagel (1979b) posits the dichotomy of the subjective view and 'the view from nowhere' (that is to say, the objective one). But the latter is not, as we saw, properly a view at all, not simply taking a good look at things. This was illustrated in the suspended bucket example. Looking only supplies evidence; objectivity is reached through interpreting the evidence presented to me as a subject and then judging my own interpretation of that evidence. It is not at all the case that in order to include the 'subjective' or phenomenological dimension in our account of human reality, one "invents a new element of objective reality," the ego, mind, or self, as Nagel (1979b:211) puts it. There is no need for invention because, in appropriating the dynamism of human questioning (grounding science), one affirms one's capacity to know how things are and to affirm value, in other words, one's agency.

The reorientation in the presentation of basic philosophical questions would focus on the development of the person as subject (see Bracken, 2009). And scientific theory, in this new approach, is understood not as pronouncing on what we are in contrast to our common-sense experience. Science is, rather, one way in which the compact consciousness of primal society, undifferentiated between natural and personal causes (rainstorms being given anthropomorphic explanations suited to human events such as wars), becomes differentiated in our subjective consciousness. Theory becomes a tool in the world of the person, who is the source of theory as a human project. Instead of asking, What is *Homo sapiens*? (as we might ask about the substance of some object, say, gold) we inquire, as Descartes (1641 and 1968) famously did, into how it is be a conscious subject, in particular what it is to ask questions about oneself.

Somewhat tangential to our argument, I can refer here to the critical remark of a reviewer of an earlier version of this chapter, namely that the APA stylistic convention discouraged the use of personal pronouns such as 'I', 'we' and 'our' in academic writing. Humanising higher education, on the other hand, would call for the rejection of this depersonalisation of scholarship (and, in all probability, depersonalising the classroom situation). When it comes to humanising basic philosophical questions Lonergan's remark is worth quoting:

> Who is a man? Who is to be a man? The answer is 'I', 'We'. That use of the first person supposes consciousness. What has to be a man is not just any instance of rational animal. It is one that is awake. Moreover, insofar as he is concerned with being a man, he is aware of potential triumph or potential failure, and aware of his own freedom and responsibility (Lonergan, 1993:81).

If we begin from the self-conscious subject, as he does, we have the possibility of a philosophy that is truly humanising; art, religion, and language can be seen distinctly human phenomena (as is democracy), the way the self-expressive subject objectifies itself. What is humanising is the bringing to greater awareness of the active role of the creator of these human phenomena. A good example of this is the way the authors of fictional narratives have become, more recently, less hidden from the reader, as Wood (2008) explains. But the conditions for such humanising can be neglected in a culture, to its detriment.

Traditional-religious expressions of wisdom

Simply to introduce traditional-religious expressions of wisdom without the framing guidance of the questioning subject would be to court a mocking scepticism. 'Why is there death?' the sage is asked in Kenyan philosopher Odera Oruka's research project into traditional religious wisdom (see Presbey, 2002). 'To make space for the young,' comes the sage answer. But what about desert areas, where there is no shortage of space? The question is an irritation to the sage!

Traditional wisdom can also be expressed in proverbs. The isiZulu proverb, *umuntu ngumuntu ngabantu*, a person comes to be themselves through other persons, has been a cornerstone of our discussion so far. We have taken it as expressive of a traditional African worldview. But other proverbs could be invoked. 'When elephants fight, the grass gets crushed underfoot.' This well-known proverb invokes the idea that social harmony is achieved through the Big Man except when there is more than one; and it is an idea that seems to envisage patronage or even corruption at odds with the primordial solidarity and the ethical norm (that of *Ubuntu*, humanness) invoked in the former proverb. The presentation of any traditional religious worldview is not straightforward.

In Chapter 5, it was argued that the appropriation of the traditional wisdom need not find this lack of precision as a problem. At the same time, there must needs be a dialogue of traditional and modern. The way into a philosophy that is not alienating and allows for dialogue between modern scientific and traditional religious worldviews, is, I am arguing, through the questioning subject. All pre-scientific cultures raised questions about the meaning of life, about death, about life and morality. The questions are articulated through myth. Examples abound, and there are many well-known ones from the Bible and the Qur'an. However, I want to take, first, an Ancient Near-Eastern myth, the Mesopotamian story of Gilgamesh, and second, two African traditional myths. All three are concerned with death and the human anxiety of approaching death. In the first story (Pritchard, 1958:74, slightly modified), the hero Gilgamesh has been on a quest for the source of eternal life, a tree, and is returning with a branch of the tree.

This plant is a plant apart
Whereby a man may regain his life's breath.
I will take it to ramparted Uruk,
I myself shall eat it
And thus return to the state of my youth.

After twenty miles they prepared for the night.
Gilgamesh saw a well whose water was cool.
He went down into it to bathe in the water.
A serpent sniffed the fragrance of the plant;
It came up from the water and carried off the plant.

Gilgamesh sits down and weeps
His tears running down over his face.

So, some external evil force is responsible, in a kind of accidental way, for our present state of alienation from the fulfilment of our deepest desires. (Similarities are apparent with the more well-known biblical myth (Genesis 2-3) of the first man, Adam, tasked with a mission regarding 'the tree in the middle of the garden').

Two different African myths about death tell how humans appeal to the god on the matter of death, with animals as the intermediaries (from Beier, 1966:56-59). The first has the toad as evil manipulator of the message to the god: humans, he tells the god, have no wish to return to life after death. But the second story thinks that death has something to do with human failings:

When death first entered the world, men sent the chameleon to find out the cause. God told the chameleon to let men know that if they threw baked porridge over a corpse, it would come back to life. But the chameleon was slow in returning and Death was rampant in their midst, and so men sent a second messenger, the lizard.

The lizard reached the abode of God soon after the chameleon. God, angered by the second message told the lizard that men should dig a hole in the ground and bury the dead in it. On the way back, the lizard overtook the chameleon and delivered his message first, and when the chameleon arrived the dead were already buried.

That is why, owing to the impatience of man, he cannot be born again.

The take-away message from these myths has to do with the need to unpack what is implied in speaking of human responsibility. This will supply us with the key for rearticulating traditional-religious knowledge in a way that allows it some manoeuvrability in the contemporary secular context.

How to position traditional-religious knowledge in a more humanised higher education

The difficulty of positioning traditional-religious knowledge in higher education arises from the policy in secular democratic societies of relegating religions to the margins of the open, public discourse. Gauchet, as discussed above, argues that the appropriation of human powers of understanding and responsible choice, has to do with a lengthy process of reflection on religion. This has issued in a non-super-naturalistic frame of understanding the world, and a non-hierarchical set of social arrangements. It was argued above that if this is the case, there is, implicit in the values of a humanist society, a critique of both a fundamentalist understanding of religious faith, as well as a reductionist view of religion as confined to an ignorant, pre-secular past. In its educational policy the democratic state has, I am suggesting, a responsibility regarding what goes on in religious bodies. And this idea is grounded on the way that all education involves a personal journey - of the kind that seems to be at the heart of the traditional-religious narratives.

As starting point in unpacking this personal dimension in education we can draw attention to our awareness of sense experience and, at the same time, our equally self-evident experiences of our acts of inquiry, insight, and reflection on our insights and conceptualisations. How we react to this awareness of these processes throws up a dialectic to do with the opposing principles on the questions of what is knowing, what is reality, and what is objectivity (Lonergan, 1992). All three questions are bound to arise, because of the duality of human knowing, which is a given.

Lonergan's own description of this duality will clarify the terms of the dialectic. He takes the instance of a kitten and notes the role of the kitten's consciousness as a technique for attaining biological ends. What does he mean by this?

> The kitten's consciousness is directed outwards towards possible opportunities to satisfy appetites. This extroversion is spatial: as it is by the spatial manoeuvres of moving its head and limbs that the kitten deals with means to its end, so the means also must be spatial, for otherwise spatial manoeuvres would be inept and useless. The extroversion is also temporal.... Finally, the extroversion is concerned with the 'real' (1992:276).

A realistic painting of a saucer of milk might attract the kitten's attention but it cannot lead to the cat lapping; in other words, to the successful achievement of its biological needs. The painting is not 'real'.

This is the world of immediacy that is the whole of the newly born infant's world. With the acquisition of language, however, we also live in a world mediated by meaning (Langer, 1996). We can live by being oriented not simply by the pressing demands of our biological needs for their satisfaction but also by our responses to values. We can think, because we can, unlike the pre-linguistic toddler, grasp things 'in the mind' without grasping them with the fingers or the mouth. By invoking their names, we can simply hold them in mind without them being present. We can also question whether or not what we have experienced is in point of fact what we have supposed it to be. Our intention here is not circumscribed by the needs of the biological organism: will it or will it not meet those needs? Rather, it is open-ended, and aims at what is true.

Philosophy, for Lonergan (1992), is tasked with showing how this constitutes a source of confusion and how one would break the duality of one's knowing. For both kinds of knowing have their point; elementary knowing is not mere appearance while the other reaches reality. Elementary knowing proves its point by survival, while any attempt to dispute the validity of intellectual knowing involves the use of that knowing. It must go beyond the realm of experience to the realm of asking questions about our experience, whether or not we do know in this non-biological sense, and it involves further reflective questioning about our answers in order to press towards some judgement.

Lonergan explains that the dialectic issues in a moment of 'conversion', which he describes as

a radical clarification of an exceedingly stubborn and misleading myth concerning reality, objectivity, and human knowledge. The myth is that knowing is like looking, that objectivity is seeing what is there to be seen and not seeing what is not there, and that the real is what is out there now to be looked at (1972:238).

But, this myth overlooks the difference between the world of immediacy (the world of the senses, experienced by the infant) and the reality of everything we experience through the meaning we find in the world. The world of the infant is but a tiny fragment of the world mediated by meaning. So we cannot just 'look' at reality; we need to learn how to be a critical adult, thinking about the evidence, judging our understanding. Knowing is not just seeing. Nor is objectivity reached through seeing alone (but through seeing, understanding and judging). And the real is not just what we can touch and see: it is what we aim at getting to know through being attentive, being intelligent, and being reasonable in our judgements (see McCarthy, 1990). The dialectic, in other words, calls for a personal response.

It is in this sense that existentialists pointed out that modern philosophy had forgotten the subject. Kierkegaard begins to formulate the categories of interiority, the 'subjective' way to the truth (see Romano, 2019). It involves a personal journey, he emphasises. And this should have important implications for how academic inquiry is understood at universities. How could there be this journey unless it was specifically catered for?

Given the effort required to understand human self-transcendence, nothing less than a systematic treatment of the issues raised above is needed in the academy. In the absence of this, simplistic answers are likely to be propagated, uncritical picture-thinking in religions, and in the human sciences a dismissal with sarcasm of the claim of traditional-religious knowledge to make a positive contribution to our common public life.

In summary, I have argued that the academic standards of higher education when properly understood, reveal that it is personal knowledge that is at the heart of academic inquiry. I have presented Lonergan's idea that the basic appropriation of one's subjectivity (and intellectual powers) entails an awareness of an existential dialectic. The dialectic calls for a personal development, one that can only be framed in the humanities, and guided by the kind of philosophical approach canvassed above.

Traditional-religious knowledge, suitably framed, is one way into this kind of understanding. However, contemporary culture, to a large extent, works with a model of knowledge which disinherits these intellectual traditions. And this leaves institutions of higher education impotent to challenge social structures which fail to enhance human flourishing. Central to humanising higher education is the integration into the curriculum of the kind of knowledge we have been concerned with in this chapter, the heritage of a society with both secular and pre-secular cultural elements. I have unpacked the provenance of a global tendency towards a de-humanised kind of higher education by means of key turns in European intellectual history, and illustrated the possibility of a proper dialogue with ordinary pre-modern kinds of self-understanding. In this way, I hope to have contributed to a way of framing further work, with other examples, on humanising educational systems.

Chapter Fourteen

Teaching Philosophy and Religion: Can African Traditional Culture Offer Something of Value?

What characterises the dominant global culture is a kind of autism, the loss of a well-articulated sense of self, a reluctance to spell out its core values and aims. A good education system, on the contrary, helps the learner precisely to articulate their *sense of self* in ever more adequate ways, and so become more self-aware and self-directing. In the context of African traditional culture, this will mean engaging with the pre-philosophical expressions of self-understanding, which will have to be thought through in the context of modernity. The differentiation of consciousness that is at the heart of our ability to do this, however, is only articulated within a philosophical framework that has not lost the foundational idea of the presence to self of the questioning subject. In what follows, I develop this contention (i) for general philosophy, (ii) for ethics, (iii) for the philosophy of religion, (iv) for theology, and (v) for how philosophy is presented in an African cultural context. In this paper, I attempt to show the underlying unity of these topics and in this way, make my point more effective.

Introduction

I think that African traditional culture has something of value to offer global society, in particular in its dominant form. This is nothing new, but I want to summarise a project of promoting this 'something of value' in the way philosophy, and religion, are taught in Africa. The 'something' I am talking about is the idea and value of being a human person, and becoming more of a person, through the community of others. An extended discussion of this idea was given in Chapter 2, and I am not here going to revisit this specific understanding of African traditional thought. Rather, my aim is to work out its implications for how a culture where this is so, can contribute to teaching philosophy and religion. Because what characterises the *dominant* global culture, on the other hand, is a kind of autism, the loss of a well-articulated sense of self, a reluctance to spell out its core values and aims. A good education system, on the contrary, helps the learner precisely to articulate their sense of self in ever more adequate ways and in this way become more self-aware and self-directing. So far as South Africa is concerned, the project seeks to make a contribution to the transformation of higher education, as envisaged in Chapter 6, 'The Knowledge Experience,' of the 2008 Ministerial Report on transformation in higher education, which explicitly mentions Thad Metz's '*Ubuntu*' research project at the University of the Witwatersrand (Wits), which addresses the dimension of "epistemological transformation," to do with "a priori assumptions and a worldview" (Report, 2008:91).

It is with this in mind that I have been researching the framework in which philosophy is approached in the dominant model in the English-speaking academia. My target in this inquiry is wide-ranging: general introductory philosophy, ethics, the philosophy of religion, and the African context. My aim in this paper is to show the underlying unity linking these topics, and in this way, to strengthen my overall case. I begin by identifying (very roughly, of course) in each case a dominant approach in the field and offer a critique of this approach, based on the need for growth in self-knowledge in the student. In the discussion of the African context, I point to the unhelpful trend of allowing this a space *alongside* the given set of topics in the field, whereas the student needs precisely to be guided to unify these. The unifying thread behind these pieces of research - each topic by the nature of things only sketched in this unifying paper - might not, however, be immediately evident and I want in this paper to bring this to the fore.

An example: Religion in a secular age

As a first example, I can refer to teaching religion in the context of a secular culture and to the need for a normative self-understanding of our human nature. In this case, and for the case of teaching philosophy to students with some contact with a traditional African cultural background, my goal is to obviate leaving the student with a bifurcated mind. That would be the case if the religious section in the former case or the traditional section of beliefs in the latter case, were, at the end of the course of study, left untouched by any critical questions. There would likely be a similar uncritical belief (not held with any *really informed* conviction) in 'scientism' (the notion that only the products of the sciences produce truths, strictly speaking) in the one case and 'Western individualism' in the other. In dealing with the philosophy of religion, that is to say, what must be emphasised is the need to speak of religion in terms that are intelligible in our own secular and scientific culture (Taylor, 2007; Akyol, 2011; Johnston, 2009).

In general, my approach is based on the idea that the dominant global culture is in some sense 'autistic', Marilynn Robinson's (2010) way of putting it, lacking in a sense of self, or reluctant to articulate the substance of its ideas about persons and values. This is also a key or framing idea in Shutte (1993, esp. Chapter 4). In each area discussed below, this intuition of Robinson will be verified.

Let us take, typically, someone who takes their religious tradition seriously. They are trying to grapple with how to understand the idea of a god who is both eternal, timeless, and also 'in touch' with our own time-constrained lives, of relevance for ourselves. The researcher in question, who shall remain nameless, believes in scripture (but one could equally think of other persuasions, the edicts of the Pope, for example). God, the researcher notes, seems to be acting in the world. She adds that:

> God's creation of the heavens and the earth, his response to Abraham's plea for his nephew Lot, and the dividing of the waters so Israel could escape the Egyptian army are three Old Testament examples among many.

A second example could be found in someone who takes African traditional wisdom seriously. A few years ago, I visited a special section at the Botanical Gardens in Durban on indigenous plants and the uses they are put to in traditional societies. Various ailments can be cured, it is explained, by certain plants. And of one plant one reads that it is (not was) applied when the person wishes to thwart their opponent in court.

In both cases, the appreciation of the religious-traditional approach has not been integrated with the framework of a secular and scientific culture. The need for such integration is nothing new, however it has become more pronounced. In general, that is the task of the university that is embedded in a plural culture. For dialogue within the university framework has objective (though not static) standards of scholarship, of argumentation, its inheritance from its origins. I am referring to the distinction between common-sense ways of talking and arguing, and theoretical, that was at the origin of the development of philosophy as a discipline amongst the Ancient Greek thinkers. For the latter, problems arose because common-sense notions of justice and so on could not stand up to the kind of scrutiny that Socrates was putting to them: theories of justice were needed to sort out the manifest contradictions Socrates was happy to point out (Plato, *The Republic*, Book 1). Such a distinction has become commonplace. 'The sun rose this morning' is true. 'The earth's rotation placed us again into contact with the rays of the sun' is also true. It makes no sense to ask now: how is the true statement about the dawn compatible with the possibly true or purported statement about the earth's rotation! For, the latter assumes that we are adopting a different framework, not a common-sense one but a theoretical one. It assumes a distinction between two kinds of discourse. But, in both our examples, the writer purports to be asking philosophical questions (or theoretical questions) but without taking note of the distinction inherent in such questions between different kinds of writing and of truth. We can refer to the pre-philosophical approach as that of 'compact consciousness', in other words, undifferentiated (Lonergan, 1972: 302-305). The radical dependence of the universe on a non-finite power can be defended (as Aristotle did) through philosophical reasoning; not so the event of the dividing of the waters so Israel could escape Egypt. The efficacy of a plant in healing makes perfect sense; not so its efficacy in helping to get a favourable judgement in court. Both the latter can however *be made sense of* by means of the appropriate framing and contribute to our understanding of ourselves and the universe. One can make sense of the 'rising of the sun' and the 'six-day creation story'. In line with this, biblical scholars distinguish different kinds of writing and hence, truth in the narrative, myth, legend, history, poetry, parable, and so on.

My contention here is this. In Chapter 5, I introduced Lonergan's notion of the differentiation of consciousness that is at the heart of our ability to think through these traditions in the context of modernity. This notion will, however, only be properly articulated in a philosophical framework that has not lost the foundational idea of the presence to self of the questioning subject. In African traditional thought, this idea comes to the fore in how persons are seen by virtue of their nature as capable of growing in self-understanding and spiritual power. Each person is related to the transcendent with which they share a spiritual nature and growth comes about through what they receive from God, the ancestors, and fellow human beings, parents and grandparents and others who influence their lives to the good.

In what follows, I develop this contention (i) for general philosophy, (ii) for ethics, (iii) for the philosophy of religion, and (iv) for how philosophy is presented in an African cultural context.

Teaching philosophy in general

In general philosophy, my approach is to meet in open ground, the dominant trend in philosophy in the English-speaking world. For each central framing question put forward in the textbooks, one can counter on its own terms. But my strength comes from a flanking movement against this well-disciplined but ultimately myopic force in the academia. The myopia is linked to what can be termed its autism, and its result in overlooking the contribution of a long tradition in the understanding of human persons; in particular, the notion of self-transcendence (other terms may be used). An alliance can be made in this approach with existential phenomenology and its critical thematisation of subjectivity in a way that consciously seeks to avoid a dualism of subject and object, mind and thing (Luijpen, 2000; Charles Taylor, regarding

Merleau-Ponty and Heidegger, and Haldane, 2012:683, turning to Wilhelm Dilthey). With this in mind, David Walsh attempts a thorough reformulation of the modern philosophical tradition from Kant through Heidegger, Levinas and Derrida, speaking of "the shift of perspective that has been under way in modern philosophy against the subject-object model whose dominance has been so great that the countermovement has scarcely been noticed" (Walsh, 2008:4). So the critique I am putting forward, although very much a minority position, is not at all simply my own! Amongst phenomenologists the position of Jean-Paul Sartre (1969, Part Three) is somewhat of an exception, seeing no chance of transcendence of the kind we have suggested; for him, one's identity is necessarily constricted by one's relation to the other. But, *pace* Sartre, we *can* grow through bodiliness and our intersubjective relations (for example, Macmurray, 1999b; Ver Eecke, 1975; Shutte, 1993, Chapter 7). Philosophy, fortified by this key idea about our human capacity, can be a kind of aid to a critical self-appropriation, as Lonergan puts it (1970, Preface). There is no doubt that the need for this is widespread in our culture, as the growth of self-help sections in bookshops, squeezing out philosophy in a more technical sense, testifies to, as well as the rise of 'coaching' as a lucrative profession. Yet, there can be a more systematic and critical way of doing this, that links to the human sciences, and to the dialogue or Socratic mode of discussion that is a bulwark against this area falling into simply 'preaching'.

The origins of modernity can be partly traced back to the picture of the universe that has entrenched itself in our imaginations with the dominance of science. Newton's mechanistic model is no longer the paradigm in science. We still think (in a way!) of a world in which our intentions, our aims, our (subjective) grasp of things determines outcomes. But this is taken, by science-influenced thinkers, as unjustified, as folk-psychology (as it is put in the popular introductory textbook, Smith and Jones, 1986). We do things, in our own minds, for reasons. But the reality (science is supposed to be telling us) is otherwise: "science, and especially physics," claims cognitive scientist David Spurrett (2008:159), has shown us "that the actual universe is alien to our default conception of the world."

More accurate, it is argued, is to hold to a non-purposive 'blind' causally determined world of objects interacting in some way determinable by an algorithm.

The key confusion here is over the notion of objectivity. Here, it is as well to precis the discussion in Chapter 4 on the idea of an African philosophy of mind. Let us put aside any dubious unproven and perhaps culturally biased picture of 'man' (we can think of Plato and Aristotle, at the origin of the argument for some human capacity for transcendence). Rather, consider the assumptions about objectivity that are tied into the picture drawn above associated with modern science. Objectivity is reached, it is thought, when subjective elements are put aside. That's the empiricist Hume, in a nutshell: our beliefs, he thinks, arise in us "through causes and effects by a secret operation, and without being once thought of"! (*Treatise*, Book 1, Part 3, Section 8). He can hold to this prima facie strange idea (that our ideas arrive in our minds as unconsciously as the billiard ball is conscious of arriving in the pocket), because of a picture of reality as 'out there': remember, our inner world is or seems to be an anomaly, in a world uncovered by science. If this is the case, then knowing is simply a form of *reacting* to this reality - as it no doubt sometimes is, as I react spontaneously to swerve to avoid the pedestrian. But this overlooks another kind of knowing, the typically human one of *actively* asking questions and evaluating alternative answers one holds in mind as possibly plausible. Is there a self, one might ask, capable of agency, as Hume, and after him, Daniel Dennett (2004:199) have doubted? Consider the evidence, put forward an explanation of the evidence, reflect on your ideas and come to some judgement: aiming at and reaching perhaps some objectivity. Isn't this what we understand by knowing? (Lonergan, 1970: Chapter 10) And it is precisely *not* putting aside subjective elements but using these to the full that is necessary if one is to reach objectivity, as much objectivity as is possible in this particular question. The capacity for agency, one might conclude, is real. But this capacity is not at all an object 'out there', not an object of any science. In the African philosophical tradition we are considering here, on the other hand, agency is specifically normative: in thinking it through the ethical dimension is always prior. In other words, being placed in relation to others one (ideally) adopts a critical sense of one's own subjectivity, attitudes, and choices.

We can now spell out the shift in how the basic philosophical questions should be framed. It is convenient to follow the set of questions, or issues, put forward in Nagel's (1979) classic of introductory philosophy (other texts could be used, e.g. Pinchin, 2005) in the English-speaking world. The first question concerns the problem of knowledge, framed as, Can we get from 'in here'- our mind - to 'out there'? This is only a coherent question if one assumes the aim of knowledge is to get to what is 'out there'. If by 'out there' is meant simply what is the truth of the matter (rather than simply imagined) then the problem dissolves into the development of reasonable judgements. But if by 'out there' is meant what does not involve the subject, then it is a misleading concept of the real. In the process of trying to reach knowledge, the aim is to a reasonable judgement of the accuracy or otherwise of one's ideas in the light of the data furnishing evidence. The aim is the appropriation of one's capacity for a heightened self-presence and cognitional self-transcendence. In other words, the framing question has to do with the fulfilment of one's humanity - in our African suggestion this is captured in the term *Ubuntu*. How is this possible, how is it linked to the human sciences, and how has our understanding of it changed since the rise of modern science? These are, contrary to Nagel, the more interesting questions.

Do other minds exist? asks Nagel. This is an offshoot of the above problem: if we assume, with Descartes, some special exceptional inner knowledge of one's own self - what about other selves (i.e. as opposed to their obviously real *bodies*)? But if the capacity for self-consciousness develops only through others, the reality of the self is not at all an 'out there' reality of an object (let us call that 'material reality'). It is affirmed at one and the same time as real and precisely as a norm (I can achieve it more and more), unlike the case when one affirms any material object as real, which is in itself value-neutral. So the self is affirmed not as alongside other 'objects', as atoms and molecules and any kind of body is, but shareable, as we discover in intersubjective causality, the sharing of ideas and the personal influence of one person by another. (See the classic two-volume analysis of this by John Macmurray 1999a and 1999b; the African traditional notion of the person and of intersubjectivity dovetails with analyses such as this one).

Is there an intractable problem of free will? If every event has a cause, then, so too, must so-called free choices. And if an action is caused, it is determined. What is 'intractable' here is that our whole social setup, in particular our legal system, seems to assume the capacity for free choice and responsibility, i.e. precisely *not* being determined. But, again, this 'problem' all depends on the framing of the question, and the slogan conceals an ambiguity between *an event having a cause* and *an action having a reason*, which is a common enough distinction. In other words, as is the case with the other central (confused) questions of introductory philosophy, we can question how this issue is framed. In each case we can uncover a norm; a norm of being human, lost in the paradigm of the dominant modern approach to philosophy. (Particularly well analysed in the now unfortunately neglected school of Dutch and Flemish phenomenology: see Strasser, 1965; Kwant, 1969; Van Peursen, 1956; Bakker, 1964). Yes, there is a problem of moving from essential human freedom to actual human freedom, which could be framed as a problem of free will, though not an 'intractable' one. 'Free will', otherwise understood, could, on the other hand, seem to suggest a magical power of choice operating apart from the conditioning factors uncovered by the human sciences, by psychology and sociology and ethology – but this would miss out on the crucially important inquiry into how our *capacity* for free self-disposition translates into a real, effective, *ability*. In the discussion (Chapter 4) on the Philosophy of Mind in the Context of African Tradition, reference was made to Wittgenstein's remark in the *Tractatus* (2001) that there is nothing of *philosophical* interest in this question, an analysis of the will which could furnish a norm for human action. But that simply indicates, again, an autism of the kind we have been highlighting, and to which we can again point, as a valuable counterbalancing approach, to the African philosophical notion of the person being present to themselves through being present to others.

Teaching ethics

The shape of an ethics influenced by African culture and tradition has been drawn in Chapter 3. My purpose here is to draw out the implications for teaching ethics. The suggestion I am making is to draw on the pre-modern philosophical tradition in order to reintroduce the understanding of the human person as able in some way to creatively react to the determining influences of biological, psychological and sociological factors, to transcend. The dominant categories in terms of which we debate the human person in modern philosophy are inadequate to this task, as we have argued. This is not to say we can't pick out dualist, essentialist and gender-biased aspects of, say, Aristotle's understanding of human nature (as also in the African traditional concept). Aristotle's approach, again, was unhistorical, whereas we see persons as cultural products. The point, however, is to note the failure of modern philosophy adequately to deal with the resultant problem of ethical relativism, where ethics is seen as an epiphenomenon of culture. And where no answer can be given to the critical question, Why be moral? (if I can get away with not being moral), because remaining unthematised is the orientation by virtue of our human nature towards ever fuller participation in a universe of real values. And here again we can detect a resonance with the African cultural idea of real personal growth through fuller embeddedness in the human, and transcendent, community.

Again, I can finger the lack of a sense of real self-knowledge at the root of the inadequacies of modern ethics. More precisely, I can refer to the separation of reason from emotions, facts from values, the 'is' from the 'ought', intellect from the will. We have already seen this problem arise in discussing 'free will': Kant's ethics 'solves' this problem by arguing we must act 'as if' we are free - but I am pointing to the crucial growth of self-knowledge, of one's natural hierarchies of desires, as the matter, the content, of any adequate ethics. In an ethics of principles only, this is left out. It is judged that no trans-cultural notion of normative human nature can found ethics (no 'ought' from an 'is'). But, this means that the problem of *motivation* is left out of the discussion (as Smith, 1994, pointed out in his book-length discussion). We can only discuss ethics with those who can agree on the basic principles. The foundation of these (say, justice, equality) is off the page. John Skorupski (2007:140-141) puts it well: "It is not that people in 'Western' liberal democracies show a lack of moral concern about urgent moral issues such as poverty, oppression, global warming. I am raising a different question. Are we living off certain ideals without really being willing to defend or revise them, or even scrutinise them?" What is missed, in a science-influenced approach to ethical inquiry, is the appropriation of one's agency and the virtues constitutive of such appropriation, which is a matter of self-understanding, of one's inner life (Cronin, 2006). And this involves taking a step of commitment, at least of involvement (Johann, 1975). As illustration of the step, we can consider Freud's scientific - 'objective'! - description of the kiss, as the meeting of the mucous membranes at the entrance to the digestive tracts, and compare this with a fuller account, with what really matters at the level of intentions, the discernment of the inner life of the agents, whether (this is crucial) her lips, are non-responsive (pursed at the mouth) or responsive (slightly open?).

Being unable to thematise our subjectivity and agency, any foundation for ethics seems somewhat arbitrary. A common move is to take as foundation a list of basic individual human rights - which is admittedly culturally founded, and linked to the values of tolerance and equality. But this ethical approach will be unable to dialogue with particular cultural and religious traditions, and - crucially - to discriminate between their - objectively! - more helpful and less helpful aspects. The upshot, well brought out by Johann (1988), would be a politics of domination rather than one of deliberation and consensus. It is of grave concern for our project of contextualising philosophy in Africa. In particular, as pointed out by Paulus Zulu (2013), this framework is inadequate to think through an ethic of transformation which does not betray our deepest values. "A rights based culture alone," he writes, "is not a sufficient condition for democratic accountability." What is needed is "recognition of a basic moral value that exists independently of power politics and so cannot be subjected to moral expediency" (Zulu, 2013:41-42).

Teaching the philosophy of religion

So far as concerns the philosophy of religion, and also theology, my suggestion is to build on our capacity for creative action. In the absence of a sense of this foundational notion, philosophical reflection on religious faith has, in the English-speaking world, turned to conceptual analysis (for example, Davies, 2004; Murray and Rea, 2008). The starting point here is our idea of the god (written as 'God', capitalised, since in this tradition the god is thought of as personal and hence *named*) as omnipotent, eternal, all-knowing, compassionate, omnipresent. At the same time, the subject matter of the inquiry is focused almost exclusively on *belief*, i.e. the intellectual attitude that is one dimension only of religious faith, involving as this does both a commitment of the will, and a crucial emotional and existential dimension too. The reason for this thin version of faith is not difficult to see: it is the corresponding thin version of objectivity that has accompanied the rise of modern science and scientific method. The only objectivity possible, on this truncated view, is achieved through excluding so far as possible subjective elements, objectivity as knowing what's 'out there' and not including any elements (such as 'the self') which cannot be verified in that way. However, in our view, which grounds all knowledge - including scientific knowledge - on *self-knowledge*, objectivity is not to be *contrasted* with subjectivity but is the fruit of authentic subjectivity, of attentiveness to the data, of habitual practice of asking intelligent questions of that data, and of a commitment to not go beyond what is reasonable in judging any suggested interpretation as plausibly true, or unlikely to be true. It is this fuller notion of subjectivity that was developed by Hegel's phenomenology and before him appealed to by Kant, and in both cases applied to *how we frame* our understanding of religion (for example, Kant, 1960). With exceptions (e.g. Pattison, 2001; also Armstrong, 2009), this approach to religion is very much in the shadows of contemporary philosophy of religion.

By modelling religious faith on the kind of knowledge (of what is 'out there') characteristic of the sciences, the object of the faith is seen as *competing* with scientific knowledge (Ward, 2006). And coming a very poor second to the latter. The evidence (in this sense of evidence) for the existence of the god is thin. There are also problems in the integrity of one's intellect; it is as if one has to suspend disbelief when it comes to supposed divine interventions in the natural, empirically verified, order of things. Furthermore, there is the problem of evil: if the god is all-powerful and compassionate, evil should not exist, and the conclusion is either that the god is not all-powerful, or that the attribute of compassion is incorrectly applied to the god (in which case one should not worship such a being).

On the other hand, if one takes as proper object of inquiry the attitude of religious faith at the existential level, at the level of taking up one's life as a whole, including one's attitude to oneself, in an inevitably personal overarching narrative, then the god is seen as sourcing this capacity (for self-transcendence) not as rivalling any intra-universe force. And as a consequence, as McCabe (2005b:6) points out, cannot be conceived of 'interfering' in the world's natural processes - the idea of 'miracles.' The object of inquiry is not at all something 'out there' but that does not imply that it is merely something 'in here', i.e. only mental or imaginative. What establishes the plausibility or otherwise of such an object of faith is the cogency of the argument, in the same way as the plausibility or otherwise of the existence of 'the self' is established. And there is a long tradition of such arguments, beginning with Aristotle's cosmological argument for a 'prime mover'. In the narrative in which one places oneself, there is likely to be place for special, decisive, moments which are especially revealing of the presence of the god, but this does not imply *intervening* divine action, rivalling the natural forces. (See Stoeger, 2008:225, explained in Giddy, 2011, and the further critical remarks of Verhoef, 2012). Furthermore, given, in our conception of religious faith, an affirmation of the integrity of the universe, there is no question of wishing away the negativities which are part of the evolving and developmental nature of the world (Swimme and Berry, 1994). There is also scope for seeing 'evil done' as an underachievement of our human potential, a privation of the good, and hence calling for an existential response of patient forgiveness, the faith in the god giving a motivation for this attitude. It is, again, the African philosophical approach which can be seen to fit in with this idea: both the notion of our 'place' by nature in the universe, and the specific moral value of including the other, can provide a more adequate framing orientation to ethical inquiry than that associated with the dominant philosophical paradigm.

The contribution of African traditional thought

It is not difficult to see the import of all this for the contribution of African traditional thought to introductory philosophy and theology. In any effective teaching, the cultural background of the learner is crucial (Ndofirepi, 2011). But we have to distinguish between content and method. All traditional-religious expressions of ideas about our reality as a whole, written up in proverbs and myths, can and should be subject to critical questioning, and the tools for this, including the key principle of non-contradiction, were developed by the Ancient Greek thinkers in response to *their* early form of modernisation. This is philosophical method, properly speaking.

However, the bias of modernity has been in the *content* of what is taken as proper subject matter. The bias has been to think of *any* expressions of an orienting understanding of the self as lacking in objectivity. The problem, to say it again, is the loss of the sense of the presence to self of the subject. If one thinks that it is only the objects investigated by the sciences that merit the attribute of being really real, this 'self-presence' must be simply made-up, not real. But, of course, science as an activity is not possible without it: we can only thereby actually *set up* standards for getting at the truth of things, by reflecting on how we do come to know things as they really are. This presence-to-self can't itself be an object of scientific inquiry. Hence, a philosophical outlook which bypasses this idea, will also neglect to subject to critical inquiry ways in which such presence-to-self grows and is developed, in interaction with others. And we can note that traditional African culture might very well fill this gap, articulating through some such idea as that of *Ubuntu* precisely how it is through our interaction with others and participation in communities that we achieve greater self-knowledge and begin to adopt a more adequate hierarchy of values.

I can point to a corollary of the autism, the lack of a sense of self-knowledge, in the contemporary global culture, namely the understanding of 'the modern' as subtracting from the whole set of objects of belief (spirits, gods, miracles, etc.) of a previous age, to get to the natural (material, bodily) residue underneath! On the contrary, I argue, along with Charles Taylor (2007:151–154), for an understanding of academic standards as *deriving* from an appropriation of human subjectivity that has its roots in what Karl Jaspers termed the 'axial age' of the major religious traditions (the prophets in the Hebrew religion, the Upanishads and Gautama Buddha in the Indian culture, for example), where outward conformity is criticised in favour of an inner authenticity of faith.

The myth of the real as what is 'out there', a myth accompanying the rise and dominance of the sciences in our global culture, is a permanent obstacle in human understanding. This is because every individual has to move from the world of immediacy of the infant, oriented by biological needs, to the world mediated by meaning. With the acquisition of language one is able to grasp things 'in the mind' without grasping them with the fingers or putting them in the mouth. By invoking their names we can hold them in mind, and we can consider whether or not what is in the mind corresponds to how things really are, we can exercise our powers of reflective judgement. Of course, the infant 'knows' that the breast is now at last here in its grasp. But there is another kind of knowing, through asking questions and suggesting answers, and the confusion between the two, reinforced by the myth of a material universe (atomic or otherwise) accompanying modern science, is cleared up through what Bernard Lonergan (1972:238ff) calls 'intellectual conversion'. (Along similar lines are the well-known critiques given by Michael Polanyi, 1962 and Nicholas Maxwell, 1987). For the infant's elementary knowing, the real is whatever I come up against 'out there'. But the 'second objectivity' that is pertinent to adult living is a quality of *being reasonable*, an actualisation of our intellectual capacities. It is moving to a new level, from sense experience to being intelligent to reflective judgement of the probable accuracy of our ideas. These transitions are growth moments. The existentialist writers, protesting against a loss of the self in modern thought, stress the personal nature of the quest for truth, the 'subjective' way. For Kierkegaard (1968:181), the highest truth is what he terms 'subjectivity'. Such intellectual growth - heightening one's critical grasp of one's set of ideas, in particular, through the systematic methods of the natural and social sciences - needs to be structured into a university curriculum. This happens not *within* any science (where the conversion is implicit only) but rather in the humanities.

Finally, one may note the vision of my own university, the University of KwaZulu-Natal, to promote itself as 'the premier university of African scholarship'. If this slogan is to have any meaning, it will have to imply the promotion of the kind of inquiry that matures and develops the student's capacity for self-appropriation; for growth in self-understanding and in responsibility. This approach is taken up in the next chapter on the idea of African scholarship. And, if what I have argued in the course of this chapter is plausible, then this will imply the promotion of the humanities at the University; a re-orientation that is against the global stream and might very well cost the University in terms of prestige, and of course, money. For example, the Development Bank of South Africa report on transformation in higher education notes that "increasingly... the trend has been to approach higher education investment from the perspective largely of the promotion of economic growth and the preparation of students for the labour market and as productive workers for the economy" (Badat, 2010:43). At the moment, it is not clear that the University understands the trade-off involved in the desire to give proper recognition to the African culture, and to students who straddle these cultures.

Chapter Fifteen

The Idea of African Scholarship

We are arguing for the facilitation of the African traditions of ethics in the wider global context. Part of this might involve what has been termed 'African scholarship', and the University of KwaZulu-Natal - my own university - has had for some years as its motto, "The Premier University of African Scholarship." It has drawn up a programme of action towards reaching this ideal, 'The UKZN Transformation Charter' (www.ukzn.ac.za). Nowhere, however, is it explained what is meant by 'African Scholarship' nor how it has a place in a university. The aspiration to "promote African scholarship in every discipline," to quote the charter, seems to betray a lack of inquiry into the ways in which the current dominant 'identity' (a word the document also uses) of universities could (or should) be enlarged, the shift of priorities I argue for in this chapter.

Once again, MacIntyre's notion of a social practice can assist in making sense of what is at issue here. Thinking of an academic discipline in terms of a social practice helps in formulating what the ideal captured in the slogan 'African scholarship' can contribute. For every practice, as has been pointed out a number of times, is threatened by the attractiveness of goods external to the practice - in particular, competitiveness for its own sake - and to counter this, virtues of character are needed. African traditional culture prioritises a normative picture of the human person which could very well contribute here to upholding the values internal to scholarship. In this chapter, I argue that this idea can be seen developed in Tempels' pioneering work on African traditional thought. Contrary to Matolino, I find Tempels' understanding of the transactional process of becoming more of what you are by virtue of the human insertion in nature, to be a useful example of African scholarship. It has links with a Thomistic philosophical framework but adds something to this in bringing out the intersubjective conditions for the augmentation of any particular 'force.' Finally, I interrogate the lack of clarity in the dominant modern philosophical framework on 'objectivity', a theme already broached in this book, which cripples its capacity to facilitate dialogue with other cultures, specifically the African. And I conclude with an example of the usefulness of this kind of scholarship in challenging the dominant understanding of justice.

Philosophy as a social practice

There is a normative tradition in any academic discipline, which we can best understand as a social practice, a "coherent and complex form of socially established cooperative human activity," a concept - referred to in several sections of this book - that is central to MacIntyre's attempt, in *After Virtue*, to recapture some objectivity in ethical discussions (1981:175). Key here is the idea that the practice has objective standards gauging the quality of the performances of the participants: these, continuing the definition above of a practice, are specified as "goods internal to that form of activity [which] are realised in the course of trying to achieve those standards of excellence which are appropriate to, and partially definitive of, that form of activity." In other words, you can't be a proper participant without understanding those 'internal goods' and appreciating them as of true value. If a child learning the internal goods of playing chess, learning to enjoy it, then cheats, "he or she will be defeating not me, but himself or herself" (1981:176). "Defeating" here means that one diminishes oneself somehow by cheating. The difference is between winning a game and winning a life. For our purposes we can think of a good academic versus a career academic, something blurred when a university becomes excessively concerned with measuring 'productivity', a tendency, we shall see, reinforced by a misunderstanding common in 'Western' philosophy of the standard of 'objectivity'. It is because there are real, objective, values at stake here in the practice, values enhancing our life together, that the way the practice is understood can be creatively developed over time: that conceptions of the internal goods can be "systematically extended" - to round off MacIntyre's definition of a practice. This means that any tradition - say, African traditional ways of arriving at knowledge - can be extended through a confrontation with alternative traditions, not simply placed alongside these. Cultural relativism can be avoided because the dominant academic tradition, to the extent that it is truly authentic, i.e. embodies real objective human values, can learn from the alternative African traditions. MacIntyre's notion of a social practice can be seen as framing our discussion of human values because it points not only to the fact of essential human freedom (the capacity to share a conceptual world associated with a practice and to act for reasons of its internal goods) but also to the development of the virtues to make that freedom effective.

This notion was developed at length in Chapter 6 and, as mentioned, already brought to bear on a number of applied topics. Within the context of a social activity, participants find meaning and reasons for achievement in ideals of character necessary to the success of the enterprise. In a murder trial I attended (Cape Town Magistrate's Court, September 2011), the magistrate asked the lawyer for the defence if, in the absence of 'financial instructions' (i.e. without being paid), he could proceed with the case. He replied, "I could not apply my legal mind, your Worship." If a good internal to the profession is one appreciated for itself and not simply or only for the sake of other goods (monetary compensation, in this case), then this lawyer seems prima facie to be lacking in true professionalism. Ethics needs this context of social practices if it is not to be mere pious words: participants find the values worthy of being upheld. Outside of this context, little remains to motivate individuals to pursue goals of justice and fairness, for example - as Appiah (2010:209) points out, in his discussion of 'honour codes'. A practice is sustained by an institutional set-up with rules for the efficient allocation of the external goods of power, status and financial reward. But, whereas the internal goods are essentially shared, the external goods are allocated to some and not others: one person gets promoted to be the new C.E.O., others do not. Thus "the ideals and the creativity of the practice [and] the cooperative care for the common goods of the practice [are] always vulnerable to the competitiveness of the institution." And without the virtues of character, as MacIntyre argues, "without justice, courage and truthfulness, practices could not resist the corrupting power of institutions" (1981:181).

A commercialised society is one in which these external goods, summed up in monetary reward, have all but superseded the goods internal to the practices. Our extended example in Chapter 9 considered the pressures on a particular social practice, that of the choral, *amakwaya*, tradition. But the global society is precisely a commercialised one. In other words, individuals enter into the global society not as members of particular ethical cultures and traditions, but as units, potentially productive of a tradeable good, in a global economy. In contrast, in the pre-modern classical society, the care of the institutional arrangements, facilitating the enjoyment of the practices by participants, was the most noble of activities, namely politics, and the normative idea of membership of a polis, the set of virtues making up the ideal of being human, ensured that the rules of the practice would be taken in the spirit in which they were intended. For Aristotle, his series of lectures on *Politics* is simply Part Two of his *Ethics*.

What I am suggesting is that a culture such as the African traditional one, can contribute here by virtue of its substantive and not procedural view of ethics; in other words, because it sees people in a normative way - we can refer here to the idea of *Ubuntu*. A pertinent example here would be the development of the tradition and set of values in the Roman Catholic tradition that found expression at the Second Vatican Council (1962-5). The reformers here battled it out and gained ascendency over those opposed to reform - they forgot, however, that the promotion of these goods internal to the social practice needed institutional arrangements. It was the 60s, and the reformers were reacting against excessive juridical approach to the institution. But as a result of this neglect, the new vision could be undermined by those factions opposed to it - in particular, the rules governing the composition of the Pope's inner circle, the Curia, had remained unchanged. The abhorrence of 'juridicism' was articulated in particular by Bishop De Smedt (Hill, 1988:112). Similarly, appropriate structures would have to be implemented so as to promote the revised vision of the philosophical tradition that is being suggested in this paper, through the contact of this tradition with African traditional culture, if 'African scholarship' is to have any purchase. For example, the Humanities, locus of the express articulation of the human virtues that are at issue here, would have to be given greater priority than at present in the university. The particular importance of the discipline of philosophy was canvassed in Chapter 12.

The project of African philosophy: A question of culture

Whatever the shortcomings of Placide Tempels' pioneering attempt to characterise the conceptual framework of African traditional thought, he succeeds in giving a first indication of how values in African culture are grounded on what human beings potentially are. And this surely needs to be taken seriously, both because this seems to be what is needed if moral judgements are to be more than relative to culture; and secondly, because it offers an alternative to the dominant Western procedural conception of values, which disallows, I am arguing, dialogue with substantive ideas about human flourishing.

For this reason, I am in disagreement with Bernard Matolino (2011), whose disparagement of Tempels' argument that "there is a certain African essence" (2011:337), seems largely a matter of throwing doubt on the project in general of uncovering and re-expressing a culture's normative idea of what it is to be human. Support for Matolino can be found in Section 1B of Mosley's 1995 collection, *African Philosophy, The Critique of Ethnophilosophy*, which has essays by Wiredu, Hountondji, Appiah, Mosley, Owomoyela and Irele. Irele, for example, argues that the whole project of finding an 'African essence' was a reaction against "the rationalizations by which Western ideologues sought to justify European domination of other races" (1995:266). Any attempt to deal with this impressive list of critics is beyond the scope of this chapter. I want simply to point to one useful summary account of the debate, that of Jean-Godefroy Bidima. Bidima agrees that one can indeed question Tempels' motives, for he did appear to formulate a way of civilising Africa, which was more acceptable to the inhabitants: *"Tempels applique là une grande ruse coloniale!"* (1995:12), a great colonial trick, Bidima's concern however is not with the motives for, but with the substance of, the argument, and Tempels, he points out, is following in his project a set of ideas associated with 'negritude', already before 1945 initiated by French-speaking native Africans such as Cesaire and Senghor. Amongst African writers who find Tempels' methodology and his hypothesis useful, Bidima mentions Diop, Senghor, Kagame, Mbiti, Mulago, Lufuluabo and others (1995:13).

Bidima goes on to discuss various philosophical frameworks and their usefulness for thinking through African cultural ideas - hermeneutics, the Frankfurt School, and so on. Ndaba (2001), mentioned by Bidima, has argued, as I am doing here, that some philosophical frameworks lend themselves to the project of African philosophy better than others - whereby 'better' is meant more fruitful for the project of engaging with traditional ways of thinking about life that are characteristic of a large number of African people. It is important to make explicit the frameworks in which the various matters of substance are discussed. The discussion in Chapter 11, of the African ecclesial response to secular public policy, is pertinent. A framework of thinking may dominate without being a subject of interrogation by those within that framework. The example I gave was of the bifurcation of political parties in Lesotho, deriving from historical circumstances to do with the split in the Christian church in Europe in the sixteenth century. We need a teaching ethic of transformation, which means making students aware of their socio-epistemic community, and through this, opening them up to insights into our shared humanity (cf Praeg, 2011:356-357).

Tempels' project has as much to do with revealing to Europeans their unarticulated framework as it has with articulating an African traditional worldview, and is to that extent indeed worthwhile, at least in principle. Tempels is judged by Matolino (2011:332) to be a 'racialist', by which he means, following Appiah, that he thinks that of members of a particular race we can say that they "share certain traits and tendencies with each other that they do not share with members of any other race." But this attitude - in Tempels' case and that of the very many other African philosophers who think that one can do 'ethno-philosophy' - might better be described as that of 'culturalism'. In his use of the term 'Bantu' - as in Biko's use of 'African' in his essay, *Some African Cultural Concepts* (1978:40-47) - what is being referred to here might equally well be termed 'culture' as 'race'. Tempels is not particularly concerned here with the 'relatively stable genetic breeding pools', Neville Alexander's classic definition of race. Tempels is a 'culturalist', but then so is anyone prepared to speak of 'Western culture', or 'African traditional culture', or 'Native American culture', and so on, simply referring to a set of ideas and values and ways of behaving that characterise that group of people. If Tempels is a racialist, so is, for example, Biko.

Ela, again, speaks of the need to affirm the particular cultural personality of the black African (1963:61). To wish away any such attempts at characterising human beings this way is to wish away the development of culture and tradition. In the face of the questioning of traditional values by the new generation, in particular the Sophists, Plato tried to justify why it is important to act justly, by means of his theory of what it means to be a human being, namely that it is to be ruled by reason. The theory attempts to describe an 'essence' of what this is. Only a nominalist - denying the reality of anything's 'nature' - would think the project futile. This is because nominalism is closely linked to what I am suggesting is a truncated view of objectivity in modern philosophy, namely one which only allows objects of the sciences the status of 'objective', a framework referred to as 'naturalism'. JP Moreland (2000:67) writes that "throughout the history of philosophy, many have advanced the idea that there is a connection between naturalism and nominalism."

It is clear that Tempels thinks that Western culture has been seeing itself as normative, in an uncritical way: vis-à-vis African culture it is thought of as "an All against a Nothing" (*Als het alles tegenover het niet*) (Tempels, 1959:169). This is what he tasks himself with correcting: "the universally accepted picture of primitive man, of the savage...living before the full blossoming of intelligence, vanishes beyond hope of recovery before this testimony" (1959:168). Matolino, to do him justice, does grant that this is Tempels' aim, the idea that "a disdainful view of the

African system is born out of a lack of understanding of who these people are and what makes them tick" (2011:336).

An existential and dynamic philosophical framework: The idea of transactional growth

We can now look at an example of African scholarship in action, and it is useful here to stay with that of Tempels, in an attempt to see how the internal goods of this particular social practice, the philosophical tradition, may be, in MacIntyre's phrase, "systematically extended." It is only if there is indeed a human capacity for self-reflection and self-repositing, an 'essence' if you like which goes beyond any particular set of cultural ideas and values, that a social practice could extend itself in this way. This makes the 'ethno-philosophy' project worthwhile, re-thinking cultural ideas in dialogue with changed circumstances. I will argue below that because of its truncated view of 'objectivity', which elides the possibility of this picture being plausible, the dominant approach of modern philosophy disqualifies itself from this kind of inquiry, in other words from doing African scholarship in the sense in which we have described it. According to Tempels, the metaphysical substratum for the Western philosophical tradition is that of 'being', while for the African traditional mind it is 'active force'.

It has to be said, in parentheses, that Tempels is referring here specifically to the dominant trend in Western philosophy. This is not to deny other trends exist. A classic analysis of how the non-dominant critique of the static concept of being in favour of a metaphysics of dynamic becoming, or act of being, was developed by Aquinas, is that of Etienne Gilson (1941, Chapter 2). Komprodis' 2006 collection, *Philosophical Romanticism*, in particular, the section titled, *The Living Force of Things*, also points to a counter-tradition in Europe.

For Tempels, force is not something 'out there' simply to be observed in a neutral way; rather it is at once a reality and a value: things find their fulfilment, their natural end, in the actualisation of what they potentially are. And since persons are part of nature - not standing over against nature, their actualisation is also a value for us. Union with how nature is, is a value. And nature tends towards the augmentation of force. Nature and persons are seen as very much more integrated than is the case for the Western thinker. There is a spirit ('living force') which runs through the whole of the cosmos, and Matolino quotes Tempels as describing this, the "divine force, celestial or terrestrial forces, human forces, animal forces, vegetable and even material or mineral forces" (cited in Matolino, 2011:338). The way of thinking of things is not what they are but how they act: force is not an accidental predicate of some or other static being, thought of in a 'neutral' way apart from how it acts, or develops itself in and through its environment. Rather, "force is the nature of being, force is being, being is force."

There is no need to elaborate on Tempels' ideas: the gist of his thinking has been canvassed in Chapter 3. Matolino's (2011) critique of the idea of 'force,' as we saw, can be answered by pointing to the model of how one person can influence another, in a way that 'frees' them. This idea has little to do with the idea of being 'magical', as Matolino would have it.

Intersubjective conditions for growth and the attitude of trust

'Force,' as understood here, is also not something held to out of fear – Matolino's second point of criticism. Tempels' metaphysical grounding of his ethics makes this clear.

> Just as Bantu ontology is opposed to the European concept of individuated things, existing in themselves, isolated from others, so Bantu psychology cannot conceive of man as an individual, as a force existing by itself and apart from its ontological relationships with other living beings and from its connection with animals or inanimate forces around it. The Bantu cannot be a lone being. It is not good enough synonym for that to say that he is a social being. No; he feels and knows himself to be a vital force, at this very time to be in intimate and personal relationship with other forces acting above him and below him in the hierarchy of forces. He knows himself to be a vital force, even now

influencing some forces and being influenced by others'
(1959:103).

The growth of force occurs through the positive influence of
others who are more 'persons' than oneself.

> The child, even the adult, remains always for the Bantu
> a man, a force, in causal dependence and ontological
> subordination to the forces which are his father and mother.
> The older force ever dominates the younger. It continues to
> exercise its living influence over it.... Nothing moves in this
> universe of forces without influencing other forces by its
> movement. The world of forces is held like a spider's web
> of which no single thread can be caused to vibrate without
> shaking the whole network (1959:60).

Tempels emphasises the normal, not mysterious or mystical,
nature of this transaction of forces, far removed from
superstition. "One force will reinforce or weaken another. This
causality is in no way supernatural in the sense of going beyond
the proper attributes of created nature. It is, on the contrary, a
metaphysical causal action which flows out of the very nature
of a created being" (1959:59). Lower forces cannot of their own
act on human persons, so there is no cause to fear occult, pre-
personal or hostile forces. Sophie Oluwole, on the other hand,
is one philosopher prepared to disagree, as already mentioned
in Chapter 5 in the discussion of the importance, in interpreting
traditional knowledge, of understanding the 'differentiation of
consciousness'. It is an open question, she argues, whether or
not witchcraft in this sense, is possible. She cites the example of
someone who could not be woken up from a coma, until the fly
was released from the bottle (1995:366).

Augustine Shutte's understanding of interpersonal causality
has been a key theme throughout this discussion of ethics in the
context of the African philosophical tradition. The influence of the
more developed person on the less developed, it was argued, is of
such a nature that freedom is enhanced rather than diminished
by such influence. The influence cannot at all operate without the
consent of the other, hence there are no grounds for confusing

this with the idea of witchcraft. This is not clarified in Tempels, perhaps only hinted at.

Blocking the African project: A bias in modern philosophy about 'objectivity'

Tempels presents African traditional thought as if it were intelligible simply as alongside 'Western' thought. But epistemic biases are to be expected in the way philosophy is often presented. I want to hypothesise a problem with 'Western' thought insofar as it systematically elides the crucial notion of the presence-to-self of the subject – and a fortiori, the idea of growth in one's personhood – a lack highlighted by the existentialists, Kierkegaard suggesting that philosophy is being presented as if there were no subject for whom the philosophy was a kind of self-knowledge. My suggestion focuses on the ambiguity of the notion of 'objectivity'. The emphasis in the early modern period, with the rise of science, was all on observation as key to objectivity. Observation replaces deduction as the royal road to knowledge, deduction from truths supposedly established by the authority of Aristotle, for example. Within the framework of this new, massively influential shift, Descartes tried to retrieve some space for our own inner minds by saying we have immediate access to their content, which can be posited as real alongside the physical world verified in the sciences. Hume followed the new method in science more consistently, concluding that both mind and self are imagined fictions. Kant disagreed in part with Hume, arguing we can't know we have minds or selves, but must act 'as if' these exist. The neglect of the subject, the person and her growth, in philosophy, was an inevitable consequence and continues to this day, both in philosophy and in the social sciences, often dominated by a Kantian-inspired social constructivism. But only if our capacity for self-actualisation is a proper object of our understanding (not disqualified by failing to be observable), could alternative expressions of such human capacity, such as that of African traditional thought, be taken seriously. In a sense, the move being suggested here goes back to the origins of philosophy in classical Greek thought: in his celebrated cave metaphor Plato describes human knowing as an existential journey, a journey of personal growth.

We have, throughout this book, drawn on the ideas of the Canadian philosopher Bernard Lonergan, also, like Tempels, trained in Thomistic metaphysics. As we have seen, he identifies a duality in human knowing giving rise to an ambiguity over the notion of objectivity. He notes (1992:276) the kind of 'objectivity' characteristic of any biological organism confronting and tasked with dealing with what's 'out there'. And he contrasts this with the attainment of objectivity through our capacity to reflect on and evaluate the accuracy of our ideas, how we suppose things to be. The organism - and this is the case with the new-born infant too - lives in a world of immediacy, dominated by biological ends. With the acquisition of language, we however also live in a 'mediated' world - encountered not in terms of biological needs but through meaning. We can think, because we can, unlike the pre-linguistic toddler, grasp things 'in the mind' without grasping them with the fingers or the mouth. By invoking their names we can simply hold them in mind without them being present. When your dog pricks up his ears on hearing your name spoken in a conversation while you are still at work, he looks around to identify you. But your name is being used here not at all to point to you but to bring you to mind. The dog plays no active part in this - or any other - conversational world. If we focus only on the former sense of 'objectivity' we might think what is real are 'bodies', i.e. 'out there' (Lonergan, 1972:238-239). But more coherently, what is real is whatever we come to critically judge actually is the case on the basis of the evidence - 'bodies', to be sure, but also, for example, minds, atoms, transactional forces, and so on. This capacity to live in this larger world of reality has to be discovered for themselves by each person. What needs to be brought to the fore is how one grows in one's very personhood, understanding this as a journey, as Plato depicted it in his simile of the prisoners set free to move out of the cave, moving from a less encompassing to a more encompassing world. Indeed, the systematic evidence-based inquiry into things out there by modern science is properly thought of as a development of precisely these powers of self-reflexivity. To the extent that modern Western thought overlooks this, restricting knowledge proper to what can be affirmed within the sciences ('scientism'), the influence of the African traditional normative idea of the human person, growing in the crucial virtues that define personhood, may very well contribute to the discipline having its set of internal goods 'systematically extended'.

Conclusion: The example of justice

In the African traditional thought-world, social connectedness is a higher value than that of procedural equality (cf Jacobsen-Widding, 1997). This is because, as we have seen above, the effective human ability to act ethically (to be a full person) is fully dependent on the action of others on one, and one's own receptivity to this. To the extent to which this is neglected (say, by marginalising these inquiries at universities), the ideals of equality and justice will remain just that: ideals, without real purchase in people's agendas. In this conception, doing justice is always qualified by the nature of the agents in question: doing justice to a child is different to doing justice to an adult. There is scope in this alternative, metaphysical, idea of justice for linking human ethics with a sense of the importance of paying attention to the ecology: doing justice to the environment as it naturally is. Matolino thinks Tempels' characterisation of an African ethic is unhelpful. Could Tempels not see, he asks, that all peoples, in this case African peoples, can indeed "go beyond their culture to see timeless values such as equality, justice and fairness" (2011:340, my emphasis). But nowhere does Matolino argue for these as indeed timeless values. Perhaps he considers it obvious. But we could ask about the value of social connectedness. And what about human flourishing, and personal growth, and community? What about participation in the life of the being that we can suppose is at the origin of the universe and accounts for it existing rather than not existing? What about these as timeless values? Tempels introduces, long before MacIntyre (1998) (from a similar communitarian point of view) asked about 'Whose Justice?' an alternative conception of justice. "Evil and injustice towards ancestors consist in making an attempt against their vital rank. This occurs when a younger person makes a decision off his own bat, or disposes of some piece of clan property without recognising the elders..." (1959:142). Our attitude to all human life must proceed from the respect due to that which is the supreme gift of God. "In this respect every injustice, every attempt against human life (against its vital power which fathers persons and things dependent upon it) is a stupendous evil..." (1959:143). It is clear from this, that abstract justice is not, for good reasons, here at the top of the ethical agenda. There is no doubt that the African traditional conception of justice - like any conception, including the modern Western - needs developing. In particular, with the greater individualism accompanying the development of society, the participation must be not rigid but intelligent, based on insights into our nature as developing, interconnected, persons. In our Africa-influenced vision of things, introductory philosophy should be framed by means of a conception of personal growth, growth of the self-conscious, deliberate, responsible, questioning of one's set of beliefs and attitudes to one's self. With this foundation, alternative concepts of justice can be evaluated and possibly harmonised. For example, Garrett Barden, as we saw in Chapter 5, has argued that underlying practices both of witchcraft in medieval Europe and of consulting the king's chicken's entrails (*benge*) in African traditional cultures, lies the idea that questions for intelligence about the best interpretation of evidence, need to be separated from judgement as to the accuracy, the reasonableness, of such interpretations, the idea of separating the prosecution from the judgement of the jury. The foundation of justice lies in just people - who do not exist as atoms but as encultured - people who have developed the intellectual and moral powers of being persons. Purely procedural or formal concepts of justice omit this crucial aspect. This would apply, for example, to the otherwise praiseworthy 'global civics' project of Hakan Altinay (2011). And without this notion of the person's capacity to become more of a person, more self-aware, more integrated, there can only be formal principles of justice. The dominant way philosophy is framed - in which what is truly objective knowledge is confined to 'things out there' - disallows this foundational notion.

The upshot of my conception of African scholarship is that introductory philosophy must (a) draw on the cultural background of the students; (b) present itself as an existential journey; and (c) be in the form of a dialogue with the dominant tradition, and its internal goods. In effect, it should be liberatory. Robert Doran (1990:38-41) stresses this aspect of Lonergan's analysis of the growing, more integrated subject and agent, with reference to Paulo Freire's methodological pedagogy of the oppressed. Doran's argument is that the postmodern context has heightened the importance of Lonergan's approach, a context "constituted by the necessity of choosing between, on the one hand, the anticipation of a post-historic homogeneous State incrementally moved forward by terrorist and counter-terrorist violence, and on the other hand the anticipation of a truth above and beyond divergent points of view, a truth that, while preserving the sharpest sense of subjectivity, provides access to a new organic civilisation on a transcultural or world-cultural basis" (1990:155-156). This is what is envisaged with the concept of philosophy presented here. Another way of phrasing it is to speak in terms of philosophy as 'narrative', which allows for dialogue with non-Western cultures - very much along the lines developed by Fasching (2011) so far as concerns religious ethics. I hope I have done enough to indicate a certain bias in the dominant way of framing philosophy and to motivate a rethink that would allow for the project of African scholarship - in the tradition-extending sense I have described - to get off the ground.

Chapter Sixteen

'Philosophy for Children' in Africa

In this chapter, I argue that a critical touchstone is needed if the traditional wisdom in Africa is to be sifted, and that this can be found in the idea of the questioning and responsible subject. This approach was canvassed in Chapter 5 in the discussion of how traditional-religious ideas may be enculturated in a culture of science. Traditional proverbs and myths, whether African or not, reveal a growing sense of responsibility but philosophy, I argue, can contribute the principle of non-contradiction and the foundational norm of responsibility. The principle and the norm can be found to be at the heart of the modern scientific enterprise and can in principle ground a dialogue between African traditional and modern European value systems.

Introduction

It is useful for our purposes to take as starting point Ndofirepi's (2011) well-researched and balanced argument for a hybrid approach to teaching critical thinking to high-school learners in Africa. The framework he suggests for teaching philosophy at schools is an African traditional one, using proverbs and myths. These, he argues, need to be complemented by a sifting process if the learners are to be provoked into critical thinking. He agrees with Makinde that "the philosophical task is to receive the messages of the past and to carefully adjudicate what is worthy of passing on to the present generation" (cited in Ndofirepi, 2011:252). He does not suggest that the traditional proverbs can be simply left as they are: rather, he says, they 'are vehicles to drive a point home'. His point is simply that the learners will derive the most benefit from the philosophical teaching if this is seen to be somehow cognate with the traditional wisdom, rather than left outside of this teaching. He agrees with Gyekye that "philosophical concepts... can be found embedded in African proverbs..., customs and traditions of the people" (in Ndofirepi,

2011:251), and with Bodunrin that there is no reason why proverbs, myths of gods and angels and social practices could not be proper subjects of philosophical inquiry. But the critical engagement with these comes precisely from the 'community of inquiry' that is the classroom situation. The learner must transform "primarily unreflective systems of beliefs... into more reasoned, objective and justified thoughts" (Ndofirepi, 2011:250). This is well put and, I think, a good starting-point but, speaking as a professional philosophy teacher in Africa, more needs to be said. In particular, what is needed are criteria for doing the sifting, if the learner is not to be left, which is not at all Ndofirepi's wish, with a bifurcated mind, or else an easy relativism. I have already, in the discussion of the role of traditional-religious ideas in humanising education (Chapter 13), given examples of traditional pre-philosophical thinking which illustrate the problem. Here, I can simply point to these, and, in addition, unpack the importance for philosophical thought of how Socrates brought into the core of European philosophy, the principle of non-contradiction.

Ndofirepi says "Philosophy for Children in Africa should draw its content and methodology from African beliefs and philosophies of life' (2011:249); I agree here in terms of content but disagree regarding methodology. The confrontation of traditional thinking with a more critical one was the beginning of philosophical method, strictly speaking, as this has been handed down from the Ancient Greeks. This is a heritage to which all learners are entitled.

A framework for appropriating traditions

Traditional thinking uses common sense. If a pre-philosophical questioner asks, Why do we bury the dead? the answer, quite adequate for the time, is: That is what we do. It is common sense. It is the confrontation with other cultures with other ways of doing things, that spurs the development of criteria for a more sophisticated answer. In some cultures, the ancient Greeks discovered, the custom is to burn the dead; and in yet another, the pious act is to eat the one who has died! 'Common sense' is common only as long as the culture is relatively isolated from other cultures. A more sophisticated answer will be in terms of some or other theory explaining why something is the case. In Book One of *The Republic*, Plato gives the example of the understanding of justice. What is justice? The common-sense answer is easy: Justice is giving back what you owe. So far so good. But what about the case when you have borrowed an axe from your neighbour, and this very man is now chasing his wife in anger: is it just, now, to give back what you owe? Tricky cases such as this (it cannot be the *good* thing to do to give back what you owe in this case) indicate the need for a theory explaining what justice is, a more adequate definition, and Plato does this in an extended fashion.

Examples such as the above provokes Socrates to invoke the criterion of non-contradiction. Justice is giving back what you owe; but in this case, it is *not* the just thing to give back what you owe. That seems to be contradiction. A (justice) is B (giving back); but also A is not-B. In his dialogue with his interlocutor Callicles, Socrates gets him to agree that it is better "that the majority of mankind should disagree with and oppose me, rather than that I, who am but one man, should... contradict myself" (Plato, *Gorgias*, 482). It is the principle on which he will advance his ideas: get your opponent to see that what they are claiming is self-contradictory. If I want to claim, It is raining, and I also want to claim, It is not raining, I am, in effect, claiming nothing. I need to revise or rephrase my claim.

I have mentioned, above, Gail Presbey's (2002) article on the method of Odera Oruka in unpacking traditional sage philosophy (Chapter 13). Why is there death? the sage is asked. To make room for the new generation, comes the sage answer. And in sparsely populated regions, such as deserts, where there is no shortage of room? Traditional wisdom is given in proverbs, but proverbs contradict one another. Too many cooks spoil the broth; but: Many hands make light work. Look before you leap; but: He who hesitates is lost.

We could do something similar with African proverbs. The proverb, *Umuntu ngumuntu ngabantu*, (roughly, a person is a person through other persons), is often taken for granted (e.g. Metz, 2007b:332, discussing his 2007a), as identifying something at the heart of the African traditional worldview. However, in an interesting study, Christian Gade (2010) has shown convincingly that this is not something that occurred, at least in South Africa, before 1990, and in fact, he argues, such identification is largely due to one specific book, that of Augustine Shutte's *Philosophy for Africa* (1993), although this idea rose to prominence in the Truth and Reconciliation Commission under the influence of Desmond Tutu. "To my knowledge, *Philosophy for Africa* is the first book in English which explores the identity belief embedded in the proverb *umuntu ngumuntu ngabantu*" (Gade, 2010:72). He also notes that there are more than twice as many Google search results (in July 2010, namely 742) for this book over its main rivals for contemporary *Ubuntu* philosophical literature in South Africa, namely Ramose's (1999) *African Philosophy Through Ubuntu* and Bhengu's (1998) *Ubuntu: The Essence of Democracy*. "To me, the act that a large number of texts refer to Augustine Shutte's *Philosophy for Africa* makes it plausible that this book might be an important part of the reason for why *Ubuntu* has become linked with the proverb '*umuntu ngumuntu ngabantu*'" (Gade, 2010:73).

Other proverbs could very well have said something perhaps contrary. When elephants fight, the grass gets crushed underfoot. Could this well-known proverb not illuminate the heart of African culture, seen as one in which the Big Man prevails, and harmony is achieved through him, except when there is more than one Big Man. Indeed, studies of corruption in contemporary African states sometimes have recourse to this idea as explanatory (for example, Sikku Hellsten, 2006; cf also the discussion in Chapter Two). Of course, in English, there is also the saying that 'no man is an island; everyone is part of the main,' which would indicate something quite different to the idea expressed in the common moral advice, 'Stand on your own two feet,' which seems to promote a strident individualism. Finally, it is evident that the term *Ubuntu* or *umuntu* might, when identifying different members of *Homo sapiens*, be contrasted to *umlungu* (meaning a white person) - not at all something that could act as a universal moral idea! And *Ubuntu* is also sometimes interpreted to refer to an ethics where a person's worth is whatever the community deems it to be. For example, Gade shows, some take *Ubuntu* to adhere only to those who have been initiated into the community, for example through circumcision and clitoridectomy. This would also mean ancestors lose this status when they are forgotten (Menkiti quoted in Ramose, 1999:91). In all these cases there are choices to be made as to what proverb really expresses the kernel of the traditional wisdom, and what exactly it means. Furthermore, it is to be expected that any principle of such sifting is bound to be controversial. Shutte's 1993 book is a case in point. He claimed, as described in Chapter 1, that some philosophical frameworks are more suitable for this kind of dialogue than others; in particular, Analytic philosophy was found wanting. To which a colleague, as we saw, hastened to attack it as "a very bad book on an extremely important topic," failing to meet "universally recognised standards of argumentational rigour" (Holiday, 1994). Later, it was criticised for assuming a white South African could presume to speak authoritatively on African traditional thinking: the preposition 'for' in the title seemed to indicate a paternalism on the part of the author; why, moreover, should African thinking only be 'authenticated' by reference to a Western philosophical framework (More, 1996). Ndaba (1999), on the contrary, was in broad agreement with Shutte.

Such controversies are extremely illuminating and point to a further role for African traditional thought that Ndofirepi also alludes to, namely, that it may offer itself as a contribution to global thinking. The controversy also suggests the way forward for the framing of philosophy education for teachers in Africa. For what Shutte, Ndaba, and many others are alluding to is the loss of a sense of the subject and agent in the dominant contemporary style of philosophy; in particular, in the English-speaking world. The sceptical approach does not allow the questions we are asking to get off the ground. We are aiming at a critical appropriation of the tradition or traditions, i.e. at a more nuanced and less contradictory set of ideas.

But in the dominant philosophical approach, there is no sure starting point for this kind of task. For, objectivity, it might be claimed, is reached through the sciences - and traditional understandings of the human condition, and of values, are thought of as having only subjective status. The connection between traditional views of life and philosophical thinking, is broken. Eloquent support for this critical interpretation of the dominant trend in contemporary philosophy can be found in the novelist Marilynne Robinson's Terry Lectures at Yale, published as *Absence of Mind* (2010).

Any standard textbook in philosophy will reveal the problem. Our discussion in Chapter 4, on African Philosophy of Mind, is pertinent. Thomas Nagel's popular *What Does It All Mean?* (1987) was exampled as mainstream. The list of topics presented by Nagel as standard are these: how do we know anything; other minds; the mind-body problem; the meaning of words; free will; right and wrong; justice; death; the meaning of life. The basic underlying philosophical question, it would seem, is whether or not there are good reasons for holding onto the idea of the mind, i.e. something non-material, in particular, with the rise of neurophysiology, contrasted with the brain. I seem to have access to my own mind (and hence am assured of its reality), but what about other minds? The scientific point of view seems to doubt the existence of anything non-material - every event has a cause, so how can free will exist? And what status can be given to moral values, to right and wrong? They are not objects of scientific inquiry, so perhaps they are simply agreed-upon rules for behaviour. But then how would we *criticise* any given set of such rules?

Basically, the problem is the loss of the sense of the presence to self of the subject. 'Scientism' names the view that only objects investigated by the sciences merit the attribution of being really real. But - to anticipate here a more developed argument below - all scientific inquiry presupposes and must assume such presence to self, which allows one to set up standards for judging whether any hypothesis or theory one holds might be possibly true. It cannot itself be an object of scientific investigation. It is only because one knows, is aware of the fact that, one holds such a theory or hypothesis that one can ask whether or not it corresponds to how things *actually are*, and to test it.

The irony is that the prestige of the method of the sciences disallows the idea of any such non-scientific object of the real world. This self-contradictory and self-destructive standpoint has given rise to the postmodern scepticism about knowledge. This conclusion about the upshot of modernity is worth studying. Nevertheless, such scepticism is, given our aim, unhelpful. In African traditional thought, we are offered ideas about the normative status of being a person, *umuntu*, and about the grounds of this capacity to be a person, a person's *seriti* or *isithunzi* (literally, shadow, but by extension, influence or power). If the approach we have termed 'scientism' means these are excluded from exploration, then there will be a gap between the framework of the traditional-religious person, and that of the science-influenced person, even when these two frameworks exist in the same person. The traditional-religious is then not going to develop or find its insights expressible in terms more appropriate to our secular culture. In contrast, in what follows, I will assume a broadly *non-sceptical* position and ask of those issues raised in the myths and proverbs the conditions of possibility for affirming the human capacity to reach some deeper objectivity and also to act responsibly; that is to say, on the basis of our judgement as to the real worth of alternative courses of action.

I now turn to my proposal. For these purposes, I draw freely on some of the discussions earlier in this book - based on papers written for a different audience, namely university colleagues. It must be noted that I am keeping my eye on the ball, which is the normative end of developing in the learner a deeper sense of what it means to be a responsible participant in contemporary society, such as it is. In other words, I am not approaching the topic of philosophy from some neutral point of view common to all practitioners of 'Philosophy' in the list of philosophical topics, in the manner of Thad Metz's annotated bibliography (2011), which interestingly enough, omits the 1993 Shutte book.

Philosophy through myths

The way into a philosophy which is not alienating and allows for dialogue between modern scientific and traditional religious worldviews, is through *the questioning subject*. All prescientific cultures raised questions about the meaning of life, about death, about life and morality. We can see this expressed in myths.

Examples abound, and earlier in Chapter 12, I drew attention to the questions being posed (and inadequately answered) in the Ancient Near-eastern myth of Gilgamesh, to do with our understanding of death and loss. Similarly, in the case of African traditional narratives, the same question is raised in a number of myths and two examples were given above. The 'problem' of death, it was suggested there, arises from some external evil force (the toad) but might also have to do with some human failing (undeveloped virtue of patience). Better known to school learners would be the biblical stories in Genesis 1 - 11, the stories of Adam and Eve, of Cain and Abel, of the Flood and of the Tower of Babel. In each case, what is natural in human striving is seen to be somehow out of reach or problematic. Adam of course desires eternal life - the tree in the middle of the garden - but, it seems, has to wait on God's gift; and in each case Jahweh gives a sign that this natural desire put there in creation, will be met: Adam is clothed not with leaves but with skins; Cain is given a sign to protect him; the rainbow is the promise that it is God's will not to destroy the human race; and what might build human civilisation, it is suggested, is the lineage of Abrahamic faith, to be the subject matter of Genesis 12 and following. Of course, here we have to do - in the minds of ordinary folk - with multiple and misleading interpretations alien to the project of human growth and responsibility.

But the advent of modern science has itself not been without its problematic attitudes to human responsibility; in particular, insofar as accompanying science has been a myth (we have called it 'scientism') about a fully impersonal universe, determined by factors apart from human moral efforts. This needs interrogation as much as do the traditional, pre-scientific narratives. In the following section, I want to suggest that this outlook, unhelpful for our project, is not at all a necessary one.

Science and the norm of responsibility

Modern science in early modern Europe was born not without a struggle. Faced with extra-scientific determinations of truth, from religious and traditional authorities (church and philosophical - Aristotle was the authority), science posited observation as key to knowledge proper. But it was Newton who introduced the key notion of 'inertia' as explanatory tool for understanding the physical movement of objects. It is not at all, he argued, that things have a natural tendency by virtue of their nature to move to certain ends (Aristotle), the stone 'wanting' to be at rest on the ground: no, the movement of objects is solely due to the impact of other objects on them (gravity, in this example). But, in this, Newton can be seen as 'murdering' matter, taking the natural life out of them. And hence, making the world seem more *alien* to our normal end-governed behaviour, to our human world. We became aliens in a world of matter. Philosophers henceforth were to ask, as foundational question, can how we experience things be at all how they are out there? (answer: not really).

The impact of Copernicus on world-consciousness needs to be recalled. To be told that how we observe things, the sun running its diurnal course from the East to the West, is in fact incorrect; this threw our confidence in reaching objectivity into disarray. We couldn't any longer be satisfied with common sense as control over our thought patterns.

Observation was posited as crucial in science, not authority. But, objectivity, of course, is not reached through observation. Or at least, through observation alone. Different observers see things from different points of view. From Newton, we have the idea of solving this problem, the problem of relativism, so destructive to our project of eliciting the ethical potential of our scientific and secular age. I am referring to the thought-experiment, described above in Chapter 13, of the spinning bucket. The two observers, standing outside the bucket and standing on the edge of the bucket, see 'movement' in two different ways. The observer on the edge of the bucket, however, understands that his observation (that the water is now still) does not accord with the evidence, the concave shape of the water in the bucket when it is moving. On the basis of the evidence, he concludes that the outside observer has the more correct understanding of what is happening. No relativism.

The idea that both observers can agree on the objective truth of the matter assumes that both have the capacity to weigh the evidence and consider that they might be occupying a position which biases their perception. It is this self-awareness that is crucial and which is left out of the picture in any materialist (scientistic) view of reality, and also left unthematised in the way philosophy is presented by Nagel.

We can note here also, that we are assuming that both observers are acting responsibly. In other words, they not only have the capacity to observe attentively, to hypothesise intelligently, and to make a reasonable judgement about the hypothesis, but they are actually trying to do so. They are making an effort. The outlining of the effort required by our capacity for responsibility, is ethics. And here we have a possibility of dialogue with traditional-religious worldviews. For, what they do is precisely this: outline the necessary ways in which such responsibility is developed. For example, we might say that African traditional culture has a lot to say about how our self-understanding and our growing sense of a more adequate hierarchy of values is acquired through participation in the community and interaction with others more mature than ourselves. And that modern global culture very little: the idea of autonomy so well articulated by Kant in the eighteenth century, downgrades such other-influenced growth as undermining one's autonomy and therefore dignity. Materialist philosophers such as Marx, on the other hand, think that human behaviour is fully determined by an individual choice undermined by the influence of others. Modern-traditional dialogue is not at all a one-way street - as prophets such as Fritjoff Capra (1983) have said for some time.

Philosophy as a dialogue of worldviews

In the light of the above, we now have a framework for a productive 'community of inquiry', after the fashion spoken of by Ndofirepi. But it means joining the existentialist thinkers in appealing against the loss of the sense of the subject and agent in modern European thought.

Kierkegaard argues that truth is subjectivity, not meaning that no objectivity is possible, 'subjectivism'. He means that the full context of human existence is the personal, the ethical and engaged, not the impersonal and scientific, and must be thematised in this context. As examples of 'engaged' philosophers, the names of Marx and Sartre come to mind. Their very different views are responses to the challenge to express human transcendence without a dualism of the kind that Plato was content with, but which is much more problematic in a secular and scientific age. This transcendence, as we have suggested, refers to the capacity to make oneself present to oneself in being able to stand back and evaluate the accuracy of one's beliefs, and also the relative worth of one's desires or wants or any proposed course of action. Clearly, on the model of scientism, this is not possible. But science itself - I am summarising here the counterargument articulated in many very dense philosophical tomes, in particular Lonergan's *Insight* (1957 and 1970) - as an activity obviously *presupposes* our human capacity for self-awareness; in other words, to transcend. The only possible conclusion is that reality consists of more than the objects of scientific inquiry, strictly speaking. Such objects, for example ourselves, in this sense of having the capacity for freedom, themselves demand an explanation. Obviously, freedom cannot be brought into being nor developed by any finite causality - which would precisely take away the freedom. Those who baulk at the consequences of this, namely that there exists a *non-finite* causality, would prefer to think of human self-awareness as epiphenomenal - but this does not make sense, contradicting the very act of making a claim about this, which *assumes* self-awareness and freedom as really real.

One can draw attention here to an inevitably contentious issue. For, in the notion of responsibility as explained, here there are obvious influences of the Hebrew and Christian notion of God, as transcendent of any finite reality, and of humankind in the image of God; in other words, as sharing in this power of transcendence, but in a relation of dependence on the god, the finite transcendence being explained by and sourced by the infinite transcendence. And for a secular intellectual culture this conceptual and historical connection with a particular religious tradition puts this whole approach to philosophy under a cloud of suspicion. For a common perception - although challenged, for example by Henry (2010) - is that modern science and modern philosophy arise out of a *conflict* with the religious authorities, in particular, of this religion. And this hostile attitude has largely lasted until the present day, at least in a modified form. At the same time, the recourse of large sections of the religious population has been to take refuge, in the face of secularisation and science, in a fundamentalism of the most anti-philosophical kind. Taking up the battle with the latter, the so-called New Atheists (the philosopher Dennett (2006) amongst them) have unfortunately displayed all the marks of engaging in a battle where, in the words of Matthew Arnold, "ignorant armies clash by night."

I mention these wider issues in introducing philosophy at school level because they are bound at any rate to be raised in the classroom. The particular methods of modern science in understanding the material world can, however, be seen as developments of our ability to make ourselves present to ourselves, which is the key to understanding human persons in the approach we are suggesting. But knowledge of the subject and agent is not something which can be arrived at neutrally, in a disengaged stance, as if one were investigating the properties of some distant planet never before encountered. Writers today speak of the 'narrative' framework of any such understanding, which, in other words, is always a chapter in one's own autobiography. And if this is the framing of basic philosophical, critical, questions which is favoured in the African traditional approach, it can offer a refreshing take on modernity.

All this hints at how one might make sense of an African traditional understanding of the human person, and formulate a framework in which this might form part of a dialogue with the dominant global picture. The idea of *Ubuntu* is precisely a concept which is both factual (a person grows through others) and normative (it is good to foster those attitudes and carry out those acts which promote the sharing of one's life with others). Various writers could be used to expand on this basic idea, the idea of a transcending power running through all things, from the god through ancestors and living elders to all persons. To live is to grow, and ethics always has to do with growth in power and strength. Other interpretive frameworks are no doubt possible:

a personalist one of Polanyi (1962), reiterated by Vervliet (2009), and also Maxwell (1987). But it would miss the point if one were to stress the ethical idea of *Ubuntu* shorn of what Analytic philosopher Farland (2007:356) dismisses as its "cloudy supernatural assumptions."

However, the African traditional thinking is expressed and interpreted; what is important is that some framework is developed which enables a dialogue with competing worldviews. In the African tradition we have a concept of human flourishing which specifies much more precisely the attitudes that lead to a good human life together. And it is backed up by a metaphysics which does not see material reality as over and against human (free) reality: freedom is achieved through engagement with the world, in particular (here Sartre would disagree), engagement with others, which is not, *pace* Sartre, ultimately frustrating. Who is right?

Conclusion

I have introduced philosophy through the lens of common-sense traditional wisdom. This draws in *all* traditional cultures and does not prejudge any (and so undercuts the recourse to bringing in African traditional thought as if it were some exotic thinking that bears little relation to the modern world). This has brought to the fore the need for greater precision; in particular, in the light of the development of the theoretical standpoint. It has also pointed to the need for the practice of individual judgement in sifting through what is truly of worth in any culture.

Secondly, I have introduced the idea of the 'shock of science', disturbing the traditional wisdom, the naïve idea that how things seem to us is how they are in themselves. By means of a crucial example, I have developed the idea that recourse to relativism is not necessary. We are able to draw on our powers of critical judgement. In the third place, I have pointed to a possible critique of the dominant cultural and intellectual global trend to overlook the subject and agent. In the fourth place, I have suggested various contending philosophical anthropologies that resonate in the contemporary culture and can usefully play a role in making the student's take on their own culture more sophisticated and differentiated. I have also suggested that a rethink of a knee-jerk attitude to religion will be of great help in speaking to students struggling to come to terms with both traditional and modern cultural elements. African traditional culture is religious; and a reconsideration of the possibility of dialogue with it could very well assist the dominant religions in rethinking their self-understanding, in a way more appropriate to a secular culture made up of a plurality of approaches to life.

I have been asked about the implications of all this for framing the philosophical education of teachers. To some extent, it is a question of attitude: an openness to the African traditional thought-world. But the appropriation of these insights, I have argued, can be hampered by an inadequate philosophical framework. My own suggestion, running counter to the way philosophy is presented in the dominant global approach, cannot avoid being controversial.

Luckily, in philosophy, controversy is embraced, its method is that of a *dialogue*. It is ironical that the thinker who used to represent European philosophy, namely Aristotle, can now be evoked in order precisely to challenge it, and in particular, the scepticism that issues in what we have termed 'scientism'. Aristotle's *normative idea of the human person* has been reworked by contemporary thinkers such as Bernard Lonergan and Alasdair MacIntyre to bring in the greater sense of subjectivity that Descartes stressed so much, as well the cross-cultural context - a development in philosophy which I have taken as key to this whole book. With this framework traditional mythological accounts, which illuminate the way we can and do question our existence, are not dismissed as 'non-scientific' - since science is *itself* a particular actualisation of our norm of being self-aware questioning subjects and responsible agents.

Cultural relativism is also seen as unhelpful: learning is a journey, as Plato's simile of the cave brings out, and contemporary existentialist writers concur. If one asks for actual texts on African traditional thought, there are too many to mention and even more so comparative narratives from global religious traditions (e.g. Fasching, 2011). The easiest introduction to the appropriate *philosophical framework* is - as is evident throughout this book - in my opinion, Shutte's 1993 book and its 2001 follow-up specifically on the ethics of *Ubuntu*. Useful, too, is Sartre's brilliant but ultimately pessimistic analysis of intersubjectivity (1969, Part Three, especially Chapter 3) which will provoke the learner to come to their own conclusions.

References

Publications by Patrick Giddy

1995. Philosophy for Africa: Another View. *Social Dynamics*, 21:117-131. https://doi.org/10.1080/02533959508458593

1996. The African University and the Social Sciences: The Contribution of Lonergan's Epistemological Theory. *Method: Journal of Lonergan Studies*, 14:133-153. https://doi.org/10.5840/method19961422

1997. A Communitarian Framework for Liberal Social Practices? *South African Journal of Philosophy*, 16:150-157.

2002. African Traditional Thought and Growth in Personal Unity. *International Philosophical Quarterly*, 42:315-327. https://doi.org/10.5840/ipq200242324

2005. Does the Growth of Science in a Culture Necessarily Undermine the Tradition? In: A Shutte (ed) *The Quest for Humanity in Science and Religion*, 168-197. Pietermaritzburg: Cluster.

2005. [With M. Detterbeck] Questions Regarding Tradition and Modernity in Contemporary *Amakwaya* Practice. *Transformation*, 59: 26-44. https://doi.org/10.1353/trn.2005.0048

2007. Does Character Matter? Guardian Values in an Age of Commerce. *Theoria* 113, 53-75. https://doi.org/10.3167/th.2007.5411304

2009. Objectivity and Subjectivity: Rethinking the Philosophy Syllabus. *South African Journal of Philosophy* 28, 359-376. https://doi.org/10.4314/sajpem.v28i4.52981

2011. Special Divine Action and How to do Philosophy of Religion. *South African Journal of Philosophy* 30, 143-154. https://doi.org/10.4314/sajpem.v30i2.67775

2012. 'Philosophy for Children' in Africa: Developing a framework. *South African Journal of Education*, 32: 15-25. https://doi.org/10.15700/saje.v32n1a554

2012. The ideal of African scholarship and its implications for introductory philosophy: The example of Placide Tempels. *South African Journal of Philosophy* 31:504-516. https://doi.org/10.1080/02580136.2012.10751790

2013. Can African Traditional Culture Offer Something of Value to Global Approaches in Teaching Philosophy? *Acta Academica*, 45:154-172. https://doi.org/10.38140/aa.v45i4.1421

2016. Human Agency and Weakness of Will: A Neo-Thomist Discussion. *South African journal of philosophy* 35:197-209. https://doi.org/10.1080/02580136.2016.1167346

2019. Is the Essence of Christianity a Disenchanted World? A Critical Discussion of Marcel Gauchet. *South African Journal of Philosophy*, 38:313-329. https://doi.org/10.1080/02580136.2019.1655313

2020. Solidarity at Issue: Pandemics and Religious Belief. *Phronimon* 21 (15 pages). https://doi.org/10.25159/2413-3086/8568

2024. Decolonizing the African Churches in the Context of Secular Public Policy. In: Barreto R and V Latinovic (eds) *Decolonial Horizons. Reshaping Synodality, Mission and Social Justice*, 241-260. Palgrave Macmillan. https://doi.org/10.1007/978-3-031-44843-0_13

Other references

Acemoglu D and Robinson JA. 2013. *Why Nations Fail: The Origins of Power, Prosperity, and Poverty.* New York: Crown Currency. https://doi.org/10.1111/dpr.12048

Akyol M. 2011. *Islam Without Extremes.* London: WW Norton.

Alfaro J. 1975. Nature and Grace. In: K Rahner (ed), *Encyclopaedia of Theology. A Concise Sacramentum Mundi*, 1034. London: Burns and Oates.

Altinay H. 2011. Why a Global Civics? In: H Altinay (ed) *Global Civics: Responsibilities and Rights in an Interdependent World*, 1-19. Washington, D.C.: Brookings Institution Press.

Amin S. 1989. *Eurocentrism.* R Moore (transl). London: Zed Press.

Anscombe GEM. 1970. Modern Moral Philosophy. In: WD Hudson (ed), *The Is-Ought Question*, 175-95. London: MacMillan. https://doi.org/10.1007/978-1-349-15336-7_19

Appiah K. 1992. *In My Father's House: Africa in the Philosophy of Culture.* London: Methuen.

Appiah K. 2005. *The Ethics of Identity.* Princeton: Princeton University Press.

Appiah K. 2010. *The Honor Code.* New York: WW Norton.

Aquinas St Thomas 1964. *Summa Theologica*. Dominicans of the English Province (transl). Allen, Tx: Christian Classics.

Aquinas St Thomas 1993. *Commentary on Aristotle's Nicomachean Ethics*. C Litzinger (transl). Notre Dame: Dumb Ox Books.

Aristotle. 1966. *Nicomachean Ethics*. Sir David Ross (transl) London: Oxford.

Aristotle. 1981. *The Politics*. TJ Saunders and TA Sinclair (transl) Penguin Classics.

Armstrong K. 2006. *The Great Transformation*. Anchor Books.

Armstrong K. 2009. *The Case for God. What Religion Really Means*. London: The Bodley Head

Bacon F. [1620]1905. *Novum Organum*. R Ellis and J Spedding (transl) London: Routledge.

Badat S. 2010. The Challenge of Transformation in Higher Education Training Institutions in South Africa. Development Bank of SA. www.dbsa.org/Research/Higher Education and Training, 43.

Baker D. 2005. Of Mercenaries and Prostitutes: Can Private Warriors be Ethical? Paper given to the School of Philosophy and Ethics, University of KwaZulu-Natal.

Baker J. 2021. https://www.washingtonpost.com/opinions/2021/11/23/ josephine-baker=-pantheon-france-colonialism

Bakker R. 1964. *De Geschiedenis van het Fenomenologisch Denken*. Utrecht: Het Spectrum.

Barden G. 1972. The Intention of Truth in the Mythic Consciousness. In: P McShane (ed) *Language, Truth and Meaning*. Dublin: Gill and Macmillan.

Barden G. 1990. *After Principles*. Notre Dame, In.: University of Notre Dame Press.

Beier U. (ed) 1966. *The Origin of Life and Death. African Creation Myths*. Heinemann.

Bellah R. 2011. *Religion in Human Evolution. From the Palaeolithic to the Axial age*. Cambridge, Ma.: Belknap. https://doi.org/10.4159/ harvard.9780674063099

Bhengu M. 1998. *Ubuntu: The Essence of Democracy*. Novalis Press.

Bidima J-G. 1995. *La Philosophie Negro-Africaine*. Paris: Presses Universitaires de France.

Biko S. 1978. *I Write What I Like*. A Stubbs (ed) London: Heinemann. https://doi.org/10.5070/F783017356

Bloom A. 1987. *The Closing of the American Mind*. New York: Simon and Schuster.

Bodunrin PO. 1995. Magic, Witchcraft and ESP: A Defence of Scientific and Philosophical Scepticism. In: A Mosley (ed) *African Philosophy*, 371-386. Englewood Cliffs, NJ: Prentice-Hall.

Boghassian P. 2006. *Fear of Knowledge: Against Relativism and Constructivism*. Oxford: Oxford University Press.

Bracken J. 2009. *Subjectivity, Objectivity, and Intersubjectivity*. West Conshohocken, Penn.: Templeton Foundation Press.

Brague R. 2018. *The Kingdom of Man. Genesis and Failure of the Modern Project*. Notre Dame, In: University of Notre Dame Press. https://doi.org/10.2307/j.ctvpj74c6

Bryant C and Cobban H. 2006. Accountability in Development and Reconciliation in Africa. Paper given at 7th IDEA Conference on Ethics and International Development. Kampala, Uganda.

Breytenbach WJ. 1976. National Integration in Lesotho. *South African Journal of African Affairs* 1 and 2.

Bujo B. 2009. Is There a Specific African Ethics? In: MF Murove (ed) *African Ethics. An Anthology of Comparative and Applied Ethics*, 113-128. Scottsville: University of KwaZulu-Natal Press.

Capra F. 1983. *The Turning Point*. Flamingo.

Carrabregu G. 2016. Habermas on Solidarity: An Immanent Critique. *Constellations* 23: 507-522. https://doi.org/10.1111/1467-8675.12257

Chemhuru M. (ed) 2019. *African Environmental Ethics. A Critical Reader*. Cham: Springer. https://doi.org/10.1007/978-3-030-18807-8

Clark M. 2002. *In Search of Human Nature*. London: Routledge.

Cobban H. 2007. *Amnesty After Atrocity. Healing Nations after Genocide and War Crimes*. Boulder, Co.: Paradigm Press.

Cochrane J and B Klein. (eds) 2000. *Sameness and Difference: Problems and Potentials in South African Civil Society: South African Philosophical Studies I.* Washington DC: Council for Research in Values and Philosophy.

Coetzee JM. 1999. *The Lives of Animals.* Princeton: Princeton University Press.

Coetzee JM. 2003. *Elizabeth Costello.* London: Secker and Warburg.

Collins P. 1985. MacIntyre's Politico-moral Science. *South African Journal of Philosophy* 4: 100-106.

Comaroff J and Comaroff J. 1991. *Of Revelation and Revolution Vol 1. Christianity, Colonialism and Consciousness in South Africa.* Chicago: Chicago University Press. https://doi.org/10.7208/chicago/9780226114477.001.0001

Comaroff J and Comaroff J. 1993. *Modernity and Its Malcontents: Ritual and Power in Postcolonial Africa.* Chicago: University of Chicago Press.

Coplan D. 1985. *In Township Tonight! South Africa's Black City Music and Theatre.* Johannesburg: Raven Press.

Couzens, T. 1985. *The New African. A Study of the Life and Work of H.I.E. Dhlomo.* Johannesburg: Raven Press.

Cronin B. 2006. *Value Ethics: A Lonergan Perspective.* Nairobi: Consolata Institute of Philosophy.

Curnow R. 2012. *The Preferential Option for the Poor.* Milwaukee: Marquette University Press.

Davies B. 2004. *An Introduction to the Philosophy of Religion.* 3rd Ed. Oxford: Oxford University Press;

Dennett D. 2004. *Freedom Evolves.* Penguin.

Dennett D. 2006. *Breaking the Spell.* Viking.

Dennett, D. 2017. *From Bacteria to Bach and Back. The Evolution of Minds.* Penguin Books.

Derrida J. 1995. *The Gift of Death.* D Wills (transl). Chicago: University of Chicago Press.

Descartes R. 1968. *Discourse on Method and the Meditations.* F Sutcliffe (transl). Harmondsworth: Penguin.

Descombes V. 1994. Is There an Objective Spirit? In: T James (ed), *Philosophy in an Age of Pluralism. The Philosophy of Charles Taylor in Question*, 96-120. Cambridge: Cambridge University Press. https://doi.org/10.1017/CBO9780511621970.009

Detterbeck M. 2003. South African Choral Music (*Amakwaya*): Song, Contest and the Formation of Identity. Ph.D. thesis. Durban: University of Natal.

Doran R. 1990. *Theology and the Dialectics of History*. Toronto: University of Toronto Press. https://doi.org/10.3138/9781442682603

Dorr D. 1984. *Spirituality and Justice*, New York: Orbis.

Dorr D. 1992. *Option for the Poor. A Hundred Years of Catholic Social Teaching*. Blackburn, Vic.: CollinsDove.

Eagleton T. 2022. The Pope of Russell Square. T. S. Eliot's conservative modernism. *Commonweal*, May 26, 2022. Referenced at http://commonwealmagazine.org/pope-russell-square.

Ela M. 1963. L'Eglise, Le Monde Noir, et Le Concil. In: *Personnalité Africaine et Catholicisme*, 59-81. Paris: Présence Africaine.

Elchardus M and Siongers J. 2001. The Malaise of Limitlessness: An Empirical Study of the Relationship between Detribalization, Meaningfulness and Malaise. *Ethical Perspectives*, 8: 179-201. https://doi.org/10.2143/ep.8.3.583182

Etherington N. 1978. *Preachers, Peasants and Politics in South-East Africa, 1835-1880: African Christian Communities in Natal, Pondoland and Zululand*. London: Royal Historical Society.

Ethics Centre. 2016. *Ethics Explainer: Just War Theory* [online]. Available: http://ethics.org.au/ethics-explainer-just-war.

Etieyebo E. (ed) 2018. *Perspectives in Social Contract Theory*. Washington DC: Council for Research in Values and Philosophy.

Exdell J. 1987. Ethics, Ideology, and Feminine Virtue. In: Hanen M. and K Nielsen (eds) *Science, morality, and feminist theory*. Calgary: University of Calgary Press. https://doi.org/10.1080/00455091.1987.10715934

Farland D. 2007. African Intuitions and Moral Theory. *South African Journal of Philosophy* 26: 356-363. https://doi.org/10.4314/sajpem.v26i4.31493

Fasching D *et al.* 2011. *Comparative Religious Ethics.* Second Edition. Oxford: Wiley-Blackwell.

Ferguson J. 1994. *The Anti-Politics Machine: Development, Depolitization, and Bureaucratic Power in Lesotho.* Minneapolis, MN: University of Minnesota Press.

Ferry L. 2010. *La Revolution de l'Amour. Pour une Spiritualité Laïque* (The Revolution of Love. Toward a Secular Spirituality). Paris: Plon..

Ferry L. 2011. *A Brief History of Thought.* T Cuffe (transl). London: HarperCollins.

Foot P. 1978. Morality as a System of Hypothetical Imperatives. In: P Foot, *Virtues and Vices,* 157-173. Oxford: Blackwell. https://doi.org/10.1093/0199252866.003.0011

Foucault M. 1985. *The Use of Pleasure.* R Hurley (transl) New York: Pantheon.

Gade C. 2010. *Ubuntu* and the South African Truth and Reconciliation Process. MA dissertation. Department of Philosophy and History of Ideas, Aarhus University, Denmark. www//konfliktloesning.dk/files/ UBUNTU_2010_Chr._Gade.

Gade C. 2013. Restorative Justice and the South African Truth and Reconciliation Process. *South African Journal of Philosophy* 32: 10-35. https://doi.org/10.1080/02580136.2013.810412

Galloway P. 1995. Spiritual Healing through Psychotherapy. *Grace and Truth* 12: 47-53.

Gasper D. 2006. Working in Development Ethics: A Tribute to Denis Goulet. Éthique et Économique 4: 1-25. Available at http: ethique-economique.net.

Gauchet M. 1997. *The Disenchantment of the World.* O Burge (transl) Princeton, NJ: Princeton University Press.

Geertz C. 1994. The Strange Estrangement: Taylor and the Natural Sciences. In: T James (ed). *Philosophy in an Age of Pluralism. The Philosophy of Charles Taylor in Question,* 83-95. Cambridge: Cambridge University Press. https://doi.org/10.1017/CBO9780511621970.008

Giddens, A. 1990. *The Consequences of Modernity.* Cambridge: Polity Press.

Gilson E. 1941. *God and Philosophy.* New Haven: Yale University Pres.

Glaser D. 2001. *Politics and Society in South Africa*. London: Sage. https://doi.org/10.4135/9781446216910

Goulet D. 1974. *A New Moral Order: Development Ethics and Liberation Theology*. New York: Orbis.

Goulet D. 1995. *Development Ethics: A Guide to Theory and Practice*. New York: Rowman & Littlefield.

Graness A. 2022. The Status of Oral Traditions in the History of Philosophy: Methodological Considerations. *South African Journal of Philosophy* 41: 181–194. https://doi.org/10.1080/02580136.2022.2062986

Grayling C. 2007. *Against All Gods: Six Polemics on Religion and an Essay on Kindness*. London: Oberon.

Green Paper. 2006. www.fco.gov.uk/Files/kfile/mercenaries

Gyekye K. 1995. *An Essay on African Philosophical Thought: The Akan Conceptual Scheme*. Philadelphia: Temple University Press.

Haight R. 1999. *Jesus, Symbol of God*. New York: Orbis.

Haight R. 2004. *Christian Community in History*, Vol 1. New York: Continuum.

Haldane J. 2012. Scientism and its Challenge to Humanism. *New Blackfriars* 93: 671–686. https://doi.org/10.1111/j.1741-2005.2011.01458.x

Hegel GFM. [1806]1967. *The Phenomenology of Mind*. JB Baillie (transl) Harper Torchbooks.

Hellsten S 2006. Leadership Ethics and the Problem of Dirty Hands in the Political Economy of Contemporary Africa. *Ethique et Economique* 4, 2 (25 pages). https://papyrus.bib.umontreal.ca/xmlui/bitstream/handle/1866/3378/2006v4n2_HELLSTEN.pdf?sequence=1

Henning B. 2017. Call for Papers. Edited Anthology on Non-anthropocentric Climate Ethics. Connect.gonzaga.edu/henning/call-for-papers. Accessed 18 Sept 2017.

Henry J 2010. Religion and the Scientific Revolution. In: P Harrison (ed) *The Cambridge Companion to Science and Religion*, 39–58. Cambridge University Press. DOI: https://doi.org/10.1017/CCOL9780521885386.003

Herzog, W. (dir) 2008. *Grizzly Man*. Film. https://doi.org/10.1007/978-1-84457-551-0_31

Hill E. 1988. *Ministry and Authority in the Catholic Church*. London: Chapman.

Holiday A. 1994. Review of Augustine Shutte, *Philosophy for Africa. Social Dynamics* 20: 130-137.

Horkheimer M and Adorno T. 1972 [1944] *Dialectic of Enlightenment*. J Cumming (transl), London: Allen Lane.

Horney K. 1950. *Neurosis and Human Growth*. New York: The Norton Library.

Horton J. 2000. Relativism, Reality and Philosophy. *History of the Human Sciences* 13: 19-36. https://doi.org/10.1177/09526950022120575

Horton R. 1995. African Traditional Thought and Western Science. In: A Mosley (ed), *African Philosophy*, 301-338. Englewood Cliffs, NJ: Prentice-Hall.

Houellebecq M. 2001. *Atomised*. F Wynne (transl), London: Vintage.

Houle R. 1998. Constructing an *amaKholwa* Community: Cattle and the Creation of a Zulu Christianity. MA thesis, University of Wisconsin-Madison.

Hume D. [1740] 1969. *A Treatise of Human Nature*. Penguin.

Irele A. 1995. Contemporary Thought in French Speaking Africa. In: A Mosley (ed) *African Philosophy*, 263-296. Englewood Cliffs, N.J.: Prentice-Hall.

Jacobs F. 2005. Reasonable Partiality in Professional Ethics: The Moral Division of Labour. *Ethical Theory and Moral Practice* 8: 141-154. https://doi.org/10.1007/s10677-005-3293-5

Jacobs, J. [1977]1994. *Systems of Survival. A Dialogue on the Moral Foundations of Commerce and Politics*. London: Vintage.

Jacobsen-Widding A. 1997. 'I lied, I farted, I stole...': Dignity and Morality in African Discourses on Personhood. In S Howell (ed) *The Ethnography of Moralities*. London: Routledge.

Jansen Y. 2006. *Laïcité*, or the Politics of Republican Socialism. In: H de Vries and L Sullivan (eds), *Political Theologies. Public Religions in a Post-Secular World*, 475-493. New York: Fordham University Press.

Johann R. 1975. Person, Community and Moral Commitment. In: R Roth (ed) *Person and Community*, 155-175. New York: Fordham.

Johann R. 1988. The Development of Community. In: G McLean and H Meynell (eds), *Person and Society*, 65-75. Washington, D.C.: University Press of America.

Johnston M. 2009. *Saving God.* Princeton: Princeton University Press.

Kant I. 1960. *Religion Within the Limits of Reason Alone.* New York: Harper Torchbooks.

Kant I. [1783] 1966. *Prolegomena to any Future Metaphysics.* P Lucas (ed), Manchester: Manchester University Press.

Kant I. 1784. What is Enlightenment? https://resources.saylor.org/wwwresources/archived/site/wp-content/2011/02/What-is-Enlightenment.pdf

Kenny A. 1989. *The Metaphysics of Mind.* Oxford: Clarendon Press.

Kerr F. 1997. *Immortal Longings.* London: SPCK.

Kierkegaard S. 1968. *Concluding Unscientific Postscript.* Princeton, NJ: Princeton University Press.

Kierkegaard S. 1986. *Fear and Trembling.* A Hannay (transl), Penguin Classics.

Kiyala JC. 2022. Underlying Moral Justification of Baraza and Indaba Dialogic Institutions in African Social Ethics and Philosophy. In: JO Chimakonam and L Cordeira-Rodrigues (eds), *African Ethics. A Guide to Key Ideas*, 159-184. London: Bloomsbury Academic. https://doi.org/10.5040/9781350191815.ch-010

Kim J. 2005. *Physicalism, or Something Near Enough.* Princeton: Princeton University Press.

Kingsolver, B. 2005. *The Poisonwood Bible.* Harper Classics.

Kitcher P. 2006. Kant's Philosophy of the Cognitive Mind. In: P Buyer (ed), *The Cambridge Companion to Kant and Modern Philosophy*, 169-202. Cambridge: Cambridge University Press. https://doi.org/10.1017/CCOL052182303X.006

Komprodis N. (ed) 2006. *Philosophical Romanticism.* London: Routledge. https://doi.org/10.4324/9780203507377

Kung H. 1997. *A Global Ethic for Global Politics and Economics.* London: SCM. https://doi.org/10.1093/oso/9780195122282.001.0001

Kwant RC. 1969. *Sociale Filosofie.* Antwerpen: Het Spectrum;

Langer S. 1996. *Philosophy in a New Key.* 3rd Edition. Harvard Paperbacks.

LeBlanc J. 1999. Eco-Thomism. *Environmental Ethics* 21: 293–306. https://doi.org/10.5840/enviroethics199921319

Leckie R. 1995. *Hannibal*. Abacus.

Leclerc-Madlala S. 2001. Virginity Testing: Managing Sexuality in a Maturing HIV/AIDS Epidemic. *Medical Anthropology Quarterly* 15: 533–552. https://doi.org/10.1525/maq.2001.15.4.533

Levy B. 2014. *Working with the Grain. Integrating Governance and Growth in Development Strategies*. New York: Oxford University Press. https://doi.org/10.1093/acprof:oso/9780199363803.001.0001

Lonergan B. [1957] 1970. *Insight. A Study of Human Understanding*. 3rd Edition. New York: Philosophical Library. Reprinted as: Lonergan B. 1992. *Insight. Collected Works of Bernard Lonergan, Vol 3*. Toronto: University of Toronto Press.

Lonergan B. 1972. *Method in Theology*. 2nd Edition. London: Darton, Longman and Todd.

Lonergan B. 1988a. Dimensions of Meaning. In: B Lonergan, *Collection. Collected works of Bernard Lonergan, Vol 4*, Chapter 16. Toronto: University of Toronto Press.

Lonergan B. 1988b. Cognitional Structure. In: B Lonergan, *Collection. Collected works of Bernard Lonergan, Vol 4*, Chapter 14. Toronto: Toronto University Press.

Lonergan B. 1990. *Understanding and Being. Collected Works of Bernard Lonergan, Vol 5*. Toronto: University of Toronto Press.

Lonergan B. 1993a. The Theory of Philosophic Differences. In: B Lonergan, *Topics in Education. Collected Works of Bernard Lonergan, Vol. 10*, Chapter 7. Toronto: University of Toronto Press.

Lonergan B. 1993b. The Human Good as the Developing Subject. In: B Lonergan, *Topics in education. Collected Works of Bernard Lonergan, Vol 10*, Chapter 4. Toronto: University of Toronto Press.

Lonergan B. 1996. Philosophical Positions with Regard to Knowing. In: B Lonergan, *Philosophical and Theological Papers 1958–1964. Collected Works of Bernard Lonergan, Vol 6*, Chapter 10. Toronto: University of Toronto Press. https://doi.org/10.3138/9781442678415

Lonergan B. 2001. *Phenomenology and Logic. The Boston College Lectures on Mathematical Logic and Existentialism. Collected works of Bernard Lonergan, Vol 22.* Toronto: University of Toronto Press. https://doi.org/10.3138/9781442678392

Luijpen W. 2000. *Existential Phenomenology.* Duquesne: Duquesne University Press.

MacIntyre A. 1966. *A Short History of Ethics.* London: Routledge. https://doi.org/10.4324/9780203267523

MacIntyre A. 1981. *After Virtue.* London: Duckworth.

MacIntyre A. 1983. Postscript to the Second Edition. In: *After Virtue.* 2nd Edition, Chapter 19. London: Duckworth.

MacIntyre A. 1988. *Whose Justice? Which Rationality?* London: Duckworth.

Mackey J. 2006. *Christianity and Creation.* New York: Continuum.

Macmurray J. [1957] 1999a. *The Self as Agent.* Humanity Books.

Macmurray J. [1961] 1999b. *Persons in Relation.* Humanity Books.

Macmurray J. [1939] 2018. *The Boundaries of Science.* Franklin Classics.

Magesa L. 1997. *African Religion: The Moral Traditions of Abundant Life.* New York: Orbis Books.

Mangena F and JD McClymont (eds) 2018. *Philosophy, Race and Multiculturalism in Southern Africa.* Washington DC: Council for Research in Values and Philosophy.

Marks S. 1986. *The Ambiguities of Dependence in South Africa: Class, Nationalism and the State in Twentieth-century Natal.* Baltimore: Hohn Hopkins University Press.

Marshall K. 2006. Religion and Development: Wisdom and Practice, Ancient and Contemporary. Paper delivered at 7th IDEA Conference on Ethics and International Development. Kampala, Uganda.

Marx, K. 1964. *The Economic and Philosophic Manuscripts of 1844.* D Struik (ed) New York: International.

Mascall EL. 1943. *He Who Is. A Study in Traditional Theism.* London: Longmans.

Mascall EL. 1946. *Christ, the Christian and the Church.* London: Longmans, Green & Co.

Matolino B. 2011. Tempels' Philosophical Racialism. *South African journal of philosophy* 30:330–342. https://doi.org/10.4314/sajpem. v30i3.69579

Maxwell N. 1987. *From Knowledge to Wisdom*. 2nd Edition, London: Blackwell.

Mbembe A. 2020. Les métaphysiques africains permettent de penser l'identité en mouvement. *Le Monde*, December 15, 2019. Accessed August 29, 2020, from https://www.lemonde.fr/afrique/ article/2019/12/15/achille-mbembe

McCabe H. 2005a. *The Good Life*. London: Continuum.

McCabe H. 2005b. *God Matters*. London: Continuum.

McCarthy M. 1990. *The Crisis of Philosophy*. Albany: SUNY.

McDermott T. 1989. Preface. In: T McDermott, *Aquinas, Summa Theologiae. A Concise Translation*. London: Methuen. https://doi.org/10.1016/ B978-0-12-322060-8.50008-5

Meinhold P. 1975. Protestantism. In: K Rahner (ed), *Encyclopaedia of Theology. A Concise Sacramentum Mundi*, 1294. London: Burns and Oates.

Menaud L. 2001. *The Metaphysical Club*. New York: Farrar, Straus and Giroux.

Menkiti I. 1979. Person and Community in African Traditional Thought. In: R Wright (ed) *African Philosophy*, 171–181. Lanham: University Press of America.

Metz T. 2007a. Toward an African Moral Theory. *The Journal of Political Philosophy* 15: 321–341. https://doi.org/10.1111/j.1467-9760.2007.00280.x

Metz T. 2007b. The Motivation for 'Toward an African Moral theory.' *South African Journal of Philosophy*, 26:331–335. https://doi.org/10.4314/ sajpem.v26i4.31490

Metz T. 2009. African Moral Theory and Public Governance. In: MF Murove (ed) *African Ethics. An Anthology of Comparative and Applied Ethics*, 335–356. Scottsville: University of KwaZulu-Natal Press.

Metz T. 2011. *An Annotated Bibliography of African Philosophical Texts*. Oxford Bibliographies. https://doi.org/10.1093/ obo/9780195396577-0164

Meyer B. 2021. What Is Religion in Africa? Relational Dynamics in an Entangled World. *Journal of Religion in Africa* 50. https://doi.org/10.1163/15700666-12340184

Meynell H. 1981. *Freud, Marx and Morals*. New Jersey: Barnes & Noble. https://doi.org/10.1007/978-1-349-05640-8

Miaille M. 2016. *La Laïcité. Solutions d'Hier Problèmes d'Aujourd'hui*. Paris: Editions Dalloz.

Midgley M. 1984. *Wickedness. A Philosophical Essay*. London and New York: Routledge.

Midgley M. 1989. *Wisdom, Information and Wonder*. London: Routledge.

Midgley M. 1995. *Beast and Man*. Revised Edition. London: Routledge.

Miller, RW. 1984. *Analyzing Marx. Morality, Power and History*. Princeton: Princeton University Press. https://doi.org/10.1515/9780691219745

Moingt J. 2010. *Croire Comme Même*. (Believing In Spite Of) TempsPrésent.

Molefe M. 2019. The Criticism of Secular Humanism in African Philosophy. In: C Munamato (ed) *African Environmental Ethics. A Critical Reader*, 59-74. Cham: Springer. https://doi.org/10.1007/978-3-030-18807-8_5

More MP. 1996. African Philosophy Revisited. *Alternation*, 3:109-129.

More MP. 2004. Biko: Africana Existentialist Philosopher. *Alternation* 11: 79-108.

Moreland JP. 2000. Naturalism and the Ontological Status of Properties. In: W Craig and J Moreland (eds) *Naturalism. A Critical Analysis*, 67-109. London: Routledge.

Mosley A. (ed) 1995. *African Philosophy: Selected Readings*. Englewood Cliffs, N.J.: Prentice Hall.

Mullett S. 1987. Only Connect: The Place of Self-knowledge in Ethics. In: M Hanen and K Nielsen (eds), *Science, Morality, and Feminist Theory*. Calgary: University of Calgary Press. https://doi.org/10.1080/00455091.1987.10715940

Murove MF. 2009a. The Incarnation of Max Weber's Protestant Ethic and the Spirit of Capitalism in Post-Colonial African Economic Discourse. In: Murove (ed) *African Ethics*, 221-237. Scottsville: University of KwaZulu-Natal Press.

Murove MF. (ed) 2009c. *African Ethics. An Anthology of Comparative and Applied Ethics.* Scottsville: University of KwaZulu-Natal Press.

Murove MF. 2009b. An African Environmental Ethic Based on the Concepts of *Ukama* and *Ubuntu.* In: MF Murove (ed) *African Ethics. An Anthology of Comparative and Applied Ethics,* 315-332. Scottsville: University of KwaZulu-Natal Press.

Murray M and M Rea (eds) 2008. *An Introduction to the Philosophy of Religion.* Cambridge: Cambridge University Press. https://doi.org/10.1017/CBO9780511801488

Nagel T. 1979a. What Is It Like to Be a Bat? In: T Nagel, *Mortal Questions,* 165-180. Cambridge: Cambridge University Press.

Nagel T. 1979b. Subjective and Objective. In: T Nagel, *Mortal Questions,* 196-213. Cambridge: Cambridge University Press.

Nagel T. 1987. *What Does It All Mean?* Oxford: Oxford University Press.

Nagel T. 1989. *The View from Nowhere.* Oxford: Oxford University Press.

Naipaul VS. 2010. *The Masque of Africa.* London: Picador.

Nancy J-L. 2006. Church, State, Resistance. In: H de Vries and L Sullivan (eds), *Political Theologies. Public Religions in a Post-Secular World,* 102-112. New York: Fordham University Press. https://doi.org/10.5422/fso/9780823226443.003.0003

Nathan L. 1994. *The Changing of the Guard: Armed Forces and Defence Policy in a Democratic South Africa.* Pretoria: HSRC Publishers.

National Catholic Reporter. 2021. Spiritual abuse occurs more frequently than believed, Vatican official says, *National Catholic Reporter,* August 6, 2021. Referenced at https://www.ncronline.org/news/accountability/spiritual-abuse.

Ndaba WJ. 1999. The Challenge of African Philosophy: A Reply to Mabogo More. *Alternation* 6: 174-192.

Ndaba WJ. 2001. An African Philosophy for Dialogue with Western Philosophy - a Hermeneutic Project. Ph D thesis. Alice: University of Fort Hare.

Ndebele N. 2012. Love and Politics: Sister Quinlan and the Future we have Desired. Unpublished talk. Accessible at: njabulondebele.co.za/2012/12/love-and-politics. Accessed on 13 May 2021.

Ndofirepi A. 2011. Philosophy for Children. The Quest for an African Perspective. *South African Journal of Education* 31: 246-256. https://doi.org/10.15700/saje.v31n2a278

Niccol, A. 2005. *Lord of War*. Film. Fort Myers, FL. Entertainment Manufacturing Company.

O'Neill O. 1996. *Towards Justice and Virtue*. Cambridge: Cambridge University Press.

Oluwole S. 1995. On the Existence of Witches. In: A Mosley (ed), *African Philosophy: Selected Readings*, 357-370. Englewood Cliffs, NJ: Prentice Hall.

Pattison G. 2001. *A Short Course in the Philosophy of Religion*. London: SCM.

Pewa ES. 1984. 'The Chorus.' A Re-Africanisation of Hymn-singing in Schools and Churches. BA Honours thesis. University of Natal.

Phillips R. 1930. *The Bantu are Coming*. London: SCM.

Pinchin C. 2005. *Issues in Philosophy. An Introduction*. 2nd Edition, Basingstoke: Palgrave Macmillan. https://doi.org/10.1057/9780230376588

Pinker S. 2012. *The Better Angels of our Nature*. Penguin.

Pithouse R. 2001. Fanon and the Persistence of Humanism. In: P Giddy (ed) *Protest and Engagement: Philosophy after Apartheid*, 9-34. Washington, D.C.: Council for Research in Values and Philosophy.

Plato. 1961. *The Collected Dialogues of Plato*. E Hamilton and H Cairns (eds). Princeton: Princeton University Press. https://doi.org/10.1515/9781400835867

Polanyi M. 1962. *Personal Knowledge*. Chicago: Chicago University Press.

Polkinghorne J. 2003. God, Science and Philosophy. In: T Bartel (ed), *Comparative Theology. Essays for Keith Ward*, 110-1119. London: SPCK.

Poole R. 1991. *Morality and Modernity*. London: Routledge.

Poole R. 1999. *Nation and Identity*. London: Routledge.

Praeg L. 2011. Philosophy, and Teaching (as) Transformation. *South African Journal of Philosophy*, 30: 43-359. https://doi.org/10.4314/sajpem.v30i3.69581

Presbey G. 2002. African Sage Philosophy and Socrates: Midwifery and Method. *International Philosophical Quarterly*, 42: 177–192. https://doi.org/10.5840/ipq20024223

Pritchard JB. (ed) 1958. *The Ancient Near East*. Vol. I. Princeton: Princeton University Press.

Prosch H. 1966. *The Genesis of Twentieth-century Philosophy*. New York: Allen and Unwin.

Prozesky M. 2009. Well-fed Animals and Starving Babies: Environmental and Developmental Challenges from Process and African Perspectives. In: MF Murove (ed) *African Ethics. An Anthology of Comparative and Applied Ethics*, 298–307. Scottsville: University of KwaZulu-Natal Press.

Ramose MB. 1999. *African Philosophy through Ubuntu*. Mond Books.

Ramose MB. 2006. The 'Science' Question in African Traditional Religion. In: A Shutte (ed), *The Quest for Humanity in Science and Religion*, 256–276. Pietermaritzburg: Cluster Publications.

Report of the Ministerial Committee on Transformation and Social Cohesion and the Elimination of Discrimination in Public Higher Education Institutions. 2008. www.vut.ac.za/new/index.php/ docman/doc_view90-/MinisterialReport

Republic of South Africa (RSA) 1996. Constitution of the Republic of South Africa No. 108 of 1996 [online] Available at https://www.gov.za/ sites/default/files/images/a108-96.pdf

Robinson M. 2010. *Absence of Mind. The Dispelling of Inwardness from the Modern Myth of the Self*. New Haven, CT: Yale University Press.

Romano C. 2019. *Etre Soi-même*. (Being Oneself) Paris: Gallimard. https:// doi.org/10.14375/NP.9782072819216

Roth R. (ed) 1975. *Person and Community*. New York: Fordham University Press.

Sagar K. 2005. *Literature and the Crime against Nature*. London: Chaucer Press.

Salazar H. (ed) 2019. *Introduction to Philosophy: Philosophy of Mind*. Rebus Community. Accessed June 15, 2020, from https://press.rebus. community/intro-to-phil-of-mind

Sartre J-P. [1943]1969. *Being and Nothingness*. H Barnes (transl), London: Methuen.

Sartre J-P. [1948. *Existentialism and Humanism*. P Mairet (transl), London: Methuen.

Schutz A and Luckmann T. 1973. *The Structures of the Life-World*. R Zaner and HT Engelhardt (transl), Evanston: Northwestern University Press.

Shutte A. 1993. *Philosophy for Africa*. Cape Town: University of Cape Town Press. Reprinted as Shutte A. 1995. *Philosophy for Africa*. Milwaukee: Marquette University Press.

Shutte A. 1984. The Spirituality of Persons. *South African Journal of Philosophy* 31: 54-58.

Shutte A. 2001. *Ubuntu. An Ethic for a New South Africa*. Pietermaritzburg: Cluster Publications.

Shutte A. 1981. *Spirituality And Intersubjectivity*. Unpublished Ph.D. thesis. Stellenbosch: University of Stellenbosch.

Shutte A. 2006. Religion in a Scientific and Secular Culture. In: A. Shutte (ed), *The Quest for Humanity in Science and Religion. A South African Perspective*, 29-62. Pietermaritzburg: Cluster Publications.

Simpson P. 1988. *Goodness and Nature*. Dordrecht: Nijhoff.

Singer P. 1999. Reply to Costello. In: JM Coetzee, *The Lives of Animals*. Princeton: Princeton University Press.

Skorupski J. 2007. Normative Ethics. In: Petersen T and Ryberg J (eds), *Normative Ethics: Five Questions*, 131-142. Automatic Press.

Skota, T. 1930. *The African Yearly Register. Being an Illustrated National Biographical Dictionary (Who's Who) of Black Folk in Africa*. Johannesburg: RL Essen and Co.

Smith J. 1994. *The Moral Problem*. Oxford: Blackwell.

Smith P and OR Jones. 1986. *The Philosophy of Mind*. Cambridge: Cambridge University Press.

Solms M. 2019. The Hard Problem of Consciousness and the Free Energy Principle. *Frontiers in Psychology*. https://doi.org/10.3389/fpsyg.2018.02714

Spurrett D. 2008. Why I Am Not an Analytic Philosopher. *South African Journal of Philosophy* 27: 151-163. https://doi.org/10.4314/sajpem.v27i2.31509

Stoeger W. 2008. Conceiving Divine Action in a Dynamic Universe. Russel R, Murphy N and Stoeger W (eds), *Scientific Perspectives on Divine Action*, 225-247. Vatican: Vatican Observatory Publications.

Strasser S 1965. *Bouwstenen voor een Filosofische Anthropologie*. Antwerpen: Paul Brand.

Swimme B and Berry T. 1994. *The Universe Story*. Harper Collins.

Szablowinski Z. 2020. Religion (Un)wanted in a Secular Age. *Heythrop Journal* LXI: 595-606. https://doi.org/10.1111/heyj.13047

Taylor C. 1989. *Sources of the Self*. Cambridge, Ma.: Harvard University Press.

Taylor C. 1994. *Multiculturalism. Examining the Politics of Recognition*. Princeton, NJ: Princeton University Press.

Taylor C. 1997. Foreward. In: M Gauchet, *The Disenchantment of the World*, ix-xv. Princeton: Princeton University Press.

Taylor C. 2007. *A Secular Age*. Cambridge, Ma.: Belknap. https://doi. org/10.4159/9780674044289

Taylor, C. 2012. What was the Axial Revolution? In: R Bellah and H Joas (eds), *The Axial Age and its Consequences*, 30-46. Cambridge, MA.: Belknap. https://doi.org/10.2307/j.ctt2jbs61.5

Tempels P. 1959. *Bantu Philosophy*. C King (transl), Paris: Présence Africaine.

Tillich P. 1962. *The Courage to Be*. London: Collins.

Toulmin S. 2001. *Return to Reason*. Cambridge, Ma.: Harvard University Press.

Truth and Reconciliation Commission (TRC). 2002. *Truth and Reconciliation Commission of South Africa Final Report*, Vol 5. London: Palgrave Macmillan.

Turino T. 1993. *Moving Away from Silence*. Chicago: University of Chicago Press. https://doi.org/10.7208/chicago/9780226816951.001.0001

Turino T. 2000. *Nationalists, Cosmopolitans, and Popular Music in Zimbabwe*. Chicago: University of Chicago Press. https://doi.org/10.7208/ chicago/9780226816968.001.0001

Tutu D. 1999. *No Future Without Forgiveness*. New York: Random House. https://doi.org/10.1111/j.1540-5842.1999.tb00012.x

United Nations (UN). 1977. *Protocol Additional to the Geneva Conventions of 12 August 1949, and Relating to the Protection of Victims of Non-International Armed Conflicts (Protocol II)*. Available: https://www.ohchr.org/sites/default/files/protocol2.pdf.

Urquhart G. 1996. *The Pope's Armada*. Corgi Books.

Van Peursen CA. 1956. *Lichaam-Ziel-Geest*. Utrecht: Bijleveld.

Van Straaten Z. (ed) 1981. *Basic Concepts in Philosophy*. Cape Town: Oxford University Press.

Vatican News. 2020. Benedict Daswa. https://www.vaticannews.va/en/africa/news/2020-09/benedict-daswa.html

Ver Eecke W. 1975. The Look, the Body, and the Other. In: D Ihde (ed) *Dialogues in Phenomenology*. The Hague: Nijhoff. https://doi.org/10.1007/978-94-010-1615-5_13

Vergely B. 2019. *Transhumanisme: La Grande Illusion*. Paris: Le Passeur.

Verhoef A. 2012. How To Do Philosophy of Religion. *South African Journal of Philosophy* 31: 419-432. https://doi.org/10.1080/02580136.2012.10751785

Vervliet C. 2009. *The Human Person, African Ubuntu and the Dialogue of Civilisations*. Adonis & Abbey.

Voegelin E. 1956-74. *Order and History* Vols 1-4. Baton Rouge, LA : Louisiana State University Press.

Voegelin E. 1974. *The Ecumenic Age. (Order and History, Vol IV)*. Baton Rouge, LA: Louisiana State University Press.

Walmsley G. 2004. Integral Self-Appropriation and the Science-Religion Encounter: Lonergan's Methodological Mediation. In: C Du Toit (ed) *The Integrity of the Human Person in an African Context*, 205-264. Unisa: Research Institute for Theology and Religion.

Walmsley G. (ed) 2011. *African Philosophy and the Future of Africa: South African Philosophical Studies III*. Washington DC: Council for Research in Values and Philosophy.

Walsh D. 2008. *The Modern Philosophical Revolution*. Cambridge: Cambridge University Press.

Ward K. 2006. *Pascal's Fire. Scientific Faith and Religious Understanding*. Oxford: Oneworld.

Weber M. 1992. *The Protestant Ethic and the Rise of Capitalism*. T Parson (transl), London: Routledge. (Original work published 1905)

Weil S. [1949]2001. *The Need for Roots*. Routledge.

Wilson F. 2004. In Search of the Decent Economy. *New South African Outlook*, 6: 15-18.

Wilson M. 1986. *Freedom for my People: The Autobiography of Z. K. Matthews*. Cape Town: Africasouth.

Winch, P. [1958] 2008. *The Idea of a Social Science and its Relation to Philosophy*. Routledge.

Winch, P. 1972. Understanding a Primitive Society. In: P Winch (ed) *Ethics and Society*, 8-49. London: Routledge and Kegan Paul. https://doi.org/10.4324/9781003051138-2

Wiredu K. 1992. Moral Foundations of an African Culture. In: K Wiredu and K Gyekye (eds) *Person and Community: Ghanaian Philosophical Studies*, Vol 1, 192-206. Washington, D.C.: The Council for Research in Values and Philosophy.

Wiredu K. 1995. How Not to Compare African Thought with Western Thought. In: A Mosley (ed), *African Philosophy*, 159-171. Englewood Cliffs, NJ: Prentice-Hall.

Wittgenstein L. 2001. *Tractatus Logico-philosophicus*. DF Pears and B McGuinness (transl), London: Routledge Classics.

Wood J. 2008. *How Fiction Works*. New York: Picador.

Woodhead, L. 2004. *An Introduction to Christianity*. Cambridge: Cambridge University Press. https://doi.org/10.1017/CBO9780511800863

Yu, J. 2008. Soul and Self: Comparing Chinese Philosophy and Greek Philosophy. *Philosophy Compass* 3: 604-618. https://doi.org/10.1111/j.1747-9991.2008.00152.x

Zulu, P. 2013. *A Nation in Crisis. An Appeal for Morality*. Cape Town: Tafelberg.

www.ingramcontent.com/pod-product-compliance
Lightning Source LLC
Chambersburg PA
CBHW071015280326
41935CB00011B/1355